Cultural Foundations of Education

Second Edition

Young Pai
Susan A. Adler

University of Missouri-Kansas City

Merrill,
an imprint of Prentice Hall
Upper Saddle River, New Jersey   Columbus, Ohio

Library of Congress Cataloging-in-Publication Data

Pai, Young

       Cultural foundations of education / Young Pai, Susan A. Adler.—2nd ed.
       p. cm.
       Includes bibliographical references and index.
       ISBN 0-13-396979-7
       1. Educational anthropology—United States—Case studies. 2. Multicultural educa-
tion—United States—Case studies. 3. Pluralism (Social sciences)—United States—Case studies.
4. Educational psychology—United States—Case studies.   I. Adler, Susan A. II. Title.
    LB45.P35   1997
    370.19—dc20   96-4176
                                                                CIP

Cover photo: Anthony Magnacca
Editor: Debra A. Stollenwerk
Production Editor: Linda Hillis Bayma
Design Coordinator: Julia Zonneveld Van Hook
Text Designer: Mia Saunders
Cover Designer: Rod Harris
Production Manager: Patricia A. Tonneman
Electronic Text Management: Marilyn Wilson Phelps, Matthew Williams, Karen L. Bretz,
    Tracey Ward

This book was set in Baskerville by Prentice Hall and was printed and bound by R.R. Donnelley
& Sons Company. The cover was printed by Phoenix Color Corp.

© 1997 by Prentice-Hall, Inc.
Simon & Schuster/A Viacom Company
Upper Saddle River, New Jersey 07458

Printed in the United States of America

10 9 8 7 6 5 4 3 2 1

ISBN: 0-13-396979-7

Prentice-Hall International (UK) Limited, *London*
Prentice-Hall of Australia Pty. Limited, *Sydney*
Prentice-Hall of Canada, Inc., *Toronto*
Prentice-Hall Hispanoamericana, S. A., *Mexico*
Prentice-Hall of India Private Limited, *New Delhi*
Prentice-Hall of Japan, Inc., *Tokyo*
Simon & Schuster Asia Pte. Ltd., *Singapore*
Editora Prentice-Hall do Brasil, Ltda., *Rio de Janeiro*

To
Sunok, a wellspring of my growth,
on whom the East and the West meet
ever so gracefully,
and our grandchildren,
Vanessa, Chelsea, and Nathan,
whose lives shall be enriched
by the confluences of the two cultures

To
Natalya, Karolyn, and Ethan—
For education is about the future

Preface

Educators generally agree that education takes place in a specific sociocultural context. But we are not always clear and precise about the myriad of ways in which cultural factors influence the processes of schooling, teaching, and learning. More often than not, our insensitivity to and the lack of knowledge regarding the rule of culture in education lead to unsound educational policies, ineffective school practices, and unfair assessment of learners. Accordingly, the primary purpose of this introductory text is to examine education as a cultural phenomenon and the implications of this perspective for schooling, multicultural education, educational development, and the processes of teaching, learning, and counseling.

Cultural Foundations of Education is designed to provide educators and prospective educators with knowledge essential to making decisions about teaching and learning. It is not a methods textbook; rather, as the title implies, it is intended as a foundation for thinking about curriculum and pedagogy. We are in a time of sociocultural as well as educational change, and educators must be equipped with the knowledge and understanding necessary for effective analysis of educational issues. Teachers cannot close their classroom doors on cultural influences on education. It is our intention that this book will contribute to more thoughtful dialogue about education in its cultural context.

Use of This Text

Most of the concepts, theories, and issues presented in this text, along with their educational ramifications, will require further probing and elaboration; therefore, instructors are encouraged to introduce their own materials, experiences, and insights to these topics as well as to the influences of political, economic, and religious variables on education and schooling.

Case studies involving African American, Asian American, Hispanic American, Native American, and white American groups are presented at the end of each chapter. The contents of individual chapters will help readers analyze the cases; also, additional sources in anthropology and education, opinions of other students, and the instructor's guidance will be useful in gaining varied and alternative insights.

New to This Edition

A number of changes have been introduced to this second edition. Many sections have been updated, including the discussions of **core values** in chapter 2 and **multicultural education** in chapter 5. The extended discussion of **current reform efforts** in chapter 4 should help readers consider these efforts within the context of cultural issues. The overview of theories about the role of schooling in chapter 5 has been reorganized and extended to include a look at the **postmodern perspective.** Several end-of-chapter cases have been replaced with newer examples for student analysis. Other updates, while changing the text in only minor ways, are aimed at keeping the text connected with current trends and theories, as well as with the experiences of readers.

Acknowledgments

Our thanks to Shu Chen for her work in preparing the revised manuscript and to our colleagues at the University of Missouri-Kansas City for their ongoing support and review of this work. Comments and suggestions by the following reviewers have been most helpful in enhancing the depth and breadth of the book: Frederick J. Baker, California State Polytechnic University, Pomona; Malcolm B. Campbell, Bowling Green State University; John B. Cross, Livingston University; and Etta R. Hollins, California State University, Hayward.

Brief Contents

Contents

PART ONE

Culture and the
Educative Process

1

Introduction

WHY STUDY THE CULTURAL FOUNDATIONS OF EDUCATION?

Today there are widely divergent views of education. Some people see it as the process by which individuals are helped to become the best they can be on the basis of their ability and personally envisioned possibilities; others regard it as the development of the intellect through which learners acquire essential cognitive and social skills and perennial knowledge (truths). Still others prefer to view education as a process, fundamentally similar to that of industrial production, in which certain human behaviors are shaped and maintained so that they may become useful to the individual and others at some future time. Indeed, it is important to examine critically the relationships between these and other concepts of education, with their varied philosophical and ideological perspectives and their practical implications, for our ideas do make a difference in what we do and how we act. But the meanings of these ideas and their influence on human behaviors, thinking processes, and learning styles vary according to the society's prevailing worldview and values. This being the case, it is not surprising that each society has its own conceptions of what *liberal education, well-rounded person,* and even *basic skills* mean. Moreover, the relative worth of special goals and educative means is rooted in the social, cultural, political, and economic contexts in which people learn and educational institutions function. There is no escaping the fact that education is a sociocultural process. Hence, a critical examination of the role of culture in human life is indispensable to the understanding and control of educative processes.

3

Regardless of how education is defined, from a cultural perspective it can be viewed as the deliberate means by which each society attempts to transmit and perpetuate its notion of the good life, which is derived from the society's fundamental beliefs concerning the nature of the world, knowledge, and values. These beliefs vary from society to society and culture to culture. To put it differently, if we accept English anthropologist Edward B. Taylor's definition of culture, "the complex whole which includes knowledge, beliefs, art, morals, law, custom and any other capabilities and habits acquired by man as a member of society" (Gould & Kolb, 1964, p. 166), then we may regard education as the intentional attempt to pass on such a complex whole from one generation to another. Because educational practice is the design by which cultural contents are relayed to the next generation, the structure of the educational system, the role of the school, and the teacher-learner relationship reflect the social organization and the cultural norms of the society. For example, in a society where individuals treat each other as equals, the teacher-learner or parent-child relationship tends to be informal, and communication styles tend to be open with frequent reciprocal exchanges. On the other hand, in a culture where individuals see others as either above or below their own status (a hierarchical perspective), we are likely to find a formal teacher-pupil relationship with a communication style characterized by commands and demands issued from teachers to learners, who are seen as occupying a lower status.

In another sense, the aims and the ways of educating the young are not only influenced by the conditions of society and its culture, but they may also be viewed as responses to societal and cultural needs. This means that in a culturally diverse society such as ours, the various educational agents, especially the schools, must deal with the issues, problems, and needs arising out of the relationship between the dominant and minority cultures. In sum, no part of the educative process, neither its contents nor its products, is free from cultural influence. Educators need to realize that the processes of teaching and learning are influenced by the core values, beliefs, and attitudes as well as the predominant cognitive and communication styles and linguistic patterns of a culture. Further, the educative process, whether formal or informal, is equally affected by the socioeconomic status of the learner, peer pressures, the nature of the relationships between dominant and minority groups, and the impact of technology on the society.

As inextricable as the connection between culture and education is, education as a field of study has not always been concerned with this important relationship. Traditionally, the study of education and teacher education programs has placed much greater emphasis on the psychological rather than the sociocultural dimensions of teaching-learning processes. As well-known educational anthropologist George D. Spindler (1973) points out:

Educational psychology has clearly dominated the scene, partly because of a historical accident that institutionally wedded psychology and education rather early in America and partly because the need for tests and measurements and applied principles of learning have been particularly obvious in the educational milieu of American schools and have been appropriate for psychological applications. (p. 101)

Even in other foundational fields, the sociocultural areas that are usually called *educational sociology* are primarily concerned with the relationship between socioeconomic stratification, social change, bureaucracy, sex roles, demographic trends, and so on, in education and schooling. It is true that in the early 1900s Edgar C. Hewet wrote about anthropology and education (1904) and ethnic factors in education (1905), and a significant number of works on education and culture by such well-known scholars as Margaret Mead, Jules Henry, Clyde Kluckhohn, Solon Kimball, Dorothy Lee, and others appeared in the 1940s and 1950s. But serious attempts to utilize the tools and the findings of anthropology in dealing with matters related to general education, schooling, and teacher education did not begin until the early 1960s. Even today, cultural foundations of education are usually subsumed under educational sociology, educational psychology, or social foundations of education or even history and philosophy of education.

The fact that the study of the cultural foundations of education is not yet a clearly established, distinct discipline should not diminish its importance as practitioners attempt to examine how cultural variables affect education, teaching, learning, and the growth and development of all learners. The relevance of such a field in the study of education rests on the fact that worldviews, values, cognitive and communication styles, linguistic patterns, childrearing practices, tool making, knowledge acquisition, and the different ways in which people relate to each other are all culturally bound. They also have substantial impact on how people of all ages learn and become educated. Moreover, our knowledge of how these and other related factors influence human behavior may enable us to expose the cultural assumptions underlying the ways in which we and others think, analyze, and observe. Indeed, studying cultural foundations (bases) of education may give us a critical tool with which we can more accurately assess our work as educators and facilitate the development of more effective and just educational strategies and resource allocations so that optimal learning may be assured for all.

ANTHROPOLOGY AND EDUCATION

Given the nature and function of the cultural foundations of the education field as just described, anthropology should be considered its parent discipline and knowledge base. Anthropology, a science *(logos)* of man *(anthro)*, is concerned with describing, analyzing, and comparing the physical, social, psychological, and linguistic aspects of human behaviors as they manifest themselves in different cultural patterns. These patterns are investigated regardless of whether they exist in remote places in prehistoric times or at home today. When we consider the wide range of topics and the immensely varying spatiotemporal contexts in which investigations are carried out, anthropology may be considered the discipline with the broadest scope and the most holistic approach to understanding human behavior and institutions. Accordingly, there is no single definition of culture to which all anthropologists subscribe, albeit that "culture is the basic and central concept of this science" (Paulsen, 1968, p. 12).

The major subdivisions of anthropology consist of physical anthropology, cultural anthropology and archaeology, and anthropological, or comparative, linguistics. In addition, the newly formed field of psychological anthropology has been receiving increasing attention, because cross-cultural studies of perception, cognition, socialization, and ethnicity are believed to be significant in understanding the connections between the processes of learning, schooling, and education as cultural transmission. It is important to note that although these branches of anthropology represent different ways of studying human beings, they are really "separate but related approaches to the distinct but interrelated aspects of man" (Ianni, 1967, p. 27). When we consider that the educative process is necessarily sociocultural in nature and that cultural factors have profound impact on effective teaching and learning, anthropology should be seen as an essential aspect of any serious study of educational theories and practices.

Physical Anthropology

A major function of physical anthropology is to study human beings as biological organisms in terms of their physical characteristics and how these have evolved. Examining racial differences, inheritance of bodily characteristics, and developmental processes, as well as the relationship between human organisms and their environment, plays an important role in the field. Accordingly, physical anthropologists are keenly interested in analyzing and comparing variations in human populations or racial groups and the manifold ways in which these groups have adapted themselves to their environment. A study of how biological factors and the varied means of environmental adaptation—that is, culture—influence each other becomes a vital part of physical anthropology. Reliable knowledge of the interaction between biological (genetic) and environmental factors is a valuable source for gaining a sound insight into the ways in which human beings learn and adjust to their environment.

As an illustration, findings of physical anthropology suggest that races are to be considered categories of people grouped according to their physical characteristics for the purpose of making convenient classifications. Studies of these classifications (races) in relation to cultural distribution reveal that cultures are transmitted socially and through education rather than biologically—in other words, throughout the world people of the same race do not necessarily share the same culture. Cultural behaviors and racial traits vary independently from each other. However, there is general agreement that people's varying responsiveness to different stimulus situations does have a biological basis. This means, for example, that genetic factors do influence a person's sensitivity to sounds, colors, or shapes. But whether or not a person becomes a good musician or an outstanding visual artist depends on the relative values a culture attaches to certain art forms as well as on the individual's own abilities, interests, and efforts. Both formal and informal education play a significant role in the specific ways in which these personal capacities and propensities are developed. In this way, knowledge gained through physical anthropology about the relationship between culture and biological characteristics helps us understand the nature and function of the educative process.

Cultural Anthropology and Archaeology

Cultural anthropology deals with the investigation of cultural patterns or complex systems of human behaviors that represent people's attempts to solve the problems arising out of nature and human beings' associations with each other.

Cultural anthropologists carry out their work by tracing and reconstructing cultures of the past and by observing and comparing contemporary cultures. Archaeologists who study past cultures scrutinize buried tools, artwork, written records, and other human artifacts. These scholars have not only developed many special techniques of unearthing hidden evidence of early civilization and cultural development, but they have also utilized knowledge and tools of other sciences such as chemistry, physics, geology, and anatomy. Advancement in archaeology has led to closer relationships between anthropology and such other fields as history, paleontology, geophysics, and oceanography. Traditionally, archaeology has been considered a study of past cultures. But many of its findings are regarded as essential in understanding how modern cultures have evolved into their present states.

The work of describing and comparing today's cultures belongs to ethnography and ethnology, respectively. The primary function of ethnography is to collect data in the field through observation and interviews; the role of ethnology is to interpret the gathered information (Spindler, 1982). As with archaeology, growth in these areas has significantly influenced the emergence of several new subfields. Ethnomusicology, psychological anthropology, educational anthropology, urban anthropology, and other new disciplines have given anthropology a new image of increased relevance in today's world. Historically, cultural anthropology has been viewed as a science concerned primarily with the study of prehistoric, "primitive," preliterate, or non-Western cultures. But as anthropologists began utilizing their unique concepts, theories, and methods to deal with contemporary issues, specialists in other social sciences became increasingly interested in applying cultural anthropology in their own attempts to understand today's major institutions—education, business, religion, and so on. The interdisciplinary relationships just mentioned give us a genuinely enriching and sound basis for gaining new insights into the present condition of our society and clarity for the control of our society's future.

Central to cultural anthropology is the premise that culture is and should be viewed as a system. In other words, culture is an integrated complex of behavioral patterns, core values, and ideals of a society. This implies that people's behaviors are not random in character; rather, they have patterns and directions rooted in the fundamental ideals and values of the society. Cultures are human attempts to solve both environmental and social problems, and they may be compared with each other as alternative ways of dealing with essentially similar problems. Because human cultures, as a whole, can be viewed as a pool of problem-solving strategies and methods, societies can learn from each other. Indeed, an important role of educational institutions in any society should be facilitating the understanding and appreciation of other cultures. Through such learning experiences we may enrich our lives by adding new perspectives and problem-solving approaches to our own repertoire of ideas, knowledge, and skills.

As has already been pointed out, education is a process of cultural transmission, which suggests that the content, the form, and the process of informal learning as well as schooling in any society are influenced heavily by its culture. On the other hand, ample evidence indicates that educational outcomes may in return affect culture by influencing how people think, believe, judge, and act. For example, new knowledge about the dangers of passive smoking and the ensuing education of the public have led to the creation of new laws against smoking in public and in workplaces. Significant changes in the behaviors of and relationships among smokers and nonsmokers are attributable to this education of the public about the ills of smoking. Clearly, these events have materially changed the overall climate of offices, schools, hotels, restaurants, and other places in our society. The smoke-filled meeting rooms in most organizations have become extinct, and the militancy of nonsmokers asserting their right to clean air is not an unusual phenomenon.

Anthropological (Comparative) Linguistics

The scholars in anthropological linguistics study the origin, structure, and development of languages and their relationship to other learned human behaviors. The scope of this field includes historical and comparative analyses of modern and ancient languages and other artifacts as vehicles of communication. These investigations often focus on dialect variations, phonetic patterns, syntactical rules, and the consistency with which these elements of language are used. The varying ways in which languages reflect cultural norms, social organizations, and modes of interpersonal relationships are other important areas of inquiry.

Notwithstanding the tremendous differences in speech forms, phonetic patterns, and dialect variations in ancient and modern languages, the findings of anthropological linguistics reveal that, in general, all languages seem to do their job. That is, all languages are capable of expressing thoughts and feelings that the society considers appropriate. Hence, no language or language group should be regarded as inherently superior to any other. But this does not imply that all languages are equally functional; some may be better equipped in expressing logical and analytical thoughts, whereas others might be better suited to communicating more global or aesthetic thoughts and feelings.

Languages do enable us to express and communicate our ideas and emotions to others. However, they are more than mere tools for transmitting information, because the language we use frequently indicates our sociocultural status, educational level, and even our regional and ethnic background. Moreover, ample evidence suggests that people who use different languages not only see the world differently, but they also have different understandings of concepts considered to have manifest meanings in other cultures. For example, individuals from an authoritarian or hierarchical society may assign very different meanings to such notions as freedom, self-determination, assertiveness, and participatory democracy than those who come from an egalitarian culture. Because communication flows from higher to lower positions in hierarchical societies, people in a lower status have no words with which to compliment or admonish those who occupy a higher position. Knowledge of the relationship between language and human behavior should be extremely useful to American educators who must work with learners from divergent ethnic and social groups. This kind of knowledge must also be helpful to educators grappling with such controversial issues as the pros and cons of bilingual education, the desirability of using the black dialect in schools, or the relative merits of American Sign Language as compared to Signed English for hearing-impaired children and their parents.

Psychological Anthropology

Psychological anthropologists are either psychologists who are knowledgeable about anthropological concepts and tools of inquiry or anthropologists who are seriously interested in psychology's theories and methodology. Regardless of the practitioner's primary academic orientation, the central concern of the field is to investigate the ways in which culture and personality influence each other. More specifically, the scope of psychological anthropology encompasses the studies of perception, cognition, variations in learning processes, different approaches to enculturation, and effects of ethnic stereotyping in personality development. Human behaviors occur in sociocultural contexts from which they draw their meaning and significance. Further, whether we view personality as a unified system of human responses or as a psychological makeup that underlies overt behaviors, personality, too, develops in social and cultural environments.

More often than not, psychologists and educators have thought that perception is primarily a physiological or neurological process unaffected by cultural conditions. Yet, events and objects we observe have no inherent meanings, for the meanings are assigned to the raw perceptual data from a particular cultural perspective. For example, in the Far East writing a person's name in red signifies that the individual is deceased; in the West no special meaning is attached to writing a name in red. The color red has no inherent meaning or significance unless seen in a particular context. We learn to see, hear, and feel "things" as this or that according to the cultural norms of our own society. Similarly, although the psychological conditions for learning may be the same everywhere, the specific manifestations of these conditions are culturally bound. As an illustration, it may be true that rewarding leads to learning and punishing results in avoidance behavior. But what is rewarding or punishing to a particular learner depends on the cultural environment. Patting the top of a child's head may be rewarding in one society, but insulting (punishing) in a different culture.

Scientific studies of perception and cognition are important because they furnish us with valuable information regarding two essential preconditions for learning, namely (1) what individuals can be aware of and (2) what they do with their perceptual experiences (Harrington, 1979). Scientific investigation of perception and cognition is particularly helpful to educational inquiry, because reliable knowledge regarding how individuals experience and think about their world is necessary for a sound understanding of the learning process (Harrington, 1979).

The process of enculturation, or how the young learn to become full-fledged members of their society, is another area of concern for psychological anthropologists. Becoming a member of society requires that an individual acquire the behaviors, values, and beliefs that the group considers desirable and appropriate. Psychological anthropologists examine how one learns to act, think, and judge according to the fundamental norms of the society. In a culturally diverse society like the United States, growing into an acceptable member of the dominant society poses special problems for minority youth, who must learn the norms of the dominant culture while deciding whether to maintain or abandon their own ethnicity. This process can be extremely painful, especially if the mainstream society views minority cultures as being undesirable. It is for this reason that the effects of ethnic stereotyping on personality development and learning are key concerns of psychological anthropology.

ANTHROPOLOGY AND TEACHING

The relevance of anthropology in educational inquiry and the practice of teaching has already been intimated in this chapter's discussion of the scope and function of several subdivisions of anthropology. Moreover, because the specific implications of anthropological concepts and findings will be discussed in the remaining portions of this book, only two broad aspects of the relationship between anthropology and teaching will be examined here. One is the value of anthropology as a part of the general education of teachers; the other is the relevance of anthropological findings and methods in the professional development of teachers and prospective teachers.

A primary role of schools as specialized agents of human society is to transmit the fundamental worldviews, values, beliefs, and behavioral norms of the society to the young. In an ethnocentric society, schools tend to cultivate and reinforce attitudes that encourage learners to regard only their own beliefs, values, and ways of thinking as right and worthy of respect and admiration. Because all societies are more or less ethnocentric, most of us may be seen as products of ethnocentric education. According to Solon Kimball (1974), it is because of this kind of education that "few individuals possess the capacity to view themselves and the world around them either objectively or as parts of an interrelated system," and most individuals have been intellectually "isolated from new insights through adherence to established formulas, dogmas, or other rigid systems of beliefs" (p. 56).

An unfortunate consequence of ethnocentric education is that it robs people of respect for and appreciation of other cultural patterns and therefore robs them of the flexibility to utilize other ways of coping with a wide range of problems. Through comparative and analytic studies of other cultures, teachers can develop a broader perspective and critical understanding of these cultures and their alternative means of dealing with divergent human needs and problems. In the words of Robert Redfield (1973), anthropological studies may:

> lead the young person to look back upon his own culture from a vantage point secured in the understanding gained of other cultures and thus achieve that objectivity and capacity to consider thoughtfully his own conduct and the institutions of his own society which are, in part, a result of thinking as if within another culture. [Further, the individual will be able to] see that there are ways other than his own which are compatible with human needs and with the dignity of the individual . . . to develop the

power to think well about one's own way of life so that that way may be improved. (p. 205)

The liberalizing influence of anthropology is bound to have a positive impact on teacher education programs. Indeed, effective teaching in a pluralistic society such as America needs to be based on an understanding of the various ways in which cultural factors and conflict influence the pupils' modes of thinking, learning, communicating, and relating to others. The infusion of anthropological studies in teacher education is relevant and necessary, because by applying the insights of anthropology teachers may be helped to develop sensitivity to the varying patterns of motivation, intergroup and intragroup relationships, and the manners of relating school-taught concepts to out-of-school life (Greenberg, 1968). Ideally, the knowledge and skills to deal effectively with learning and behavioral difficulties stemming from cultural differences and conflicts should be integrated into the entire teacher education curriculum as a basis for formulating instructional strategies and resources to facilitate optimal learning for all.

USES OF ANTHROPOLOGICAL METHODS IN EDUCATION

A productive approach to applying anthropology in the study of education is to utilize the investigative methods of anthropology in educational inquiry. As might be inferred from the preceding discussions of the different branches of anthropology, anthropological studies use three major methods: (1) the field work approach, (2) the organismic approach, and (3) the comparative approach.

The Field Work Approach

The field work approach, first pioneered by Franz Boas (1858–1942), is based on the assumption that the most reliable data about cultural patterns should be obtained through objective observation of a society by an investigator who is also closely involved in the life of that society.

Ethnography and other qualitative field approaches to the study of education, such as observation and in-depth interviewing, have become increasingly popular over the past several years. The methodologies and the assumptions undergirding these approaches differ in several ways from the experimental designs that dominated research in education during much of the 20th century. Sherman and Webb (1988) identified several characteristics common to qualitative field studies. First, such studies are premised on the assumption that events can only be understood if they are seen in context. The contexts of inquiry are natural, not contrived or designed. Those who are studied are allowed to speak for themselves, to describe their perspectives and behaviors. Researchers attend to the experience as a whole, not to separate variables. In this way, researchers seek to understand experience holistically.

> . . . qualitative research implies a direct concern with experience as it is "lived" or "felt" or "undergone." . . . Qualitative research, then, has the aim of understanding experience as nearly as possible as its participants feel or live it. (Sherman & Webb, 1988, p. 7)

In this approach, the anthropologist becomes a participant as well as an objective observer. Observation in the field rather than the study of other people's reports is central to this method. While the field work approach is the most widely used anthropological method in education research, the other two approaches have also influenced research in education.

The Organismic Approach

The premise upon which the organismic approach rests is the belief that a culture should be seen as a living organism—an integrated system of institutions, folkways, and mores. Hence, a study of conditions or artifacts in any society must be done in the context of a culture as an integrated system. Because functions of the various sectors of a culture are all interrelated, changes in one area are bound to have ripple effects on the others. It is worth noting that two separate perspectives comprise the organismic approach. The structuralist view holds that societal needs provide the unifying force in people's lives. An early holder of this view was English anthropologist A. R. Radcliffe-Brown (1881–1955). The second perspective is founded on the belief that the individual's needs give the integrating thrust in human life. The best-known early holder of this view was Polish anthropologist Bronislav Malinowski (1884–1943). When the organismic approach is utilized in education, schools and classrooms may be seen as an independent culture or a social system. In this way we not only look for the characteristics that distinguish schools from other institutions, but we can also examine the influence of the school's unique values, customs, traditions, and behavioral norms on students. The effects of the school's general climate on the institution's instructional effectiveness can also be examined via the organismic approach.

Cultural Materialism

Although cultural materialism is not considered an organismic perspective, some attention should be given to this relatively new but major contemporary mode of anthropological thinking. Not unlike advocates of the organismic view, cultural materialists argue that culture should be seen as a system. As leading cultural anthropologist Marvin Harris points out, seemingly strange and irrational cultural practices in another society have rational bases when viewed as an integral part of a system. Moreover, what determines the nature of human institutions, social interactions, and even philosophies and religions is not ideals and logic but rather the manner in which the society stores and uses energy (Harris, 1968).

The East Indian belief in the sacred cows, which may seem irrational and self-defeating from the Western point of view, illustrates Harris's point. When seen as an integral part of the people's attempt to cope with the harsh ecological conditions for survival, however, the belief has a perfectly rational basis. Consider this: India is an agricultural land lacking many important natural resources, such as oil, coal, wood, and steel. In such an environment, using oxen as traction animals, their milk as a source of nutrition, and even dried cow dung as a source of fuel and floor covering material has provided an efficient and adaptive means of harnessing and using energy for survival. On the other hand, treating cattle as a main food source would have been an inefficient and maladaptive means of expending energy for livelihood. Eating beef would have deprived the people of many critical measures for living and perpetuating the Indian people. The religious significance of the cows then must have evolved from tales about their pivotal role in life that were passed on from one generation to another through informal education, for example, storytelling (Harris, 1974). In sum, the religious belief about the sacred cows did not originate from some theological or philosophical idea regarding the nature of reality, because "livelihood eventually dominates social organization, which in turn governs ideology and logic" (Burger, 1975, p. 107).

From the cultural materialist point of view, what is taught, how people learn, and how schools function are not determined by the ideals held by educators and philosophers, but rather by modes of harnessing and expending energy. Consequently, the ways of storing and using energy determine teacher-pupil, administrator-pupil, and even school-community relationships and define what constitutes usable technology, for example, computers, calculators, word processors, and other electrical or electronic hardware and software. Because cultural materialists are concerned with the efficient use of energy, they do not believe that cultures are relative or that all cultures are equally "good." Quite to the contrary, they insist that cultures can be compared with each other in terms of the efficiency with which energy is stored and used. For example, the efficiency of a culture can be measured by studying the amount of energy used in relation to the amount of food produced according to the long-term consequences. Similarly, cultures can be compared according to their use of human and technological resources in proportion to the effectiveness of their educational institutions.

It is important to note here that cultural materialism should be viewed more as a strategy for empirical study of human society than as a philosophical system such as Marxism. Marxism, also known as dialectical materialism, is founded on the assumption that the modes of producing and distributing goods determine the nature of social organization and human ideologies. Further, the dialectical process of the struggle between workers and their "masters" in a capitalistic society is believed to result in the inevitable destruction of the latter followed by the appearance of a classless society. Hence, dialectical materialism entails political activism, which cultural materialists consider inimical to an objective empirical investigation of human culture.

In respect to the place of cultural materialism in education, the specific implications of this point of view for educational plans and strategies and teacher education have yet to be worked out. However, cultural materialism as a fundamental perspective may give us a unique insight into the connection between culture and education. In an era in which technological changes are rampant and their influence pervasive, the findings of cultural materialists ought to be taken seriously for an explanation of the present and possible control of the future.

The Comparative Approach

As the term itself suggests, advocates of the comparative approach study cultures by comparing a set of data from a particular culture with similar information about other cultures. Studies in international and comparative education are examples of the comparative approach applied to educational inquiry. In recent years, many educators and the public have been interested in learning about the Japanese educational system. This curiosity comes partly from the fact that compared to our schoolchildren, Japanese pupils are significantly more proficient in mathematics and science. Some argue that Japanese children in general are better educated than American children. In investigating the relative effectiveness of Japanese and American schools, we may compare the impact of respective cultures on children's attitudes toward schooling, teachers, intellectual activities, learning, and other people. In the area of school administration, data regarding the behavioral norms for interpersonal relationships in Japanese and American cultures may tell us about the nature of administrator-teacher and teacher-pupil relationships as they impinge upon teaching-learning effectiveness. Through this kind of study, we may find that transplanting an educational measure from another culture may not be helpful to our society. On the contrary, such an action may lead us to other unsuspected but more serious difficulties. Cross-cultural studies of education can enable us to avoid counterproductive research studies and self-defeating educational practices.

Although each of the three approaches of anthropological studies just discussed has its own distinctive features, more than one approach could be used in educational inquiry. For example, in doing a comparative study of Japanese and American schools, one may use ethnographic as well as ethnological techniques in analyzing the different systems. Empirical studies of effective schools or bilingualism may follow the field work approach and the comparative method. Though not detailed here, the historical approach (comparing the present with the past) in the study of cultural development is indeed applicable to the study of educational institutions and their functions. All in all, when we consider the complex and intricate relationship between culture and education, cross-cultural approaches in educational inquiry and teacher education play a pivotal role.

Implications for Practitioners

While teachers are generally not prepared to do full-scale anthropological research, some of the skills of anthropological research can serve classroom teachers in their efforts to become more effective. For example, a teacher beginning a new job might approach the new school as a field site. Through systematic observation and listening and the use of field notes to record impressions and information, the new teacher can begin to understand the culture of the school. What are the expectations and beliefs that guide the behaviors of the participants in the school culture? What does the new teacher have to do to fit in or to avoid counterproductive practices? What are the routines of the school? How are decisions made and conflicts resolved? Who holds informal power? What routines and practices exist to support or work against effective teaching practices? If one can begin to understand the school as a system with a history, one can begin to see and understand the reasons for particular practices. This understanding can help practitioners step outside the values and behaviors of the field site that are taken for granted in order to evaluate them for their impact on teaching and learning.

The school itself is a cultural site; in addition, the students are members of cultures to which the teacher may not belong. Learning about the communities of students who are culturally different from the teacher can help him or her communicate more effectively with them. This can mean reading about different cultures, but it can also mean talking with parents and others in the community, observing the neighborhood, and participating in local events—in short, getting involved with cultural groups in nonjudgmental ways in order to better understand the learners. Even when students are members of the same race, class, and ethnic group as the teacher, they are still members of their own youth culture. Understanding young people means listening and observing in order to better see the world as they see it. While effective teachers don't act like adolescents or children, at least not on the job, they are able to understand the world from the perspective of their students and to find ways to make learning more meaningful to them. Seeing students as part of cultural systems and being willing to learn about those systems are important characteristics of effective teachers.

CASE STUDY

This case study has a twofold purpose. One is to help readers become aware of the variety and complexity of factors that may contribute to the education of an individual or a group. The other is to stimulate readers to reflect critically about the types of questions we need to raise and the kinds of anthropological methods we may use in attempting to account for the educational achievement of a particular group. Suggested discussion questions are given after the following excerpts from a *Time* magazine article.

THE NEW WHIZ KIDS: ASIAN AMERICANS

Some are refugees from sad countries torn apart by war. Others are children of the stable middle class whose parents came to the U.S. in search of a better life. Some came with nothing, not even the rudiments of English. Others came with skills and affluence. Many were born in the U.S. to immigrant parents. No matter what their route, young Asian Americans, largely those with Chinese, Korean and Indochinese backgrounds, are setting the educational pace for the rest of America and cutting a dazzling figure at the country's finest schools. Consider some of this fall's freshman classes: at Brown it will be 9% Asian American, at Harvard nearly 14%, the Massachusetts Institute of Technology 20%, the California Institute of Technology 21% and the University of California, Berkeley an astonishing 25%.

By almost every educational gauge, young Asian Americans are soaring. They are finishing way above the mean on the math section of the Scholastic Aptitude Test and . . . outscoring their peers of other races in high school grade-point averages. [According to the *Chronicle of Higher Education,* the 1987 SAT verbal scores for Asian Americans and whites are 405 and 447, respectively. Scores for the math section are 523 for Asian Americans and 489 for whites *(Chronicle,* 1987). There have been virtually no changes in the verbal scores of Asian Americans since 1975.] They spend more time on their homework, . . . take more advanced high school courses and graduate with more credits than other American students. . . .

. . . In only two decades Asian Americans have become the fastest-growing U.S. minority, numbering more than 5 million, or about 2% of the population. . . . In 1965 a new immigration law did away with exclusionary quotas. That brought a surge of largely middle-class Asian professionals—doctors, engineers and academics. . . . In 1975, after the end of the Viet Nam War, 130,000 refugees, mostly from the educated middle class, began arriving. Three years later a second wave of 650,000 Indochinese started their journey from rural and poor areas to refugee camps to the towns and cities of America.

As the children of these immigrants began moving up through the nation's schools, it became clear that a new class of academic achievers was emerging. One dramatic indication: since 1981, 20 Asian-American students have been among the 70 scholarship winners in the Westinghouse Science Talent Search, the nation's oldest and most prestigious high school science competition. . . .

Such achievements are reflected in the nation's best universities, where math, science and engineering departments have taken on a decidedly Asian character. . . .

The stereotype of Asian Americans as narrow mathematical paragons is unfair, however, and inaccurate. Many are far from being liberal arts illiterates. . . . Many Asian-American students excel in the arts, from photography to music. New York City's famed Juilliard School has a student body estimated to be 25% Asian and Asian American.

Many Asian Americans come from an educated elite in their native countries. Their children seem to do especially well. . . .

How then to explain the accomplishment of children whose refugee parents were less well educated? One claim is that Asians are simply smarter than other groups. A subscriber to this theory is Arthur Jensen, a controversial Berkeley educational psychologist. Jensen tested Asian children—500 in San Francisco and 8,000 in Hong Kong—then compared the results with tests of 1,000 white American children in Bakersfield, Calif. He contends that the children with Asian backgrounds averaged ten I.Q. points higher than the whites, and believes there are "genetic differences" in the rate at which Asians and whites mature mentally.

Most researchers are unconvinced by the natural-superiority argument. But many do believe there is something in Asian culture that breeds success, perhaps Confucian ideals that stress family values and emphasize education. . . . By comparison, . . . Laotians and Cambodians, who do somewhat less well, have a gentler, Buddhist approach to life.

Both the genetic and the cultural explanations for academic success worry Asian Americans because of fears that they feed racial stereotyping. Many can remember when Chinese, Japanese and Filipino immigrants were the victims of undisguised public ostracism and discriminatory laws. . . . "Years ago," complains Virginia Kee, a high school teacher in New York's Chinatown, "they used to think you were Fu Manchu or Charlie Chan. Then they thought you must own a laundry or restaurant. Now they think all we know how to do is sit in front of a computer." Says Thomas Law, a student at Brooklyn Law School: "We are sick and tired of being seen as the exotic Orientals."

The performance of Asian Americans also triggers resentment and tension. "Anti-Asian activity in the form of violence, vandalism, harassment and intimidation continues to occur across the nation," the U.S. Civil Rights Commission declared last year.

To be that good and face rejection is tough for anyone, but seems more difficult for many Asian Americans. . . . To some Asian Americans (and their parents), being only "very good" is tantamount to failure. In 1982, . . . a Cambodian student at South Boston High School, overwhelmed by the pressure of school and adjustment to a new country, tried to take her own life. She was one of eight Cambodians at South Boston who attempted suicide that year. . . .

Asking for help is not easy for Asian Americans. "They are likely to say that willpower can resolve problems," explains psychologist Stanley Sue, who has specialized in their emotional difficulties. He has found that the problems of these young people "are highly submerged" because they have been "taught not to exhibit emotions in public." [Psychologist Jeanne] Nidorf notes that youthful Indochinese are so conditioned to polite behavior that they hesitate to complain. . . . Indeed, the view of Asian Americans as passive and obedient is a stereotype that teachers tend to reinforce by not urging students to express themselves. . . .

Ultimately, assimilation may diminish achievement. The Rumbaut-Ima [sociologists Ruben G. Rumbaut and Kenji Ima] data from San Diego show lower grade-point averages for Chinese-, Korean- and Japanese-American students whose families speak primarily English at home compared with those whose families do not. The *New York Times* has reported that a Chicago study of Asian Americans found third-generation students had blended more into the mainstream, had a lower academic performance and were less interested in school. . . .

. . . The largely successful Asian-American experience is a challenging counterpoint to the charges that U.S. schools are now producing less-educated mainstream students and failing to help underclass blacks and Hispanics. One old lesson apparently still holds. "It really doesn't matter where you come from or what your language is," observes educational historian Diane Ravitch. "If you arrive with high aspirations and self-discipline, schools are a path to upward mobility."

Source: From "The New Whiz Kids: Why Asian Americans Are Doing So Well, and What It Costs Them," by David Brand, August 31, 1987, *Time,* pp. 42–51. Copyright 1987 by Time Inc. Reprinted by permission.

QUESTIONS

How would the answers to the following questions help you explain why Asian Americans are doing so well in school and at what cost they pay for their educational performance?

1. Asian Americans come from several different nationality groups. What common cultural characteristics could you infer from the information given in the *Time* excerpts and how are they related to the academic achievements of Asian Americans? Could such characteristics have anything to do with the Asian-American young people's choice of academic fields and future occupations?
2. What possible connection could there be between the socioeconomic status and educational backgrounds of the Asian- American parents and their children's academic achievement?

3. What possible role do religions, for example, Confucianism and Buddhism, play in the education of Asian-American youth?

4. What impact might ethnic stereotyping have on the education of Asian-American and other minority students?

5. What is your estimate of Arthur Jensen's genetic explanation of the differences in the IQ scores of Asian Americans and whites? What environmental or cultural explanations could be given for such differences?

6. If psychologist Sue is correct in saying that Asian Americans have been taught not to express their emotions, what types of teacher-student, parent-child, or adult-youth relationships might you infer from this fact? Could you draw any inferences about the nature of child-rearing practices among Asian-American families? What attitudes toward education, schooling, and teachers might develop from such practices?

7. On the average, scores of Asian Americans in the verbal section of SAT from 1975 to 1987 have been more than 40 points below the average verbal score of whites (*Chronicle*, 1987). Could this discrepancy be attributed to certain cultural factors? Could there be any relationship between the lower verbal scores of Asian Americans and the selection patterns of their occupational and academic fields?

8. If assimilation seems to lower the achievement level of Asian Americans, what could you say about the role of culture in learning?

9. If Asian-American students have done well in school, why have American schools been less successful in helping other minority young people to do better academically?

10. Even if Ravitch is correct in saying that high aspirations and self-discipline enable people to move upward through schools, could we argue that the sources of motivation for learning vary from culture to culture? If this is true, how could our schools help minority children to have higher aspirations and more self-discipline? What explanations might be given for the Asian-American young people's motivational level?

11. Which of the anthropological methods discussed in this chapter might you use to answer the question "What makes Asian Americans succeed in school?"

12. What other kinds of questions might you need to raise to obtain additional information or explain why Asian Americans are doing well in school and what it costs them?

REFERENCES

Burger, H. (1975). Cultural materialism: Efficiencies not descriptions. General Systems, 20, 107–19. This article provides an excellent summary and review of Marvin Harris's book, *The Rise of Anthropological Theory.*

The Chronicle of Higher Education. (1987, September 30).

Gould, J., & Kolb, W. L. (Eds.). (1964). *A dictionary of the social sciences.* New York: Free Press.

Greenberg, N. C. (1968). Cross-cultural implications for teachers. In J. H. Chilcott, N. C. Greenberg, & H. B. Wilson (Eds.), *Readings in the socio-cultural foundations of education* (pp. 146–152). Belmont, IL: Wadsworth.

Harrington, C. (1979). *Psychological anthropology: A delineation of a field of inquiry.* New York: AMS Press.

Harris, M. (1968). *The rise of anthropological theory.* New York: Thomas Y. Crowell.

Harris, M. (1974). *Cows, pigs, wars, and witches: The riddles of culture.* New York: Random House.

Ianni, F. A. J. (1967). Anthropology: The study of Man. In F. A. J. Ianni (Ed.), *Culture, system, and behavior* (pp. 25–48). Chicago: Science Research Associates.

Kimball, S. T. (1974). *Culture and the educative process.* New York: Teachers College Press.

Paulsen, R. F. (1968). Cultural anthropology and education. In J. H. Chilcott, N. C. Greenberg, & H. B. Wilson (Eds.), *Readings in the socio-cultural foundations of education* (pp. 12–19). Belmont, IL: Wadsworth.

Redfield, R. (1973). The contribution of anthropology to the education of teachers. In F. A. J. Ianni & E. Storey (Eds.), *Cultural relevance and educational issues* (pp. 153–159). Boston: Little, Brown & Co.

Sherman, R., & Webb, R. (1988). *Qualitative research in education: Focus and methods.* London: Falmer Press.

Spindler, G. D. (1973). Anthropology and education: An overview. In F. A. J. Ianni & E. Storey (Eds.), *Cultural relevance and educational issues* (pp. 94–115). Boston: Little, Brown & Co. For a historical overview of anthropology in education see "Theory, Research and Application in Educational Anthropology" by Elizabeth M. Storey, in *Education and Cultural Process* (2nd ed.) edited by George D. Spindler, Prospect Heights, IL, published by Waveland Press in 1987, and George D. Spindler's "Anthropology and Education: An Overview," in *Cultural Relevance and Educational Issues,* edited by Francis A. J. Ianni and Edward Storey, published by Little, Brown and Company in 1973.

Spindler, G. D. (Ed.). (1982). *Doing the ethnography of schooling: Educational anthropology in action.* Prospect Heights, IL: Waveland Press.

2

Culture, Education, and Schooling

As has already been suggested, education as a process does not stand for any specific set of activities, such as reading, writing, and figuring; rather, it signifies a deliberate attempt on the part of a group or society to transmit something worthwhile to its members. This transmission may be carried on informally by parents, relatives, and peers or formally through institutions specifically designed for instructional purposes, such as schools and churches. As one author put it, "Education is the instrument through which the members of a society assure themselves that the behavior necessary to continue their culture is learned" (Quillen, 1963, p. 50). If education is indeed a cultural process, we must first clarify the meaning of *culture*.

WHAT IS CULTURE?

Culture as a System of Norms and Control

In general terms, culture is most commonly viewed as that pattern of knowledge, skills, behaviors, attitudes, and beliefs, as well as material artifacts, produced by a human society and transmitted from one generation to another. Culture is the whole of humanity's intellectual, social, technological, political, economic, moral, religious, and aesthetic accomplishments. Although it is absurd to speak of a culturally deprived child as if there could be a child without any culture, this notion was used in the 1960s and the 1970s to describe many minority children for whom compensatory education was designed. But more of this later.

Central to the concept of culture is the fact that any culture is goal oriented.

> These goals are expressed, patterned, lived out by people in their behaviors and aspirations in the form of value—objects or possessions, conditions of existence, features of personality or characters and states of mind, that are conceived as desirable, and act as motivating determinants of behaviors. (Spindler, 1963, p. 132)

Hence, culture is more than a collection of disconnected acts and beliefs; rather, it should be seen as an integrated set of norms or standards by which human behaviors, beliefs, and thinking are organized. According to Clifford Geertz (1973):

> Culture is best seen not as complexes of concrete behavior patterns—customs, usages, traditions, habit clusters, as has been the case up to now, but as a set of control mechanisms—plans, recipes, rules, instructions (what computer engineers call "programs")—for governing of behavior. (p. 44)

Culture should, then, be viewed as consisting of the standards and control mechanisms with which members of a society assign meanings, values, and significance to things, events, and behaviors. These norms and control mechanisms are the products of human beings' unique ability to symbol, or to "originate, determine, and bestow meaning upon things and events in the external world and the ability to comprehend such meanings" (White & Dillingham, 1973, p. 1). An ordinary cow becomes a sacred cow and plain water becomes holy water because human beings give them special meanings and significance. This means that the meaning and significance of objects, events, and behavioral patterns should be understood and appreciated within a specific cultural context rather than in terms of their supposed intrinsic properties. As we shall see later, symboling, or the process by which people bestow meanings on objects and actions within a specific culture, has many important implications in education.

According to Leslie A. White and Beth Dillingham (1973), the process of symboling occurs through thinking, feeling, and acting. The corresponding products—ideas, attitudes, acts, and objects—are indigenous to a culture (p. 27). The patterns of behaviors found in various societies have no inherent meaning apart from their cultural settings, for such patterns are reflections of unique worldviews and value orientations belonging to individual societies. For example, Navajo Indians are said to have a passive view of human beings; they say that "death is taking place within John," implying that human beings belong to a world in which forces of nature make "things" happen to people. On the other hand, white Western people are said to have an active (or aggressive) conception of people; they regard the individual as an agent who causes events to occur in the world, who does "things" to his or her world. Thus, a person in Western society would speak of John dying as if dying were something that a person performs. Similarly, the lack of an appropriate expression for complimenting one's grandmother in certain Far Eastern languages reflects the hierarchical nature of social organizations that do not permit the young to commend their elders directly. In dealing with different cultural beliefs and the behavioral patterns arising from them, we must always take into account the basis of their symboling process.

There is probably no definitive answer explaining why a particular culture assigns certain meanings and worth to a given set of events, objects, or acts. But we can reasonably assume that the dominant worldview of a society is a major source of meanings and values. In turn, a prevailing worldview of a culture results from certain experiences that have enabled a group of people to successfully solve the problems of daily living. In a very important sense, a culture is a conception of what reality is like and how it works.

Virtually no aspect of human life and its processes is unaffected by culture. So pervasive is the influence of culture that even our perception of colors and shapes cannot escape its effects. As Russian psychologist A. R. Luria (1976) points out, although there are only 20 or 25 names for colors and shapes, the human eye can distinguish up to two or three million different hues and shapes. This means a person perceiving a particular color or shape must identify its primary property and place it in a color or shape category. Thus, perception is not merely a physiological or neurological process. "Seeing" a color or a shape requires making decisions about the category into which a given hue or shape is to be placed. Of course, the number and categories available to a person depend on the language system being used. As Luria puts it:

> Once we recognize that perception is a complex cognitive activity employing auxiliary devices and involving the intimate participation of language, we must radically alter the classical notion of perception as an unmediated process depending only on the relatively simple laws of natural science.
>
> We can thus conclude that, structurally, perception depends on historically established human practices that can alter the system of codes used to process incoming information and can influence the decision assigning the perceived objects to appropriate categories. (p. 21)

Similarly, perception of pain is reported to be dependent on the linguistic categories available to the person as well as the extent to which a particular culture encourages or discourages the expression of one's thoughts and feelings. What all this suggests is that people who live in a culture different from ours may "see" the world differently, for the nature of language and its uses are central to any culture.

The symboling process just discussed occurs not only in the large society but also takes place within its many subunits. These subunits may be social, political, intellectual, economic, educational, religious, racial, ethnic, or generational (chronological). Consequently, a society can be said to have many subcultures or minority cultures, such as Mexican-American culture, African-American culture, the youth culture, the school culture, and the culture of the poor, each with its own value orientations. Standards and controls of each society or group are established because they enable individuals to deal with the needs and problems arising out of their environment and their associations with others. Cultures then can be seen as different ways of coping with essentially similar problems and needs. They represent various societies' successful experiments in living, which have been developed over time. Human beings become individuals "under the guidance of cultural patterns, historically created systems of meaning in terms of which we give form, order, point and direction to our lives" (Benedict, 1934, p. 278). The culture to which one belongs, then, becomes the root of the individual's identity, because culture gives us a sense of power and confidence by giving us the basis of achieving our goals, determining what is desirable and undesirable, and developing the purpose of our life. Accordingly, to reject or demean a person's cultural heritage is to do psychological and moral violence to the dignity and worth of that individual. Assuming that cultures are various societies' successful experiments in living, it would be unreasonable to argue that any one set of cultural norms is universally good for all societies or is inherently superior to all other cultures, nor should we think that any ideas, attitudes, acts, events, or objects have fixed and absolute meaning and worth.

Culture as a Map

As fundamental as culture is to human life and society, understanding a culture, even if it is our own, does not enable us to know every detail of how a particular group of people acts, thinks, and lives. Nor can we have information about how every segment of a society functions because, as Clyde Kluckhohn (1968) pointed out, "Culture is like a map. A map just isn't the territory but an abstract description of trends toward uniformity in the words, deeds, and artifacts of a human group. If a map is accurate and you can read it, you won't get lost: if you know a culture, you will know your way around in the life of a society" (p. 35). Though we cannot know all the details of either our own or another people's cultural map, an understanding of the general terrains of the society's culture would help us to be more effective in relating to others and achieving our own purposes. For example, by knowing the cultural maps of our students, we can better facilitate the conditions for effective learning for them, because we can more accurately predict and guide the students' behaviors in teaching-learning situations.

Although culture as a map contains explicit information about the norms and controls of a society, many dos and don'ts are not expressed in a clearly observable way. These cultural standards are implicit and must be inferred through observation of certain consistent and persistent patterns of thinking and acting. For example, in American culture the belief that hard work will lead to success is explicitly manifested in the ways in which we teach our children about the importance of the work-success ethic. But the fairly widely held view that those who do not succeed are either lazy or stupid has to be inferred from the ways in which people generally treat those who do not succeed socioeconomically. In a society in which the hierarchical relationships between individuals are believed to be of central importance, many language forms and rules of conduct clearly indicate what is or is not socially and even morally acceptable. In such a culture, children's unwillingness or inability to express their feelings and thoughts in front of their parents or their refusal to maintain direct eye contact with an adult during conversation implicitly reflects the fundamental importance of the hierarchical relationships. What this implies is that we learn the norms of our culture through direct instructions about explicit cultural standards, but we also acquire our society's culturally sanctioned ways through learning certain specific behaviors. We also learn our cultural norms through the ways in which people relate to each other and in which teaching is carried on.

In regard to the importance of implicit culture and how cultural norms can be learned latently, the following words are most instructive:

> Often, what the organization does in the name of its stated goals is of less cultural import—and of less particular concern to participants—than the more latent aspect of operations. . . .
>
> . . . In schools, for example, the manifest organizational function is primarily instruction in the "Three Rs," yet the experience of schooling exposes the child to a much broader "hidden curriculum" of values, norms and social skills. A child's success in schools is as much dependent on his or her mastering the content of the hidden curriculum as it is on his mastering the formal curriculum. (Sieber & Gordon, 1981, pp. 6–7)

For educators, an analysis of the manner in which education is carried on is at least as important as the explicitly stated goals and content of education, because the means or the methods of teaching and educating also inculcate beliefs and attitudes.

More specifically, the modes of social and personal interaction in the school are affected by the cultural conditions of the larger society. The ways in which adult members of the society deal with children are likely to be reflected in the teacher's approach to evaluating students' achievements and failures. Similarly, if a culture contains contradictory beliefs and practices, these may be transmitted to students unless the school consciously and deliberately points out and reduces, or eliminates, such contradictions. For example, Americans generally believe that one should always be truthful. But many people also believe that it is all right to "cheat" a little on their income tax returns or to make campaign promises even though they may not be able to fulfill them. At an elementary school, a candidate for the presidency of the student council promised to put Coca-Cola machines in every classroom and provide longer and more frequent recess periods if he were elected to the office. The boy was elected, but the school officials regarded the boy's tactic as merely humorous and imaginative. Although the purpose of forming a student council may have been to teach children the meaning of fair play and the democratic process in operation, the school actually may have helped teach them that whatever means one uses to attain one's goal are justifiable.

CORE VALUES

There are people who believe that the primary function of our schools is to transmit societal values; others insist that the schools ought to be the agent of social reform (transformation). Still others argue that the schools should be agents of both cultural transmission and transformation. Regardless of how we view the proper role of our schools, we cannot deny the fact that, intentionally or unintentionally, the prevailing values, attitudes, and behavioral norms of our society are transmitted to the young through what schools do. It is for this reason that we need to examine the concept of core values in relation to education and schooling.

In attempting to deal with its daily problems, each society develops certain patterns of behavior and attitudes that are useful in meeting human needs and resolving conflicts between individuals and groups. When these patterns become well defined (and even institutionalized) and accepted by the dominant group within a society, they constitute what anthropologist George Spindler calls the core values of a culture. These core values become the basis for the standard with which the major institutions of the dominant society evaluate their members. These standards in turn become the criteria for giving people opportunities for advancement and other rewards. The academic as well as the social expectations our schools have of the young are rooted in the core values of our society. However, the core values of the mainstream society are surrounded by other alternative (minority) patterns that often challenge or at least radically differ from the norms of the dominant group. Consequently, the possibility of maintaining social cohesion and cultural diversity depends on the dominant group's ability to deal with value conflicts arising from divergent alternative cultural patterns.

The Core Values of American Culture

Before turning attention to forces challenging the core values constituting the American conception of the good life, traditionally referred to as the WASP (white Anglo-Saxon Protestant) or the Anglo-American perspective, it may be helpful to examine some of these core values. According to Spindler (1963), the traditional values that make up the core of the Anglo-American pattern fall into the following five general categories: (1) Puritan morality, (2) work-success ethic, (3) individualism, (4) achievement orientation, and (5) future-time orientation (pp. 134-136).

Puritan morality stresses respectability, thrift, self-denial, duty, delayed gratification, and sexual restraint. The second traditional value, the so-called *work-success ethic,* is the belief not only that people should work hard to succeed but also that those who have not become successful are either lazy or stupid or both. Hence, people must constantly work diligently to convince themselves of their worth. *Individualism,* the third value, emphasizes the sacredness of the individual, which ideally should lead to self-reliance and originality. However, it often manifests itself in a form of egocentrism and disregard for other people's rights and desires. It is this individualism coupled with the work-success ethic that leads many to view welfare programs as giveaways to people who are lazy and unworthy of help. The fourth value, *achievement orientation,* relates to the work-success ethic in that everyone should constantly try to achieve a higher goal through hard work. An individual should not be satisfied with a given position but should always seek something higher and better. The last traditional value, *future-time orientation,* is summed up in the attitude of "save today for tomorrow." The stereotyped image of the teacher as a stern drillmaster who encourages children to respect their elders, work hard for tomorrow's success, and always reach for higher and higher grades reflects these traditional values.

These five values are only broad categories that can be further elaborated on to indicate numerous implications for daily living. But, of course, it is enough to point out that the most fundamental trait of these traditional values is that they are regarded as absolute and fixed. Hence, they are believed to constitute the idealized norm of behavior for all Americans and perhaps for all humanity. It is for this reason that we may say that the holders of these values are ethnocentric.

Challenges to the Core Values

Mid-1950s to Early 1960s

As a result of complex and rapid socioeconomic, political, and technological changes in our society, a number of forces challenging the validity of these core values have arisen. According to a study of several hundred students enrolled in professional education courses and representing lower-middle-class to upper-middle-class socioeconomic status in the early 1960s, the core values of college students had shifted considerably from those of their parents. Unlike their parents, the subjects held as their core values (1) sociability, (2) a relativistic moral attitude, (3) consideration for others, (4) a hedonistic present-time orientation, and (5) conformity to the group (Spindler, 1963, pp. 132-147).

Sociability means liking people and being able to get along well with them. A relativistic moral attitude is the belief that what is moral is relative to the group to which one belongs. To be considerate of others means being sensitive to and having tolerance for other people's feelings so that the harmony of the group is not disturbed. Hedonistic, present-time orientation is the opposite of the traditional future-time orientation of Puritan morality. It is said to come from the notion that since no one can be certain about tomorrow, we should enjoy the present, a sort of "eat, drink, and be merry, for tomorrow we die" attitude. Yet even this fourth value was to be carried out within the limits of the norm set by the group. The last value, conformity to the group, emphasizes the importance of group harmony as the ultimate goal of individual members.

In the 1960s, conflicts between parents and school officials steeped in the Puritan morality and youth were unavoidable because their value orientations were so contradictory. Yet no serious confrontations occurred between those two generations because the young were more concerned with balance, adjustment, and harmony than with individualism, spontaneity, and autonomy. Since the completion of Spindler's study, increasing evidence has suggested that the value orientation of youth has continued to move even further from the value systems of their parents. Today even a casual conversation with upper grade school and junior high school children reveals their strong belief in the individual's right to privacy and freedom. The significant change in the value commitments of young people may have been partially due to the student activism and counterculture movement of the mid-1960s. And although today's adolescents and college youths may tend to conform more to adult demands and norms, the flame of their doubts about the legitimacy of the traditional core values of American society continues to burn. It is to this condition that we may attribute some fundamental changes in certain areas of young people's value orientation.

Mid-1960s to 1970

The proponents of the counterculture movement in the mid-1960s argued that although America had achieved an unprecedented economic affluence through the work-success and achievement ethics, it continued to emphasize economic success and productivity. As a result of this endless search for greater and greater affluence, even the worth of an individual was said to have been determined according to success and productivity as defined by corporations and industry. But to growing numbers of young people the long-sought economic affluence and security became simple facts of life. They were no longer legitimate objects to be achieved. Consequently, the young were convinced that the core values of the older generation, that is, the cultural values of the industrial ethic, were outdated and irrelevant to their lives.

Once the society is able to demonstrate that it can produce enough for all its members, its primary concern should not be to produce more and consume more. The supporters of the counterculture movement insisted that we develop a more just and equal means of distributing the nation's wealth so that more peoples' lives could be meaningful and leisurely. The young people of the mid-1960s were not against technology, but rather against the worship of it, because a technology-worshiping culture tends to treat people as products of a technological system and to subordinate human needs to industrial and technological needs. To the advocates of the counterculture movement, the moral imperatives and urgency behind production, acquisition, materialism, and greater economic affluence had lost their validity. At the same time, the authorities (adults) who subscribed to the traditional values had lost their legitimacy. These and other similar warnings against the dehumanization of individuals were increasingly heard in the 1980s.

For the young to believe that they had been oppressed by their elders was nothing new and perhaps is to be expected in almost any period in history. But for youth to view authority as illegitimate was something new. One of the consequences of this phenomenon was that with the declining legitimacy of the authorities there was a rise in coercive violence launched by terrified authorities to maintain their threatened power. Moreover, because the young were convinced of the illegitimacy of the Establishment and its values, they struggled against institutional conformity, centralized power, and uniformity of any kind.

The demand for radical cultural revolution by the young in the mid- to late-1960s appeared in the form of increased requests for the governed to become actively involved in political, economic, and social processes. Students also sought opportunities to participate in their own educational experience and planning. Idiosyncratic lifestyle and personal grooming were said to symbolize their revolt against uniformity, and marijuana smoking was believed to be a ritual action by which they asserted a new moral position.

The counterculture movement is no longer a potent force among America's youth. But young people's desires for privacy, autonomy, and greater involvement in participatory democracy have not changed. The younger generation today still questions the legitimacy of the traditional values, even though many are willing to conform more to the adult norm because of current insecurities related to finding and keeping jobs and because of anxieties related to the general political, social, and economic uncertainties of the time.

Early 1970s to Early 1980s

According to a 1971 survey of 1,244 students in 50 college and university campuses by the firm of Daniel Yankelovich, Inc., over 75% mentioned that they were chiefly concerned with friendship, privacy, freedom of opinion, and nature *(Kansas City Star,* 1972, p. 4). Only about 25% still regarded changing society and combating hypocrisy as their primary interest. These data seem to suggest that college students had moved away from emotional involvement in social and political causes. They appeared to be channeling their efforts to those aspects of their lives over which they could have more control. The findings also showed that these students were less willing than those in the 1960s to fight wars for any reason; 50% of the participants saw war as justified only if it were for counteracting aggression. Perhaps the greatest single erosion of relations to authority was in the "boss" relationship: Only 36% of the young people did not mind being "bossed around" on the job. Moreover, in 1971 only 39% held the belief that "hard work always pays off," whereas a 1968 survey by Yankelovich had shown that 69% believed that "hard work will always pay off" (Yankelovich, 1981, p. 7). This shift from the traditional work-success ideal was indeed radical. In regard to sex, the 1971 group generally sought a much greater degree of sexual freedom and its acceptance by their elders. In summing up the study, a majority of the participants believed that American democracy or justice did not function evenhandedly, and that a considerable degree of inconsistency existed between American ideals and practices.

A survey conducted by the University of California at Los Angeles and the American Council on Education suggested that college freshmen in 1973 tended to be more liberal and were more inclined to support greater freedom for students than their predecessors. This study polled more than 318,000 students at 579 institutions; from this population 190,000 were statistically adjusted to represent the nation's 1.65 million freshmen *(Kansas City Star,* 1974, p. 15). In general, the findings of this study did not indicate any significant changes in the young people's attitudes from those found in the Yankelovich survey.

Although it is true that the studies conducted by both Yankelovich and UCLA and the American Council on Education dealt primarily with college students, their cumulative data since 1968 indicate a major shift in the core values of a sizable segment of American youth. Data from two major national studies by Joseph Veroff, Elizabeth Douvan, and Richard A. Kulka (1981) and Daniel Yankelovich (1981) also show a significant erosion in the general public's belief in the intrinsic worth of hard work. These studies also support earlier findings showing that a large segment of Americans sought greater personal freedom and fulfillment of personal inner desires. More indirectly, the extraordinary number of "pop psychology" books on self-improvement reflected people's preoccupation with self-fulfillment in the late 1970s into the early 1980s.

Mid-1980s to Early 1990s

Surveys of freshmen in two- and four-year colleges and universities in 1988 and in 1994 revealed an interesting combination of attitudes and values. The findings from the 1988 study, which were culled from 209,627 responses, indicated that "being very well-off financially" was one of the top goals of 75.6% of those polled, "up from 73.2% in 1986 and 70.9% in 1985, and nearly twice the 1970 figure of 39.1%" (*The Chronicle*, 1988, p. 34). In the similar 1994 survey, which reported the responses of 237,777 freshmen, 73.7% of the respondents indicated that "being very well-off financially" was a very important goal (*The Chronicle*, 1995, p. A31). This inclination toward financial well-being is also reflected in the finding that over 69% in 1988 and 72.4% in 1994 said they "agree strongly or somewhat" that the chief benefit of attending college is increased earnings. It is worth noting that "becoming a business executive" was the career occupation most often preferred by respondents in the 1988 survey (13.1%). In the 1994 survey, however, becoming an engineer was the most frequently cited occupation choice (7.1%), while those expressing interest in becoming business executives had declined to 6.9%. In the 1994 survey, 12.1% of the respondents were "undecided" about their probable careers. On the other hand, "developing a meaningful philosophy of life" was selected as an important goal by 42.7% of the respondents in 1994. This is up from 39.4% in the 1988 survey, but down from 82.9% in 1967.

Politically, most students in both surveys described themselves as "middle of the road." In 1994, 52.6% of the students polled described themselves as "moderate." Although this represents a decline from 56% in 1988, only 22.4% of respondents in 1994 described themselves as "conservative" or "far right." This is a small percentage given that 1994 was a year in which conservatives made considerable electoral gains. However, only 31.9% of the respondents in 1994 said that "keeping up with political affairs" was a very important goal. This figure was the lowest recorded in the 29-year history of this annual survey of freshmen (*The Chronicle*, 1995, p. 29). Despite this expressed apathy toward politics and a political climate in the nation that suggested that many Americans wanted less regulation from the federal government, 84% of the 1994 freshmen indicated that "the federal government is not doing enough to control environmental pollution"; 71.8% said "the federal government is not doing enough to protect the consumer from faulty goods and services"; and nearly 80% said "the federal government should do more to control the sale of handguns." And despite the reports of a more conservative political climate, almost 60% of the 1994 freshmen polled said they believed that "abortion should be legal"; 70.5% agreed that a "national health care plan is needed to cover everyone's medical costs"; and 67.3% agreed that "wealthy people should pay a larger share of the taxes than they do now." On the other hand, 73% agreed that "there is too much concern in the courts for the rights of criminals," and 80.6% agreed that "employers should be allowed to require drug testing of employees or job applicants." It would appear that the views of college students by the mid-1990s reflected a mix of liberal and traditional values.

In the 1990s, the behaviors of young people continued to represent challenges to traditional core values. According to 1992 reports issued by the U.S. Department of Health, Education and Welfare (Wiles & Bondi, 1993, pp. 41–43) by age 19, 69% of all teenagers have had intercourse, one in three adolescents is a problem drinker, and 25% to 30% of all fourth graders feel some pressure to use alcohol and other dangerous drugs. Between 1980 and 1990, the average age for beginning smokers dropped from 14 to 10. In that same time period, the second leading cause of death among teenagers, after accidents, was suicide.

These statistics suggest that today's young adolescents are worried about and experimenting with sex, substance use, and other related issues at a much earlier age than their predecessors. When we consider that more than 85% of the parents of these young people claim to be moderate to conservative in their value orientation, these findings are particularly significant (Search Institute, 1983, p. 27). It would appear that there is reasonably good ground for wondering whether or not the schools and parents are able to help adolescents deal effectively with matters that are likely to have a profound impact on their lives.

In spite of the fact that several forces are challenging the validity of the traditional core values, the major institutions in this country, including the schools, continue to adhere to the traditional conception of the American way. Even the opening of employment opportunities to women and minorities does not seem to have had profound impact on the traditional core values of the mainstream society. However, what seems to have happened is that the concepts of hard work and success have been defined more in terms of productivity and efficiency as seen by corporations and industries than by individual workers. Even contemporary educational institutions frequently view effective education in terms of cost efficiency to which educational accountability is closely tied. Notwithstanding the rapid shifts in values of our young people, few school board members, administrators, and teachers critically analyze the grounds for the officially prescribed norms of behavior and learning activities in relation to the changes taking place in the young people's worldview and belief patterns. Too many educators refuse to understand the young from their own "cultural" perspective. And even when they study the young, it is usually to induce them to abandon their "barbarism" and "irrationality" so that they can assimilate or acculturate the young into the idealized norms of the grown-up world.

It would appear that as the white middle class is ignorant about minority cultures, so too are adults ignorant about the culture of childhood, adolescence, and youth. Although understanding young people's acts and values from their cultural perspective will not remove disagreement, it may help to make the conflicts less disruptive and alienating. If we are to treat conflicts in school and in the classroom as cultural conflicts, both school officials and students must abandon their ethnocentrism, that is, the attitude that youngsters are "senseless" and the attitude that "old fogies just don't understand." Educationally, this means that board members, administrators, and teachers must act not as royalty but as equal members of a society in which individuals with varied cultural backgrounds (both ethnic and generational) live together. School personnel and students should act as members of a community that creates rules as a means of effective functioning of the group and resolves conflict through inquiry. Administrators and teachers should act more as moderators than as judges.

Transmission of Values

Historically, the primary function of the American school system has been seen as the transmission of the core values of the society at large. Even today, most school personnel, as well as the public, save some ethnic minorities, accept this as the most important role of the school. But in a society where rapid scientific and technological developments occur, there are equally swift changes in the patterns of institutional and individual behaviors. Both the number and the complexity of social and moral problems resulting from such changes outstrip our ability to cope with them effectively. As an example, although our technology can manufacture automobiles that can move 125 miles per hour, we have not yet found effective means of controlling drunk driving or various types of environmental pollution stemming from industrial wastes.

In addition, the impact of rapid technological changes on culture often leads to serious discrepancies between the society's established core values and the actual ways in which people think and behave. Major institutions such as schools and churches extol the inherent virtue of being honest at all times. But the young may value honesty only in relation to what it can bring them, because their attitudes and values are significantly influenced by the contents of mass media, which mirror economic and industrial interests more than traditional core values. What all this suggests is that cultures have functionally different ways of dealing with essentially similar human problems, but not all cultures are equally functional. The degrees to which various elements of a culture are consistent and integrated with each other vary from society to society. In short, some cultures contain more contradictory norms than others, and more such discrepancies seem to be found in highly technological societies.

Many aspects of American culture conflict with one another. For example, our country is said to guarantee equal rights and opportunities to all; however, full civil rights have yet to be granted to many people. Further, although long-range socioeconomic planning is often regarded as un-American and socialistic, Americans seem to be conflicted about whether governmental planning and intervention are necessary to ensure wage, energy, and media controls. In addition, most members of the dominant American culture believe that moral principles are absolute and unchangeable, but they also insist that one has to be flexible in making value decisions, particularly in relation to business practices affecting other individuals. The educational consequence is that unless we are aware of these and other inconsistencies and their influence on children's learning, we may transmit and cultivate self-defeating qualities. For example, the school may intend to develop self-reliance, creativity, and democratic leadership, but students may become docile and submissive if school activities and climate are inconsistent with the intended objectives. Specifically, a course in social studies should not be taught in an authoritarian manner, nor should school rules be merely repressive measures.

In this time of rapid technological development, it is easy for educators to become preoccupied with the efficiency with which we can accomplish our goals and measure the outcomes. More often than not, preoccupation with efficiency leads to quantification of both the ends and the means of education. Notwithstanding the importance of technology as a tool, educators need to be especially sensitive to and critical of how our use of technology enhances or detracts from the quality of what we hope to accomplish through education.

DIFFERENCES ARE NOT DEFICITS

We become individuals through our culture. Because our culture is so much a part of what we are and what we do, we often view it as if it were an innate or absolute dictum by which all individuals must guide their lives. Ethnocentrism, the belief in the superiority of our own culture, leads us to judge others in terms of our own cultural norms and inclines us to conclude that those who do not conform to our norms must be stupid, depraved, irresponsible, psychopathic, inferior, or sinful to a point beyond all redemption. When the dominant group in a society adopts the posture that its own set of values constitutes the only idealized norm in that society, the ethnic practices or traits of minority cultures are likely to be seen as deficient patterns that must be corrected either through education or coercion. In other words, the dominant culture tends to treat the minority cultures as sick forms of the normal or "right" culture and to define differences as deficits. This attitude makes it difficult for us to see that other cultures also provide effective means of dealing with the needs and problems of their respective societies. Socially, the deficit perspective, or social pathology, model of viewing minority groups contributes to the perpetuation of institutional racism and robs our society of richness (Baratz & Baratz, 1970). At the personal level, minority individuals are made to be ashamed of their ethnicity and cultural heritage.

Although the deficit view of minorities usually refers to ethnic or racial groups, this perspective is frequently but subtly adopted in dealing with such other groups as women, the aged, the handicapped, and even children. The deficit model is used in schools and other areas of our society to justify the subordinate status of minority groups of all kinds. For example, in recent times, a trend has been toward encouraging people to choose their own roles according to talents and abilities across gender or sex role categories. But the traditional view of sex roles includes two distinct sets of culturally assigned characteristics to men and women. More specifically, "male culture consists of the knowledge necessary to operate in the marketplace and political arena whereas female culture focuses on home and family" (Goetz, 1981, p. 58). Notwithstanding the fact that the gender-specific characteristics are culturally assigned, the mainstream society frequently views the traits specifically linked to females as inferior to those belonging to males (Lee & Gropper, 1974). The distinctively female characteristics are considered deficits, because "the dominant male culture is used as an arbitrary yardstick of success and both cultures are evaluated in terms of the model achievement of one, its so-called deficits are articulated in global rather than situation-specific terms, and the logical extension of globally stated deficits is an indictment of the whole female culture as pathological" (Lee & Gropper, 1974, p. 382). As Lee and Gropper cogently conclude, the deficit view

> fails to impart a highly prized cluster of abilities: production, achievement, problem solving, and environmental mastery. But a person raised according to the code of femininity should not be judged by the standards of masculinity. If the situation were reversed, males would find themselves as unfairly indicted. Each culture should be evaluated in terms of the degree to which it has prepared its members to adapt to the conditions of their lives. By this standard the two cultures would appear to be equally adequate. (p. 385)

Another example of the deficit view concerns American Sign Language. Although ASL is the single most widely used and effective means of communication among the hearing impaired, many do not view it as a legitimate language because it does not have the same structure as Signed English or Manually Coded English (MCE) (Reagan, 1985). Yet both ASL and MCE are equally functional to the people who use them. The elderly are often characterized as being similar to an ethnic minority, for their behaviors, values, and lifestyles are not considered worthy alternatives to the dominant ways of our society (Strange & Teitelbaum, 1987).

Finally, in our society, the young are assumed to be incapable of dealing with their problems without adult intervention. They are also thought of as imperfect grown-ups who should be pushed to abandon childhood as early as possible so that they can reach the normal and the ideal state of adulthood (Kimball, 1968). Anthropologist Mary Ellen Goodman (1970) suggests that in America, the culture of childhood is defined in terms of deficiencies requiring compensatory measures (pp. 2-3). Thus, children are perceived as "adults-in-the-making" (Thorne, 1987). This view of the young is based on the questionable assumption that human beings grow sequentially toward a supposed ideal and inescapable state (adulthood) (Kagan, 1978).

The deficit view has deleterious effects on the personal development of minority individuals because this perspective usually leads to cultural imperialism, which compels minority groups to adopt only the dominant norms by rejecting the culturally distinctive practices that may have served them well. Abandoning personal cultural ways denigrates the individual's dignity and impugns the integrity of the group to which the person belongs. As we have already stressed, cultural practices that deviate from our own should not be considered deficits, because cultures represent different but legitimate ways of dealing with essentially similar human problems and needs.

Some Differences Are Not Mere Differences

The notion that a difference is not a deficit is useful in exposing ethnocentric assumptions underlying various social and educational programs in our society. But it is not without difficulty, for we are not always clear about just how far the notion should be carried. For example, are we willing to grant that because the practices of all cultural groups are said to be different but equally valid, we should make no judgment about them? If we answer yes, are we then willing to insist that the racist practices of the KKK or the Nazis are nothing more than culturally different practices? In point of fact, those who affirm the ideals of participatory democracy do not view religious bigotry and racial or sex discrimination as merely culturally different practices carried on by certain special-interest groups in America. Rather, we judge such practices to be unethical, undemocratic, and even unlawful. The fact that different cultures have different norms does not necessarily imply that values ought to be relative or that there cannot be some objective way of justifying value judgments.

The slogan "differences are not deficits" does not suggest that any and all cultural differences, regardless of their harmful effects on others, should be treated as mere differences. Nor does it imply that there are no objective and rational bases for justifying basic ethical conduct. Rather, its purpose is to remind us that cultural differences should be respected and considered enriching to human experience. Implicit in this belief is the notion that we should consider the possible consequences of our actions on others, for their deeds will eventually affect our own well-being. If taken literally, this slogan can lead to the view that any inhumane and unjust actions may be condoned and justified.

Are All Cultures Equally Functional?

No matter how strange and irrational other cultural patterns may appear to us, the very existence of the practices implies that all cultures do their job. However, this does not imply that they are all equally functional. That is, some cultures may be more effective and less maladaptive than others, and cultures may be compared with each other in terms of the degree to which they are functional. The cultural patterns producing the least number of self-defeating consequences may be considered the most functional. Cultural changes may be suggested on the basis of the effectiveness or ineffectiveness with which the prevailing patterns help the group deal with its problems. This is one objective way of judging a culture.

As an example, in an ancient Korean custom two competing villages held annual rock battles in which the men expressed their masculinity and demonstrated their fighting skills. These annual events usually identified some promising warriors, but many men were fatally wounded. Because more and more men would have been killed off if such battles had continued for many generations, the maladaptive, self-defeating practice would have been a serious barrier in perpetuating the village populations. Alternative ways of expressing masculinity and identifying promising warriors could have been suggested. Similarly, the fact that sunbathing is widely practiced for the sake of health and good looks in this country does not necessarily suggest that it is the best way of promoting health and maintaining beautiful skin. To the contrary, available scientific evidence suggests that sunbathing is likely to cause skin cancer. Again, simply because certain belief and behavior patterns have been worked out by a given culture as a means of dealing with its concerns, we should not conclude that such patterns are necessarily the best possible ways of meeting human needs in that society. Nor should we even insist that a particular practice that has worked well in one cultural setting will be equally effective in a different cultural setting.

Ample evidence exists to suggest that some cultural practices, particularly in highly technological societies, despite fulfilling immediate needs, often have counterproductive long-term consequences. The culture of a society that selects its means of problem solving chiefly in terms of its immediate utility may face many complex and unsuspected outcomes that may be self-defeating to its fundamental goals. Clearly, tenacious adherence to one's own cultural practices in a radically different cultural context may be maladaptive. We should not consider the use of self-defeating patterns as merely a matter of applying different but equally valid cultural norms. In a similar sense, the adopting of cultural practices that are contradictory to the fundamental ideals of a given society, say participatory democracy, ought not to be viewed as a matter of just following different patterns.

As Harry Broudy (1981) points out, "the social organization necessitates varying degrees of interdependence, whereas cultural diversity that claims complete autonomy for each cultural group can only result in an aggregate of groups with a minimum dependence on each other. Taken seriously and interpreted strictly, it leads to cultural separatism or atomism" (p. 232). As members of a society, we must be concerned about the consequences of acting to achieve personal objectives. The merit of our actions should be tested in terms of our personal goals, which in turn should be examined according to the fundamental principles upon which one's society is founded. In the final analysis, personal or cultural practices that are contradictory to the ideals of the society will affect everyone's life. For example, in a democratic society if one's own cultural norms sanction exploitation of others and limit their freedom and equality, such practices cannot be justified in the name of cultural pluralism, because they are self-defeating at both the personal and the societal levels. To the degree to which our actions violate the rights and freedom of others, our own freedom and rights are diminished. It is in this sense that certain practices of various cultural groups may not always be viewed as simply cultural differences and that this belief should become the basis of democratic education.

STEREOTYPES VS. GENERALIZATIONS

Human beings tend to seek to understand and simplify their experiences by sorting out and categorizing their experiences. This process leads us to draw conclusions based on examples, in other words, to develop generalizations for understanding the world around us. If, in our experience with the teachers we encountered as children, we came into contact with many warm and caring individuals, we might have learned to generalize that teachers are warm and caring people. We would make this generalization despite the fact that we had encountered only a few examples from the wider universe of *teacher.* And this generalization would be open to change as we continued to encounter more teachers. While generalizations are useful, however, stereotypes can be damaging.

A stereotype is a fixed idea, a standardized mental picture that allows for no individuality or variation. A stereotype is more rigidly held than a generalization and is less prone to change. Unlike a generalization based on experience, a stereotype is often based on misconceptions and lack of information. Stereotypes may include positive ideas about other groups, for example, that all Asian Americans are good at math or that all Jews are highly intelligent. Whether positive or negative, however, stereotypes are harmful in that they lead to inaccurate expectations and judgments. An Asian-American child who is not good at math, for example, may find that he or she does not get the help and support from the teacher that other, non-Asian, children get, because the teacher simply does not recognize that this child, in fact, is having problems with math.

Often there is enough supporting evidence for stereotypes to make them *seem* true—there are dumb blonds, rich Jews, and lazy Mexicans. Furthermore, some stereotypes have arisen because of historical circumstances. For example, throughout much of European history, Jews in Europe were forced to live in ghettoes. It is ironic, then, that one stereotype that developed about Jews is that they are clannish. Similarly, George Bernard Shaw once remarked that Americans are a funny people in that they make the Negroes [sic] lick their boots and then call them bootlickers.

It is the rigidity and uncritical acceptance of stereotypes that makes them dangerous. Generalizations are more tentatively held and open to change and individual variation. Stereotypes are more difficult to confront and change. Since they are based on ignorance and limited experience, they can be broken down with experience and information. This is particularly true with young children whose stereotypes are not likely to be as firmly set. Teachers can begin to confront stereotypes by probing for misconceptions and by providing accurate information. A teacher, for example, might ask her students to draw pictures of "boy toys" and "girl toys" and then follow this with a discussion of why they classified the toys as they did. In their discussion they might think about examples of children playing with toys not typical of their gender and consider why they might do that. Depending on the age of the children, the class could investigate how advertising influences our ideas about what toys we want. They might also move into a more in-depth examination of sex roles at home and in school. Helping young people examine the complexity of the real world can help them move away from stereotypical thinking.

EDUCATION AND SCHOOLING AS A CULTURAL PROCESS

As was pointed out earlier, every culture attempts to perpetuate itself through deliberate transmission of what is considered the most worthwhile knowledge, belief, skills, behaviors, and attitudes. This deliberate transmission of culture is called education. In nonliterate societies, the educative process is carried out in a more or less informal manner. The young learn various skills, beliefs, and attitudes from their elders as well as from their peers without having a specific time or place designated for this purpose. This informal process sometimes involves certain formal rituals, for example, puberty rites. In nonliterate societies even folkways and mores serve as instructional media. However, in a complex, literate, and technological society, most cultural transmission takes place within the confines of specially arranged environments. There the young are expected to learn certain amounts and kinds of knowledge and skills within a specified period of time from those who are specialists in these areas. This formal and more restrictive process of cultural transmission may be called schooling.

Education is a form of enculturation, the process of learning one's own culture. When this process occurs formally in an institutional setting, it is called schooling. Thus, the process of enculturation is much broader than education, because the former includes both deliberate and nondeliberate learning, such as teaching and learning through imitation, whereas the latter includes only deliberate teaching and learning activities. Schooling is a much narrower concept than education, for it necessarily involves specialists teaching within the institutions designed specifically for this purpose. Education, although deliberate, need not take place in a formal institutional setting.

In spite of the differences among enculturation, education, and schooling, all three should be viewed as a single process whereby an individual learns and manipulates his or her own culture. Enculturation and education, at least in their informal sense, are present in all cultures. Education is only one means of enculturation. Similarly, schooling is one of many ways in which a person can become educated. All this suggests that although there is no society without enculturation and education, some societies are without schooling.

SCHOOLING AS ENCULTURATIVE AND ACCULTURATIVE PROCESSES

Education in a socially and culturally diverse society such as the United States is not only *enculturative;* it is also *acculturative.* That is, while many students in our schools are learning their own culture (enculturation), minority children are attempting to grasp a new and different, that is, dominant, culture (acculturation). In a true sense, the ghetto child learning white, middle-class values from a white, middle-class teacher is learning an alien culture. In a culturally diverse society, it is important for school administrators, teachers, and counselors to realize that different behavioral, attitudinal, and belief patterns of minority children stemming from their ethnic backgrounds should not be viewed as either social or cognitive deficits. For example, teachers generally expect students to speak up only after they have been duly recognized, and students who express their thoughts and feelings spontaneously are frequently considered disruptive or troublemakers. Yet many of our schoolchildren come from cultures in which spontaneous expressions of their thoughts and feelings are encouraged. Other young people have been taught to respond to a teacher's reprimand by lowering their heads in silence. This behavior is considered quite appropriate in relating to unhappy adults in the youth's culture, but it is generally viewed as a sign of nonresponsiveness or even rebellion by our teachers. The point is not that minority children be allowed to behave only according to the norms of their own culture; it is to suggest that unless these children are taught about the differences between the dominant and their own cultures and what standards of behavior are appropriate in school, they are likely to be treated as problem cases requiring disciplinary or other special measures used for children with emotional and behavioral disorders. In fact, to many minority children, schooling in America represents a difficult and agonizing process of learning to function in an alien (dominant) culture that either rejects their ethnic heritage or gives it a low status.

Education as an acculturative process can also be viewed as the modification of one culture through continuous contact with another. Antagonism often results when one culture is dominant, and this antagonism becomes exacerbated by the dominant culture's attempt to speed up the process. When the dominant group sees minority group characteristics as deficits, the antagonisms are aggravated. Harry F. Walcott (1987) believes that "the teacher might succeed in coping more effectively with conflict and in capitalizing on his instructional efforts if he were to recognize and to analyze his ascribed role as enemy" rather than by attempting to ignore or deny the conflict (pp. 136, 173). He goes on to illustrate that in the enemy relationship, specific demands are made of enemy prisoners. But these demands are not based on common values about fair play, human rights, or the dignity of office. The relationship is based on fundamental differences rather than on the recognition of similarities. This perspective of thinking about teachers and their culturally different pupils as enemies may invite teachers to examine the kinds of differences cherished by enemies just as they have in the past addressed themselves, at least ritually, to what they and their pupils share in common (p. 149). Another helpful approach may be to have both teachers and culturally different students treat each other as visitors from extraterrestrial worlds. In this way, they cannot understand each other without asking each other the "why" questions.

To recognize that the process of schooling in America is both enculturative and acculturative is to accept the fact that many of the young in our schools are there to learn the dominant but alien culture. This implies that many learning and behavioral difficulties may come from the differences between the norms the school considers desirable and those that minority children view as appropriate. The culturally different young people in our society must learn to function according to the dominant as well as their own cultural norms, depending on their purpose and the circumstances in which they find themselves. At the same time, educators need to understand that human actions do not have inherent meanings and significance. Understanding that various cultures assign different meanings to the same action can help educators interpret seemingly strange or disruptive behaviors from appropriate cultural perspectives and, consequently, minimize learning and behavioral difficulties. It is when educators believe that all children in our schools are there to learn their own culture that the patterns that deviate from the dominant norms are treated as deficits to be eliminated.

Learning or Teaching?

According to Margaret Mead (1963), one of the important effects of the mingling of different races, religions, and levels of cultural complexity on our concept of education is the "shift from the need for an individual to learn something which everyone agrees he would wish to know, to the will of some individual to teach something which it is not agreed that anyone has any desire to know" (pp. 310–311). Melville J. Herskovits (1968) agrees that in nonliterate societies much more emphasis is placed on learning than on teaching. But he attributes this shift to the fact that in simpler societies the skills and techniques the young learn have practical application. What is learned is used in everyday life; hence, the motivation to learn comes from the immediate utility of the techniques to be acquired. On the other hand, in highly technological and culturally complex societies, individuals cannot hope to learn "just everything" needed in that society. Quite the contrary, intense specialization is necessary to make a living. In a modern society, we cannot rely on our own personal resources to learn what is required even in our own area of specialization. Nor is it reasonable to expect young learners to know what skills are needed to become a specialist in a desired area, for example, a psychiatrist. It has become almost mandatory that we rely on experienced and recognized specialists to give us accurate and comprehensive information about what ought to be learned in a given field. Experts must tell others what they ought to learn. Modern societies are so complex that even among experts we do not always find agreement about what ought to be taught.

There is no simple answer to the question of why modern education has shifted its emphasis from learning to teaching. But an important lesson lies in the slogan "learning is more important than teaching." When our attention is focused on learning, we are likely to become more concerned about providing conditions under which learning can occur. Because conditions for learning are varied, we may grow more flexible in whatever we do to facilitate learning. On the other hand, when a greater emphasis is placed on teaching, we are more likely to become preoccupied with what the teacher must do. In short, teaching may be viewed as a set of acts or routines rather than a process of facilitating learning conditions. Indeed, teaching and learning are not mutually exclusive ideas, nor can we say that one is more important than the other in any absolute sense. Further, it is doubtful that, as Mead argues, it is the shift from learning to teaching that "moved us from spontaneity to coercion, from freedom to power . . . and the development of techniques of power, dry pedagogy, regimentation, indoctrination, manipulation, and propaganda" (p. 320).

Finally, society uses education for many more purposes than the transmission of culture. In some societies, both formal and informal education serve as agents of genuine change. By providing greater educational opportunities to wider and wider segments of the population, liberating social and economic as well as political changes can be created to eliminate illiteracy and poverty and to restore human freedom and dignity. On the other hand, education can also be used by those who possess wealth and power to perpetuate the status quo. Domination over minority groups of all kinds is often achieved through proselytizing the oppressed to believe that they do indeed "belong" to the positions and classes that they occupy. In such societies, educational opportunities are so restricted that the likelihood of any significant social, economic, or political change occurring would certainly be remote. This has long been the way colonies have been maintained. The following two chapters will examine how schooling in America functioned in relation to the two uses of education just discussed and will give a broad historical overview of how the dominant society's attitude toward minority cultures has influenced schooling in the United States.

CASE STUDIES

The primary purpose of this case study is to facilitate a discussion of how the values, attitudes, and beliefs of the dominant culture may have influenced the classroom teacher's work and the latent transmission of certain values and attitudes through the classroom activities, the classroom organization, and the teacher-pupil relationship. The following is a brief description of a first-grade classroom in Huntington Elementary School. (The name of the school has been changed to preserve confidentiality.) Huntington is an upper-middle-class town in which 93% of the parents were reported to have occupations that are considered professional.

MRS. NEWMAN'S FIRST GRADE

Like most of the teachers at Huntington, Mrs. Newman was older and more experienced than Mrs. Jones and the other teachers at Smith [an elementary school in a neighboring lower-middle-class town]. She had more than 20 years of classroom experience at the elementary school level, including eight at Huntington. While Mrs. Jones was still in the process of completing her requirements for a master's degree on a part-time basis at a nearby university, Mrs. Newman had long since obtained her master's degree from a far more prestigious institution.

Mrs. Newman had lived in the Huntington neighborhood even before joining the faculty, and her own children had attended Huntington. She was highly respected by parents and other members of the Huntington faculty. Parents whose older children had been in her classes requested her for their younger ones. The principal directed the observers to her classroom, saying "She's one of the best."

Mrs. Newman's class was smaller than Mrs. Jones's, with 10 boys and 10 girls for the greater part of the year. The basic overall stability of the neighborhood and the school was reflected by the fact that only one student transferred into or out of the class during the entire year. A great many of the children had attended kindergarten and even nursery school together. Other than two black males who were bused to Huntington from another neighborhood and one girl whose mother was from Central America, all of the children were Caucasian.

During the school day, the Huntington classroom was orderly, quiet, and productive. Desks were aligned in traditional rows and children worked by themselves, poring over assignments, moving quietly from their desks to resource materials that lined the room, only occasionally poking and playing with each other. Both Mrs. Newman's instruction and the organization of the classroom were structured so as to encourage independent cognitive work. Grouping desks into clusters, as for art work or special projects, was quite rare.

It was a classroom in which everything had its place. During independent work times . . . some movement was allowed, but the style and scope of movement was clearly restricted. Resources circulated from child to child, children circulated from resource to resource, but both returned to their proper places. Children's activities were generally limited to various academic options.

Mrs. Newman allowed very little to interfere with her objective of promoting independent academic work, calling interaction between children "bothering your friends." She stated repeatedly that interaction would prevent children from finishing their assignments and producing high-quality work and that play should be saved for the playground. She made her priorities clear:

> I don't think anybody really has to look at the frogs now. I know Debbie has work to do. She has a whole SRA kit to keep her busy.

You can color when you're finished, but don't spend so much time on coloring. I found out some of my good people are just spending their time coloring.

Mrs. Newman indicated a strong sense of professional responsibility to prepare children for future schooling and she stressed reading as the key to success. She kept the classroom consistently orderly and productive toward this end, and both good study habits and high academic standards were emphasized.

Source: Reprinted by permission of Waveland Press, Inc. from George Spindler, *Doing the Ethnography of Schooling: Educational Anthropology in Action.* (Prospect Heights, IL: Waveland Press, Inc., 1988). All rights reserved.

QUESTIONS

1. What core values of the community and the larger society were reflected in Mrs. Newman's approach to her classroom work and students?
2. What values and attitudes might be transmitted to the children in Mrs. Newman's classroom? By what means might these values and attitudes be transmitted to the learners?
3. Are any aspects of Mrs. Newman's work and teaching style inconsistent with the core values of the community and larger society? If yes, what might they be?
4. Would you make any suggestions to Mrs. Newman regarding her teaching and classroom management? Why?

* * *

This is a brief account of an actual case involving a young Southeast Asian girl who was adopted by a white middle-class couple. Many details have been left out intentionally, leaving enough information so that readers can think about and discuss the general approach they might take in dealing with a similar situation by critically analyzing the assumptions implicit in the ways in which we observe and evaluate individuals from another culture. Although the case deals with the difficulties a Southeast Asian girl had in an upper-middle-class suburban school in the United States, a young white girl from a lower socioeconomic class in the same school would have had somewhat different but equally difficult problems.

LISA

After living for three years in an orphanage, Lisa, a young Southeast Asian girl, was adopted by a white middle-class family in a Midwestern city. Since the orphanage did not provide Lisa's adoptive parents with her birth certificate, nobody knew exactly how old she was. According to a nearby medical center, she was either nine or ten years old. In spite of Lisa's claim that she had had two years of schooling in the orphanage, she was placed in a first-grade classroom because she had neither an adequate command of the English language nor official documents certifying her earlier schooling.

Lisa's adoptive parents were very warm and caring people who provided her with most of the things that a nine-year-old girl would want and should have—including piano lessons. Lisa was very good in music. In fact, in less than six months after beginning piano lessons she was able to play new pieces at first reading. In addition to these "privileges," she was given a number of household chores to do. Lisa was to let the family puppy out and feed her as soon as she came home from school. She was also responsible for checking all the windows and watering house plants. In addition, Lisa was to stay in the house with all the doors locked until one of the parents came home from work. She carried out the chores well, and Lisa and her parents were very happy with one another.

At school, Lisa did not do as well. According to her teacher, Lisa was always the first child to hand in the assigned work in the class. But she did very poor work, because she could not follow the teacher's instructions. Whenever the teacher told Lisa to pay more attention to her instructions and reprimanded her for handing in poor work, Lisa consistently lowered her head in silence. She responded similarly to other adults when she was admonished by them. According to Lisa's classroom teacher, she had a disruptive influence on other children because "she bothered them a lot." For these academic and behavioral problems, Lisa had been sent to the principal's office several times.

As a result of a number of reports from Lisa's teacher, a reading specialist and a teacher of English as a second language, the principal recommended that there be a comprehensive evaluation of Lisa's performance, behavior, problems, needs, and potentials so that an individualized instruction plan could be developed. This process is usually referred to as "staffing." Lisa's staffing meeting was attended by several specialists, a teacher of English as a second language, Lisa's teacher, and her parents with an "advocate." An advocate is a person who helps the child's parents make sound and appropriate judgments about their child's education program.

Following a series of reports on social, psychological, intellectual, and behavioral aspects of Lisa, the group, except the parents and the advocate, agreed that Lisa had serious emotional problems and that she ought to be referred to a professional counselor or a clinical psychologist. The school psychologist reported that her IQ score was below the norm of her age group, and the social worker indicated that Lisa had problems getting along with other children. The group also recommended that she be sent to a school providing special education programs for children with learning and behavioral difficulties. After a lengthy discussion of how her cultural background may have influenced Lisa's academic performance and interpersonal relationships, the decision was made not to send her to special education classes. (The details of how this decision was reached have been omitted intentionally so that readers may explore various options for Lisa and choose the most appropriate instructional plan for her with the information provided herein.)

Lisa is now an above-average high school senior with many friends. She is looking forward to attending a nearby university. She has continued to study music and art, and she works part-time like many of her peers.

QUESTIONS

1. What is your estimate of the ways in which Lisa's problems were determined? Does the concept of "deficit view" apply here?
2. What are some assumptions the school personnel had implicitly used in evaluating Lisa?
3. How would you explain Lisa's problems?
4. How might Lisa have been affected had she been sent to special education classes?
5. On the basis of what has been discussed in Chapter 2, what information or knowledge as well as attitudes would you need to make intelligent decisions about Lisa's situation?
6. What might be done in teacher-education programs to prepare prospective teachers to be able to deal effectively with children from culturally as well as socially and economically different backgrounds?

• • •

The following describes the experience of an early adolescent African-American girl attending a predominantly white school for the first time.

LEARNING COMPETITION

I was sent to an integrated high school that was not in my neighborhood. I describe it as "integrated" rather than "desegregated" because no court mandates placed black children there. I was there because my mother was concerned about the quality of our neighborhood school.

There were a handful of African-American students in my seventh-grade class, but I knew none of them. They lived in a more affluent neighborhood than I did. Their parents had stable blue-collar or white-collar jobs. They had gone to better-equipped elementary schools than I had. The white students were even more privileged. Their fathers had impressive jobs as doctors, lawyers—one was a photojournalist. Most of their mothers were homemakers. In contrast, my mother and father both worked full-time. My father often even worked two jobs, yet we still lived more modestly than most of my classmates did.

In seventh grade I learned what it means to be competitive. In elementary school my teachers did not seem to make a big deal out of my academic achievements. They encouraged me but did not hold me up as an example that might intimidate slower students. Although I suspect I was a recipient of a kind of sponsored mobility—perhaps because my mother always sent me to school neat and clean and with my hair combed—I don't think this preferential treatment was obvious to other students. But in my new surroundings the competition was very obvious. Many of my white classmates made a point of showing off their academic skills. Further, their parents actively lent a hand in important class assignments and projects. For example, one boy had horrible penmanship. You could barely read what he scrawled in class, but he always brought in neatly typed homework. I asked him once if he did the typing and he told me that his mother typed everything for him. She also did the typing for his cousin, who was also in our class and had beautiful penmanship. The teachers often commented on the high quality of these typed papers.

I had come from a school where children learned and produced together. This competitiveness, further encouraged by the parents, was new to me. I could attempt to keep up with this unfair competition and "act white" or could continue to work my hardest and hope that I could still achieve.

Source: Ladson-Billings, G. (1994). *The Dreamkeepers: Successful Teachers of African American Children.* San Francisco: Jossey-Bass Publishers.

QUESTIONS

1. What "core values" were being conveyed in this classroom and how were they being transmitted?
2. In what ways were the values and attitudes represented in this classroom in contradiction with those that the writer had encountered previously in her home and in school? How would you account for these differences in cultural terms?
3. What recommendations would you give to this student? To the teacher? Why?

REFERENCES

Baratz, S. S., & Baratz, J. C. (1970). Early childhood intervention: The social science base for institutional racism. *Harvard Educational Review,* 40 (1), 29–50. See also *The Myth of Cultural Deprivation,* edited by Nell Keddie, Baltimore: Penguin Books, 1973, for more discussion of this topic.

Benedict, R. (1934). *Patterns of culture*. Boston: Houghton Mifflin.

Broudy, H. S. (1981). Cultural pluralism: New wine in old bottles. In J. M. Rich (Ed.), *Innovations in education* (pp. 230–233). Boston: Allyn and Bacon.

The Chronicle of Higher Education. (1988, January 20).

The Chronicle of Higher Education. (1995, January 13).

Geertz, C. (1973). *The interpretation of cultures*. New York: Basic Books.

Goetz, J. P. (1981). Sex-role systems in Rose Elementary School: Change and tradition in the rural-transitional South. In R. T. Sieber & A. J. Gordon (Eds.), *Children and their organizations: Investigations in American culture* (pp. 58–73). Boston: G. K. Hall & Co.

Goodman, M. E. (1970). *The culture of childhood: Child's-eye views of society and culture*. New York: Teachers College Press.

Herskovits, M. J. (1968) Education and the sanctions of custom. In J. H. Chilcott, N. C. Greenberg, & H. B. Wilson (Eds.), *Readings in the socio-cultural foundations of education* (pp. 98–101). Belmont, IL: Wadsworth.

Kagan, J. (1978). *Infancy: Its place in human development*. Cambridge: Harvard University Press.

Kansas City Star. (1972, April 13).

Kansas City Star. (1974, February 10).

Kimball, S. T. (1968). Cultural influences shaping the role of the child. In J. H. Chilcott, N. C. Greenberg, & H. B. Wilson (Eds.), *Readings in the socio-cultural foundations of education* (pp. 124–133). Belmont, IL: Wadsworth.

Kluckhohn, C. (1968). Queer customs. In J. H. Chilcott, N. C. Greenberg, & H. B. Wilson (Eds.), *Readings in the socio-cultural foundations of education* (pp. 29–38). Belmont, IL: Wadsworth.

Lee, P. C., & Gropper, N. B. (1974). Sex-role culture and educational practice. *Harvard Educational Review, 44*(3), 381–388.

Luria, A. R. (1976). *Cognitive development: Its cultural and social foundations* (M. Lopez-Morillas & L. Solotaroff, Trans.; M. Cole, Ed.). Cambridge: Harvard University Press. (Original work published 1974).

Mead, M. (1963) Our educational emphasis in primitive perspective. In G. D. Spindler (Ed.), *Education and culture* (pp. 309–320). New York: Holt, Rinehart & Winston.

Quillen, J. (1963). Problems and prospects. In G. D. Spindler (Ed.), *Education and culture* (pp. 49–52). New York: Holt, Rinehart & Winston.

Reagan, T. (1985). The deaf as a linguistic minority: Educational considerations. *Harvard Educational Review, 55*(3), 265–277.

Search Institute. (1983). *Young adolescents and their parents*. Minneapolis: Author.

Sieber, R. T., & Gordon, A. J. (1981). Introduction: Socializing organizations—environments for the young, windows to American culture. In R. T. Sieber & A. J. Gordon (Eds.), *Children and their organizations: Investigations in American culture* (pp. 1–17). Boston: G. K. Hall & Co.

Spindler, G. D. (1963). Education in a transforming America. In G. D. Spindler (Ed.), *Education and culture* (pp. 132–147). New York: Holt, Rinehart & Winston.

Strange, H., Teitelbaum, M., and Contributors. (1987). *Aging and cultural diversity: New directions and annotated bibliography*. South Hadley, MA: Bergin & Garvey.

Thorne, B. (1987). Re-visioning women and social change: Where are the children? *Gender and Society, 1*(1), 93.

Veroff, J., Douvan, E., & Kulka, R. A. (1981). *The inner American.* New York: Basic Books.

Walcott, H. F. (1987). The teacher as an enemy. In G. D. Spindler (Ed.), *Education and cultural process* (2nd ed.) (pp. 411–425). Prospect Heights, IL: Waveland Press.

White, L. A., & Dillingham, B. (1973). *The concept of culture.* Minneapolis: Burgess.

Wiles, J. & Bondi, J. (1993). *The essential middle school* (2nd ed.). Upper Saddle River, NJ: Merrill/Prentice Hall.

Yankelovich, D. (1981). *New rules: searching for self-fulfillment in the world turned upside down.* New York: Random House.

PART TWO

Culture and the American School

3

Schooling as Americanization: 1600s–1970s

THE AMERICAN SCHOOL AND ITS MISSION

It has been frequently said that no nation has had more faith in education than America. As a people, we have always believed that through education not only could we produce literate, enlightened, responsible, and productive citizens, but we could also establish a society where freedom, equality, and fraternity could be guaranteed for all regardless of sociocultural, religious, and racial heritages. It was through free public schools that America hoped to achieve these goals. But the public erroneously equated education with schooling and was convinced that through schools even the backward, the poor, and the ill prepared could be taught to become productive, loyal, and affluent Americans. In short, schooling was seen as one of the most effective agents of socioeconomic mobility.

America's faith in education went even beyond this, because schooling was also thought to be the major means of resolving social, moral, and political problems. This American dream, based on an inadequate understanding of the role of schooling in a complex socioeconomic and political order, opened the way for a massive attack against the American schools during the post-*Sputnik* era (late 1950s) as well as in the early 1980s. The schools were charged with the blame for America being Number Two in the space race

Portions of Chapter 3 have been reprinted from Morris, Van Cleve, and Young Pai. *Philosophy and the American School,* second edition. Copyright © 1976 by Houghton Mifflin Company. Used with permission.

against the USSR in the late 1950s, and they were accused of being major culprits in America's failure to maintain its economic and military superiority over such nations as Japan, Germany, and the USSR in the early 1980s. Even today many believe that better schooling will reduce, if not eliminate, substance abuse, unemployment, sexual promiscuity, and supposed general moral decay, as well as socioeconomic inequities.

It was this faith in the American school that prompted a noted historian of education, Lawrence Cremin (1961), to remark:

> The common schools increased opportunity; they taught morality and citizenship; they encouraged a talented leadership; they maintained social mobility; they promoted social responsiveness to social conditions. (p. 3)

The public school was seen as the prime agent by which native sons and daughters as well as immigrants could achieve economic affluence, higher social status, and political and religious freedom, thereby becoming patriotic and responsible citizens.

SCHOOL AS AN AGENT OF CULTURAL TRANSMISSION

Since the early 1960s various minority groups have been demanding that their own cultural patterns should not only be allowed to exist but also be encouraged to develop in their own way. They ask that full civil rights be guaranteed and that social, economic, political, and educational equality be provided for all, regardless of gender, ethnic, religious, or racial background. These demands are rooted in the belief that America has consistently attempted to assimilate minority cultures into the dominant, WASP culture (see "The Core Values of American Culture" in Chapter 2). Moreover, the groups believe that the awarding of socioeconomic rewards, such as social status and income, has been based on the extent to which minorities conformed to the WASP norm. To members of minority groups, perpetuating this cultural imperialism, which regards cultural difference as a deficit, is clearly contradictory to democratic ideals. Minorities have also contended that the American school, as a special agent of the society at large, has promoted Anglo-superiority by teaching children that to be American is to be white, if not also Anglo-Saxon and Protestant. In spite of the criticism that significant reforms in socioeconomic, political, and educational institutions have not been fully achieved, the American school and its personnel have come a long way in becoming sensitive to the rights and needs of minority groups since the days of the 17th-century Puritans.

In this and subsequent chapters we will examine critically the ways in which American society and the school have dealt with questions regarding cultural diversity and issues related to the education of the culturally different during several broad historical periods. A discussion of the Puritan perspective will cover the years from 1647 (when the first major school law, known as the Old Deluder Satan Act, was passed) to about 1870, the beginning of an influx of immigrants with non-Anglo-Teutonic backgrounds. Americanization as Anglo-conformity and the melting pot ideal will be examined as related to the periods from 1870 to the 1920s and the 1920s to 1965. The early 1920s are significant because during these years several legislative measures sought to limit or eliminate the immigration of nonwhite and non-European people into the United States. It was not until 1965 that the laws were changed and quotas in favor of European countries were abolished to provide equal immigration opportunities to all races and nationalities. The impact of President Lyndon B. Johnson's Great Society program on the American school (1965–1970s) and the issues concerning cultural pluralism and multicultural education (early 1970s–1990s) will be discussed in this chapter as well as in Chapter 4.

QUEST FOR HOMOGENEITY: THE PURITAN PERSPECTIVE (1647–1870)

Because school was viewed as a primary facilitator of Americanization, its major mission was to enculturate the children of the WASP community and to acculturate the children of those who did not have the same heritage. This involved changing not only their behavioral and language patterns but also their belief systems and thinking styles to conform to WASP norms. Schooling as Americanization meant helping children learn to think, believe, and behave according to the white Anglo-Saxon Protestant ways while divesting non-WASP children of cultural practices that differed from the mainstream. The view of education and schooling as an Americanization process, explicitly fostering conformity to the dominant culture and hostility toward cultural diversity, can be traced to the Puritans' view of their destiny and mission in life. This Puritan perspective has had a lasting impact on the educational policies and practices as well as the social, political, economic, and religious lives of the people in the United States. For this reason, it is important to understand how the Puritans saw themselves and their work.

The Puritans of Massachusetts Bay Colony did not view themselves as either ordinary immigrants from the continent or fortune-seeking adventurers. Rather, they were convinced that they were given a special mission in God's grand plan for the world. As Cremin (1977) points out, this belief "proved enormously energizing. It suffused colonial politics and commerce with a zealous sense of righteousness, and it bound together the institutions of colonial education with a heady sense of purpose, as the colonists went about the work of creating and sustaining Zion" (p. 10). Clearly, the Puritans were committed missionaries who believed their purpose was to carry out

God's will by converting everyone to their own religious perspective. Hence, "the configuration of education in seventeenth-century Massachusetts operated insistently to nurture Puritans; the diurnal life of trade, commerce, and speculation operated no less insistently to nurture Yankees" (p. 23). The Puritan worldview rested on the belief that there was only one set of idealized norms to which all had to conform. Deviations from such norms were to be regarded as deficits, abnormal conditions to be eliminated.

More specifically, and as Carlson (1975) argues, the Puritans believed that their God-given mission was to become an exemplar to the world by establishing the best religion (their brand of Protestantism), the best government (the republican form), and the best society (the middle-class society) (p. 4). They were convinced that these goals could be accomplished by maintaining the purity of their beliefs and way of life. Cultural diversity was seen as harmful to national unity. The Puritans steadfastly believed that the purity of their ways could be assured and cultural heterogeneity be overcome through education. Hence, they "were not tolerant of any violation of their social norms. They were quick to condemn and punish any who dared to challenge the authority of their institutions or to break the rules" (Pulliam, 1987, p. 39). This intolerance toward diversity and the quest for uniformity affected the nonwhite minorities more than any other non-Anglo-Teutonic people. White skin was thought of as a necessary condition for becoming a "normal" and acceptable member of the dominant society, and "the white people of the United States considered themselves superior to the 'Twanies,' the 'niggers,' the 'Chinks,' and the 'Japs,' [and] despite all his problems, the lowest peasant from Europe—Roman Catholic, Eastern Orthodox, or Jewish—was in a better position on first landing in the United States than a Protestant Negro whose ancestors trod American soils in colonial times. While Indians suffered attempted genocide and the Chinese experienced immigration restriction, the largest group of non-Caucasians in America was kept at a social distance from the 'superior' whites" (Carlson, 1975, p. 13). Despite dominance by the Anglo-Teutonic people, the Puritans did acquire important knowledge and useful skills for surviving in the New World through cultural contacts with other nonwhite and European groups.

In spite of some cultural, linguistic, and religious differences, the Americanization of immigrants through education did not pose a serious problem in the Puritan era, because most of them came from the British Isles or other European countries with Anglo-Teutonic backgrounds. But because the Puritans were so unquestionably convinced that cultural diversity would lead to national disunity and divisiveness in people's beliefs and values, much of their educational efforts focused on the centrality of conformity and uniformity in the growth and security of the nation. Neither the worth of cultural diversity in national development nor the importance of a person's unique cultural heritage to personal growth are found in the educational thought of such influential leaders as Benjamin Franklin (1706–1790), Noah Webster (1758–1843), James Carter (1775–1845), and Horace Mann (1796–1859). On the contrary, Noah Webster argued that the spelling and pronunciation of the American (English) language should be nationalized as a way to combat the British influence on the new nation. He also believed that all aspects of the schools in America should be "American." Franklin, Carter, and Mann all championed the cause of equal education, which they believed would lead to the creation of a one-class—middle-class—society without social or economic disparities.

At first glance, the thoughts of these three men resemble the contemporary notion of equal educational opportunity, which affirms the value of cultural diversity and the individual's ethnicity. But a closer examination suggests that the kind of education they proposed would lead to a society of only one class and one common culture. "Economic, social, ethnic, and religious diversity were to be subsumed under one democratic system of education which would unite all the people into a single indivisible nation. Education was to be used as the chief instrument for assimilating the foreign born into the mainstream of American life and culture" (Pulliam, 1987, pp. 87–88). Puritan schools did contribute significantly in building a society of a single culture, the WASP culture, but their approach to education also fostered intolerance and hostility toward diversity and the rejection of distinctive cultural heritages. People who spoke, thought, believed, and acted differently than the dominant group were viewed with suspicion and their integrity demeaned, for they were said to pose a potential threat to national unity and prosperity. Clearly, a primary purpose of the American school was to establish cultural homogeneity through conformity to the WASP norms. Any deviation from these norms was considered inimical to the fulfillment of America's God-given mission of establishing the best society, the best religion, and the best form of government.

KEEPING AMERICA AMERICAN (1870–1920s)

The immigrants who reached American shores after 1870 differed markedly from their predecessors, for they came from southern and eastern Europe, Asia, and South America. These newcomers, without the Anglo-Saxon or Teutonic heritage, had more than a little difficulty adjusting to the English language and Protestant orthodoxy that dominated public schools. Establishment of ethnic settlements by these new immigrants and their attempts to maintain the manners, customs, observances, and languages of the old countries presented a new problem and a challenge to educators and government officials. But rather than rethinking their Americanization policy and the goal of education in an increasingly culturally diverse society, the nation's educators simply reaffirmed their belief in Americanization as Anglo-conformity. Thus, an educational historian, Ellwood P. Cubberly (1909), remarked:

> Our task is to break up these groups or settlements, to assimilate and amalgamate these people as a part of our American race, and to implant in their children, so far as can be done, the Anglo-Saxon conception of righteousness, law and order, and popular government, and to awaken in them a reverence for our democratic institutions and for those things in our national life which we as a people hold to be abiding worth. (pp. 15–16)

As Milton M. Gordon (1964) pointed out in *Assimilation in American Life*, the large majority of the dominant cultural group was Anglo-Saxon in orientation and they "presumably [were] either convinced of the cultural superiority of Anglo-Saxon institutions as developed in the United States, or believed simply that, regardless of superiority or inferiority, since English culture has constituted the dominant framework for the development of institutions, newcomers should expect to adjust accordingly" (pp. 103–104). As in the Puritan era, this meant that being American and democratic was equated with conforming to the Anglo-Saxon pattern of language, morality, and behavior, and the immigrants were to give up their own cultural forms.

An implicit assumption underlying this view was that, if minority group members conformed to the WASP norm, prejudice and discrimination would disappear. But, of course, rejection, segregation, and prejudice did not disappear for those nonwhite ethnics, even if they did succeed in adopting the Anglo-Saxon pattern. Hence, "the kind of life proper for America [was] regarded as a matter to be decided altogether by the Anglo-Saxon and by those who became assimilated" (Berkson, 1969, p. 55). It was clear that the members of minority groups should do all the changing. The sooner they divested themselves of their own ethnic traits the better. This view of Americanism as Anglo-conformity was held not only by those who came from WASP backgrounds but also by some non-Anglo-Saxon immigrants. Thus, both the majority and minority groups adopted the deficit view. Further, being nonwhite, it was implied, meant having a permanent deficit condition. Enactment of such legislation as the Chinese Exclusion Act of 1882, California's antimiscegenation law of 1878 prohibiting intermarriages of white with blacks or "Mongols," and the National Origin Act of 1924, which effectively halted the immigration of nonwhites, reflected the view that to be American was to be white. This racist view of *American* is best summed up in President Calvin Coolidge's remark to Congress in 1923 that "America must be kept American."

Schools in America went through many changes during the years from 1870 to the early 1920s, yet the belief that minority cultures represented deficit conditions to be eradicated by the schooling process remained unquestioned. Among the major forces responsible for these changes were industrialization and urbanization of America's cities as well as rapid developments in the mass media of communication. Almost as profound as the impact of the technological changes and the sociopolitical pressures of the times was the influence of new educational thought. As early as 1902 John Dewey insisted that every school be a microcosm of society, that is, containing the same sorts of elements and activities (enterprises) as found in the society at large. Dewey believed that the school could become a force for social reform by enabling individuals and the society to make their lives increasingly efficient and effective. Hence, children were to learn through experiences and grow progressively to higher and higher levels under the careful guidance of the teacher. In general, Dewey was concerned with eliminating social, class, racial, and cultural differences as barriers to building a democratic community in which all could enjoy freedom and equality and in which every individual was valued for his or her intrinsic worth. Dewey thought that schooling was to have a harmonizing effect on different groups, but he failed to deal specifically with the value and the role cultural background has in enhancing a person's life and identity.

As pointed out in the preceding chapter, all societies attempt to transmit and perpetuate their culture through both formal and informal education. In this sense, it is not only reasonable but proper for American society to expect its schools to Americanize the young. Americanization should be an important mission of the American school. However, when *American* is so narrowly defined that certain individuals and groups are excluded from becoming full-fledged citizens because of their racial, cultural, and religious backgrounds, then schooling as Americanization becomes inconsistent with and contradictory to the ideals of participatory democracy for which this nation stands.

THE MELTING POT IDEAL (1920s–1965)

Following the massive influx of immigrants from all over the world between 1870 and the 1920s, both native-born Americans and newcomers to the country realized that simple Anglo-conformity was not feasible. Hence, around the turn of the century Americanization as Anglo-conformity took on a more liberalized form as the melting pot ideal. According to this view, ethnic differences "melted" into a single "pot" would produce a synthesis—a new homogeneous culture that was not Anglo-Saxon, Jewish, Italian, or Asian. Advocates offered the melting pot ideal as an alternative means of establishing a viable nation by challenging the belief that anything that weakened the Anglo-Saxon pattern would result in national disaster. They argued:

> A nation is great, not on account of the number of individuals contained within its boundaries, but through the strength begotten of common

ideals and aspirations. No nation can exist and be powerful that is not homogeneous in this sense. And the great ethnic problem we have before us is to fuse these elements into one common nationality, having one language, one political practice, one patriotism and one ideal of social development. (Mayo-Smith, 1904, p. 78)

In a more dramatic vein, Israel Zangwill (1909) glorified the ideal in his play "The Melting Pot":

It is in the fire of God round His Crucible. There she lies, the great Melting-Pot—listen! Can't you hear the roaring and the bubbling? There gapes her mouth—her harbor where a thousand mammoth feeders come from the ends of the world to pour in their human freight. Ah, what a stirring and seething! Celt and Latin, Slav and Teuton, Greek and Syrian—black and yellow—Jew and Gentile.

Yet, East and West, and North and South, the palm and the pine, the people and the equator, the crescent and the cross—how the great Alchemist melts and fuses them with his purging flame! Here shall they all unite to build the Republic of Man and the Kingdom of God. Ah, Vera, what is the glory of Rome and Jerusalem where all nations come to worship and look back, compared with the glory of America, where all races and nations come to labour and look forward!

Peace, peace to all ye millions, fated to fill this continent—the God of our children give you peace. (pp. 184–185)

Many poor and illiterate immigrants acquiring fame and fortune supported the melting pot ideal. When we consider the number of non-Anglo-Saxon individuals who contributed to American civilization as scholars, scientists, industrialists, philanthropists, and artists, it would appear that the melting pot has produced a new and unique culture. Yet these individual contributions to American technology, science, art, and literature seem to have made little or no difference in what are generally accepted as the core values of American culture. As Gordon (1964) suggests, in some respects the melting pot was "realized," for "American cuisine includes antipasto and spaghetti, frankfurters and pumpernickel, filet mignon and french-fried potatoes, borscht, sour cream, and gefüllte fish [and even egg rolls and teriyaki] on a perfect equality with fried chicken, ham and eggs, and pork and beans" (p. 128). But he cautions that it would be a mistake to infer from this that Americans see themselves as "a composite synthesis of widely diverging elements," noting:

The American's image of himself is still the Anglo-American ideal it was at the beginning of our independent existence. The national type as ideal has always been, and remains, pretty well fixed. It is the Mayflower, John Smith, Davy Crockett, George Washington, and Abraham Lincoln that define America's self image. (p. 128)

From the 1920s to the early 1960s neither school policies nor instructional materials deviated from the Anglo-American ideal upon which the American educational goals, principles, and practices of the preceding era were founded. In reality, what has happened in the melting pot conception of Americanization is that all varieties of ethnicities were melted into one pot, but the brew turned out to be Anglo-Saxon again. To put it more bluntly, "our cultural assimilation has taken place not in a 'melting pot' but rather in a . . . 'transmuting pot' in which all ingredients have been transformed and assimilated to an idealized 'Anglo-Saxon' model" (Gordon, 1964, p. 128).

The process of melting into the Anglo-Saxon model was not only difficult for nonwhite ethnic minorities; it was impossible. They may have adopted the Anglo-norm, but the blacks, the reds, and the yellows could never become white. Racial discrimination made it extremely difficult, if not impossible, for these groups to participate meaningfully in the democratic process or even to assimilate into the mainstream culture through intermarriage. It is indeed ironic that Americanization as Anglo-conformity and its more liberalized melting pot ideal resulted in the same end, that of forcing the ethnic minorities to divest themselves of the cultural elements central to their identity. In sum, the promise of a new synthesis—a unique and homogeneous American culture from the melting pot—was a myth. It was an illusion because

> given the prior arrival time of the English colonists, the numerical dominance of Anglo-Saxon institutions, the invitation extended to non-English immigrants to "melt" could only result, if thoroughly accepted, in the loss of their group identity, the transformation of their cultural survival into Anglo-Saxon patterns, and the development of their descendants in the image of the Anglo-Saxon American (Gordon, 1964, p. 136).

What the melting pot myth did was to reinforce the enthnocentrism of the majority and convince ethnic minorities that their ethnicity and cultural heritage were illegitimate and hence needed to be abandoned. Educationally, children of the dominant group were robbed of the opportunity to enrich their lives by learning about and appreciating other cultures as different but effective alternative ways of dealing with essentially similar human problems. On the other hand, masses of ethnic minority children learned to be ashamed of their cultural heritage. Nonwhite children had to live with the awareness that at best they were second-class citizens. But a more pervasive and pernicious effect of the melting pot myth was that children of all groups were given a picture of the American society that was neither realistic nor consonant with the fundamental ideals found in the U.S. Constitution.

The 1920s and 1930s were a time of educational reform and new ideas, often in the name of social reform and expanded democracy. However, neither the concept of the "social reconstructionist school" of Harold Rugg nor

William Heard Kilpatrick's "project method" in the 1920s and the 1930s gave serious thought to the ways in which cultural variables affect how and what children learn. In principle, nothing in Rugg's concern for the learner's freedom, self-expression, and creativity or in Kilpatrick's interest in learning as inquiry would have been inconsistent with or contradictory to the notion that cultural factors do play an important role in the teaching-learning processes. But the Anglo-Saxon model, that is, the deficit view, was so pervasively and deeply ingrained in the larger society and in education as a discipline that the need for a critical cultural analysis of education and the schooling process in America probably did not occur to either Rugg, Kilpatrick, or their contemporaries.

Not surprisingly, a similar educational perspective continued into the late 1950s. Even in *The Pursuit of Excellence,* a report prepared by the Rockefeller Brothers Foundation in 1958 as a response to *Sputnik,* a serious discussion about the relationship between American education and ethnic minorities was conspicuously absent. James B. Conant's 1959 report, *The American High School Today,* which was seen by the public and educators as a means of implementing what was recommended in *The Pursuit of Excellence,* suggested a comprehensive curriculum. Conant's "comprehensive high school" was to include a good general education program (English, American literature, composition, and social studies) for everyone. Electives in vocational and commercial or other work-related studies were to be provided for non-college-bound young people, while advanced work in foreign languages, mathematics, and science was to be made available to the academically gifted. Conant did recommend improving the quality of education for blacks so that they could become integrated into the socioeconomic mainstream. Although this suggestion was based on providing blacks with learning environments similar to those of white middle-class youth, he made no mention of the ways in which different cognitive and learning styles and other cultural factors might have helped develop alternative ways of helping blacks to do better educationally. The possibility that studies of other cultural patterns, both at home and abroad, could have added richness to the learners' life and self-image did not occupy a significant place in his report.

Following *The Pursuit of Excellence* and Conant's report, public school personnel, scholars, and private foundations sought to achieve educational excellence through innovative approaches to teaching and academic subjects such as the physical and biological sciences, mathematics, and the social sciences. By the beginning of 1960 the schools were doing more things for more people than ever before, for

> the schools . . . were transformed significantly. . . . Vocational training was introduced as a principal component of the junior and senior high-school curriculum; social studies programs sought to connect the school's substance to local community activities; physical education and the arts made

their way into the curriculum; a substantial extracurriculum developed, organized largely around student athletics, student journalism, student government, and student clubs; and the materials of study and instruction changed to reflect a greater concern for the individual child and his progress through the various academic subjects. (Cremin, 1977, pp. 100–101)

In the 1954 Supreme Court decision, *Brown v. Board of Education,* the court mandated desegregation of public schools within a "reasonable time" because "separate but equal" education was considered inherently unequal. But most of the literature on educational reforms, curriculum and instructional theories, and pedagogy up to the late 1950s was based on the implicit assumption that all effective learning occurred when the Anglo styles of thinking, learning, and communicating were used and the learners lived in a white middle-class-like environment. Indeed, the picture of the American society, its norms, and its history still remained overwhelmingly Anglo-Saxon. The fact that the school operated according to the majority's norms, and so the young needed to function according to these norms for success in school and society, is beyond dispute. But for educators and scholars to have not even explored the possibility that other ways of thinking, learning, acting, and judging may have helped the culturally different to learn more effectively was culturally ethnocentric, intellectually myopic, and educationally tunnel-visioned at best. As Carlson (1975) rightly argues, through all of the changes the American school went through from 1870 to the early 1960s, "in keeping with the public's expectations, the schools worked hard to purge all real differences in the name of national unity [and educational excellence]" (p. 134).

As Diane Ravitch (1983), a historian of education, points out, by the early 1960s "there was a broad perception . . . that the United States was in the grip of an 'urban crisis'" because of "the changing racial composition of the cities" (p. 147). About 56% of the black population (12.1 million) had moved to major urban areas in search of better economic, social, and educational opportunities. Although some were successful in improving their lot, many found their lives in large cities to be filled with as much or even more poverty, unemployment, poor education, and racial discrimination as they had encountered in their earlier southern rural areas. But as Ravitch (1983) correctly notes, "the 'urban crisis' atmosphere had political implications, for it galvanized the impulse to take action against poverty and to respond to black grievances and make possible a breakthrough on the long-stalled issue of federal aid to education" (p. 148).

As we will see later, the movement of the southern blacks into major northern cities, coupled with a dramatic and massive influx of immigrants from Asian and Latin American nations after 1965, was to alter drastically the racial and cultural makeup of the population of the country and its schools.

According to demographic projections, one of every three schoolchildren will be from an ethnic, racial, or linguistic minority by the year 2000 *(Education Letter,* 1988, p. 1). Not surprisingly, these changes in our demographic landscape and in our educational institutions, in turn, were to challenge the ways in which educators viewed the "what" and the "how" of the teaching-learning and the schooling processes. But more of this later.

In keeping with the increasing concern for the elimination of poverty in the early 1960s and the acceleration of the civil rights movement, President Lyndon B. Johnson introduced his Great Society programs, including educational measures. Special provisions, such as the 1964 Economic Opportunity Act and the Elementary and Secondary Education Act of 1965, allocated federal funds for education on the basis of the number of poor children in school. These new legislations were viewed as the avenues through which full civil rights and economic, social, political, and educational equality were to be assured for the poor and ethnic minorities. Numerous projects and programs were also designed to promote better understanding of the significant roles played by various minority racial and cultural groups in the development of this country.

However, the massive War on Poverty did not fully achieve the promise of America becoming a Great Society without poverty or injustice, save some instances of modest socioeconomic gains made by limited sectors of the society. Educationally, a dearth of clear evidence shows that these special efforts have not had significant impact on the cognitive growth of minority children, on their image of their own ethnic identity, or on the ways in which the schools meet the educational needs of the ethnic minorities in contemporary America.

THE GREAT SOCIETY PROGRAMS (1965–1970)

In principle, the notion of the Great Society was founded on the implicit assumption that America was to be a society in which parity of power prevailed among all groups. This was to be achieved through providing social and economic equality, which was to be accomplished by ensuring equal access to education for all races, ethnicities, and genders. But such a society is not possible without what Alfredo Castaneda (1974) called "cultural democracy"—a system in which both the dominant and minority cultural groups share common national concerns, values, and attitudes and which also allows minority cultures to maintain themselves and grow in their own unique ways if not endangering others. As Banks (1981) aptly puts it, "this can happen only when structurally and economically excluded ethnic and racial groups feel included into society and view themselves as legitimate citizens of the nation state" (p. 240). Indeed, "the school can play a significant role in legitimizing the cultures, values, and life-styles of minority groups and in helping them to gain a sense of inclusion into the fabric of society" (pp. 240–241).

Yet the Great Society programs concentrated primarily on educational programs to help poor and minority individuals improve their cognitive skills so that they could find better jobs. Neither politicians nor educators recognized the significance of the inextricable relationship between the parity of political and economic powers and the principle of cultural democracy. Hence, "while American public education has continually attempted to keep alive the principles of political and economic democracy, it has been antagonistic to the principle of cultural democracy, the right of every American child to remain identified with his own ethnic, racial, or social group while at the same time exploring mainstream American cultural forms with regard to language, heritage, values, cognition, and motivation" (Castaneda, 1974, p. 15).

Thus, compensatory education, an important part of the Great Society programs, was conceived primarily in economic terms. It was considered a means of helping the educationally disadvantaged children of the poor and ethnic minorities to acquire the necessary cognitive skills (reading, writing, and computational skills) that would eventually lift them out of their low socioeconomic status through finding and keeping better-paying jobs. For this reason, many of the compensatory education programs came from legislation related to economic opportunity. Though numerous programs were made available to children in preschool to secondary school, our discussion of compensatory education will focus on Project Head Start, which had annual budgets of about one billion dollars in recent years (Levine & Havighurst, 1989). Examining Head Start and its outcome is particularly important because the project contained a number of elements that have influenced and will continue to influence the ways in which American children, particularly those in minority groups, are educated. From the cultural foundations perspective, the elements deserving careful scrutiny are (1) the deficit model of viewing minority groups and the concept of cultural deprivation, (2) the use of nonstandard English, and (3) the use of standardized intelligence (IQ) tests in psychoeducational assessment and placement of schoolchildren, especially those who come from poor and minority families. As we will see, there are those who are deeply convinced that the presence of these factors in compensatory education has worked against the establishment of cultural democracy by reinforcing the ethnocentric and culturally imperialistic aspects of schooling in America.

Project Head Start: Boon or Bane?

As has already been pointed out, Project Head Start, which began in the summer of 1965, was an important aspect of the War on Poverty. Its primary goal was to provide preschool education for "culturally deprived" children. By

1994, it had served over 13.8 million children (ACF, 1995). The project established "child development centers" where children of 4, 5, and 6 years of age were provided with sensory, cognitive, and social experiences that would help them develop adequate language and the perceptual and attentional skills and motivations needed to succeed in school. These experiences involved field trips and the use of a wide variety of objects and books, as well as work with individual teachers and volunteers. In addition, the centers provided physical examinations, dental care, and free meals. Although a high proportion of the children in the program were black, the project was integrated in both the North and the South in conformity with the Civil Rights Act. The entire project was based on the implicit assumption that massive intervention in the lives of "culturally deprived" children and their families would help the young to succeed educationally and socioeconomically. Accordingly, the primary purpose of the project was to help poor children grow intellectually, socially, and emotionally. However, much greater stress was placed on children's cognitive growth than on other areas. In keeping with this emphasis, project success was viewed in relation to increases in the children's proficiency in the use of standard English and in their IQ scores.

As worthy as the project's goal was, a 1970 evaluation of Project Head Start by the Westinghouse Learning Corporation and Ohio University ("Illiteracy," 1970) and other subsequent studies (e.g., Bronfenbrenner, 1974; Caruso & Detterman, 1981) suggested that many of the cognitive (IQ) gains achieved by the Head Start children were "washed out" by the end of the second or the third grade once the program was discontinued. Bronfenbrenner (1974) did point out that cognitively oriented programs involving tutors who worked with children and parents had the greatest impact on the children's cognitive growth. He further added that massive ecological interventions (social and economic reforms) were necessary to make the project effective. Yet he provided no evidence to suggest that IQ gains would be sustained even if the programs were discontinued.

A general conclusion of the previously cited evaluations was that non-Head Start children performed equally well on IQ tests and in school by the end of second or third grade. To some, this implied that Project Head Start as an early intervention had very little, if any, lasting effect on children's intellectual or emotional growth. In a controversial article, psychologist Arthur Jensen (1969) went so far as to insist that the early intervention programs failed because they were unable to raise the IQ scores of Head Start children. As he continues to argue, "in the general mental ability that a person manifests over an extended period, the genetic part of the variance of that ability in the population is consistently greater than the environment part" (p. 108). Some advocates of Project Head Start held that Jensen's article gave the federal government an excuse for reducing its support of the early intervention programs. But in spite of these strong criticisms, other researchers reported that the Head Start children not only retained significantly higher IQ gains than non-Head Start children of comparable backgrounds but also that the former as a group performed substantially better in school than the latter (Schweinhart & Weikart, 1977). Still others insisted that the program yielded certain intangible, nonquantifiable emotional and social benefits for the Head Start children and that these children, as compared to others, tended to be more aggressive, assertive, and sociable. Further, Head Start had positive impacts on families and communities by encouraging parental involvement, providing jobs and services, and coordinating community social services (U.S. Department of Health and Human Services, 1984).

Was Project Head Start and compensatory education a boon or a bane? A dilemma in attempting to answer this question is that no body of definitive evidence either confirms or rejects the claim that Head Start or other compensatory education programs had lasting impacts on the educational development of poor and minority children. Of course, considering the massiveness of the Head Start program, it may seem reasonable to think that the jury is still out on the project's success or failure. Yet it is doubtful that we will ever obtain definitive evidence to show how effective or ineffective the project has been because a reliable and comprehensive evaluation is probably not possible. Two major reasons account for this predicament. One is the fact that the programs varied widely in their purpose, scope, format, and content, as well as in the competence of the teachers involved. Consequently, as Levine and Havighurst (1984) suggest, the goals of compensatory education were not only poorly defined but also often shifted, because it was "a major national issue involving fundamental values in society . . . and everyone [could] agree on the goal of equal educational opportunity stated at this level of generality, but disagreement occur[red] as soon as the goal [was] stated in operational terms" (p. 247). The other major reason was the lack of standardized evaluation schemes, which should have been an integral part of the project from the beginning. More technically, the difficulties and weaknesses in the evaluative studies of compensatory education programs "can be summed up in three broad problems: (1) inadequate sampling, (2) failure to establish comparable experimental and control groups, and (3) techniques of data collection that make reliability and validity suspect" (Ornstein, 1978, p. 364). The difficulties of assessing Head Start were worsened during the 1980s when funding for Head Start was greatly reduced, resulting in a significant decline of onsite monitoring (Zigler & Muenchow, 1992, p. 223).

As equivocal as the evidence for or against the success of compensatory education programs was, some have denounced the programs by arguing that the entire notion of compensatory education was founded on the deficit view of minorities, which regarded cultural, linguistic, cognitive, and affective as well as behavioral differences as pathological conditions to be eliminated (Baratz & Baratz, 1970, p. 34). Consequently, compensatory education was a culturally imperialistic attempt to make all poor and minority children emulate white middle-class children and, as such, was incapable of producing cultural democracy.

Because of the deficit model, even attempts to present a balanced picture of minority cultures in America through ethnic and non-Western studies did not lead to substantial changes in the ways in which non-Anglo cultures were depicted in instructional materials. For example, Michael B. Kane's *Minorities in Textbooks,* written in 1970, indicated that of 30 standard textbooks in American history, American problems, and civics, two history texts and eight civics texts completely omitted material on Asian Americans. Eleven American history and five social problems textbooks mentioned only Japanese Americans. Although this survey dealt with only one segment of minority groups in this country, the result indicated the extreme paucity of balanced and representative materials on ethnic groups in contemporary America. FitzGerald (1979) decried the distorted portrayal of blacks, Asian Americans, Hispanics, and Native Americans in 111 history textbooks. These same texts also presented the United States "as an ideal construct. . . . a place without conflicts, without malice or stupidity, where Dick (black or white) comes home with a smiling Jane to a nice house in the suburbs" (p. 218). FitzGerald warns:

> To the extent that young people actually believe them, these bland fictions, propagated for the purpose of creating good citizens, may actually achieve the opposite; they give young people no warning of the real dangers ahead, and later may well make these young people feel that their own experience of conflict or suffering is unique in history and perhaps un-American. To the extent that children can see the contrast between these fictions and the world around them, this kind of instruction can only make them cynical. (p. 218)

In a more recent study of six textbooks in American history, Glazer and Ueda (1983) found that these books devoted only 11.6% (high) to 5.4% (low) of the total pages to ethnic groups (p. 17). When we consider that these books ranged from 726 to 842 pages, only a very small number of pages dealt with minority cultures. Much more important, Glazer and Ueda discovered that the texts portrayed ethnic minorities as victims of "tragic" circumstances such as "ignorance of other cultures, fear of strange appearance, prejudice, and unavoidable 'cultural clash' between a free-enterprise, industrializing society and populations with preindustrial forms of social and culture life" (p. 19). This meant that very little, if any, attention was given to the political role and the cultural contributions of ethnic minorities in the development of America as a nation. The history of ethnic groups may then be seen as a constant struggle between the oppressed and the oppressors. Glazer and Ueda argue that this view of history not only trivializes "the central processes that integrated American society" but also "fails to show how their [dominant and minority groups'] joint participation in historical movements created a fluid and pluralistic social system" (p. 61).

Based on the three studies just discussed, it would appear that compensatory education efforts have had no material effect on the ways in which minority cultures are presented to the children in our schools. Our efforts to help the poor and culturally different were founded on the traditional concept of Anglo-Americanism, which defines being normal, educable, and American as conforming only to the social, cognitive, and moral norms of the dominant culture. We have failed to recognize and correct these ethnocentric assumptions underlying the compensatory education projects. In Diane Ravitch's words, "in the jargon of the day, compensatory education was the answer to cultural deprivation . . . [and it] was a misnomer with an unnecessarily pejorative tone" (1983, p. 153).

Compensatory Education and the Myth of Cultural Deprivation

According to proponents of compensatory education, the inability of individuals from low socioeconomic and culturally different classes to free themselves from their deprivation was due primarily to their cognitive deficiency—inadequate language, perceptual and other cognitive skills, and lack of motivation. They argued that these deficiencies, caused by sensory and cultural deprivation, forced the children to start school with a serious handicap that made them fall academically further and further behind their more "favored" peers as they moved up the grades. In other words, early cognitive deficits and cultural deprivation would have cumulatively harmful effects with the passing years (Bloom, Davis, & Hess, 1965; Bloom, 1976). One of the most serious consequences of this situation was that the children of low socioeconomic class were trapped in their low class status.

Advocates of compensatory education insisted that the most effective means of liberating the disadvantaged from poverty and low social status was to give them the kinds of educational, social, and even sensory experiences that enabled middle-class white children to acquire the skills and attitudes believed to be necessary for a successful life in American society. In sum, poor and minority children were believed to have suffered from a lack of educability resulting from cultural deprivation, which in turn stemmed from deficient sensory and social experiences (Baratz & Baratz, 1970, p. 35). They further held that since the deleterious effects of early cognitive deficits could not be "remedied" or compensated for in a few weeks or months or by educational programs alone, they should extend the intervention programs and alter the children's own sociocultural environments, for example, by child-rearing practices. For this reason, Project Head Start was required by law to include parental and community participation and to promote the physical, social, emotional, and intellectual growth of the children. Thus, intervention in all aspects of the child's life was regarded as necessary, and the earlier the intervention, the greater the benefit. Nothing short of total effort was thought to be adequate for successful compensatory education.

If we interpret the expression *culturally deprived children* in its literal sense, it suggests that some children are without any culture. However, advocates of this concept, who attributed minority children's inadequate educability to cultural deprivation, were not insisting that these children did not have a culture of their own. "It appears, therefore, that the term [cultural deprivation] becomes a euphemism for saying that working-class and ethnic groups have cultures which are at least dissonant with, if not inferior to, the 'mainstream' culture of the society at large" (Keddie, 1973, p. 8). To put it more bluntly, children from ethnic groups had been deprived of the culture possessed by all "normal" (WASP) people. This ethnocentric assumption may be said to have come from a misconception of "the egalitarian principle—which asserts that all people are created equal under the law and must be treated as such from a moral and political [and intellectual] point of view. This normative view, however, wrongly equates equality with sameness" (Baratz & Baratz, 1970, p. 31). Hence, all members of this society were expected to speak, believe, and act the same according to a single idealized norm—the dominant pattern. It is in this sense that compensatory education was said to have perpetuated institutional racism (perhaps unintentionally) by teaching children to assimilate into the mainstream culture and abandon their own unique ethnic traits.

Because the behaviors, beliefs, and values of minority cultures were seen as deficits, those who believed in the cultural deprivation concept failed to recognize the possibility of helping minority children learn more effectively by utilizing the richness and the strengths of their cultures. With its social pathology view of ethnic groups, compensatory education—particularly Project Head Start—denied the strengths within an ethnic community and may unintentionally have promoted annihilation of a cultural system that is little understood by most social scientists (Baratz & Baratz, 1970, p. 30). As a result, the belief that to deviate from whites is to be inferior was reinforced.

It should be remembered that the critics of the concept of cultural deprivation did not deny that there was a close relationship between social class and school success, nor did they reject the fact that sensory and cultural experiences of middle-class children were key requisites for doing well in school. Moreover, they did recognize the need for poor and minority children to acquire the kinds of cognitive and social skills to perform better academically through the kinds of sensory and cultural experiences usually available in white middle-class-like environments. But the critics did object to the suggestion that the sorts of experiences had by minority children were either pathologically deviant or socially and morally illegitimate. For example, the critics found that the cultural deprivation view implicitly assumed the child-rearing practices of poor black mothers to have been inadequate (often referred to as the *inadequate mothering hypothesis*) and the sensory or perceptual experiences of poor and minority children to have been deficient for the development of intelligence. Hence, as Bernstein (1985) indicates, "if children are labeled 'culturally deprived,' then it follows that the parents are inadequate, and that the spontaneous realization of their culture, its images and symbolic representations, are of reduced value and significance. Teachers will have lower expectations of the children, which the children will undoubtedly fulfill" (p. 137).

Indeed, the social and cognitive skills that allowed these children to function well in their cultural environment probably did not provide an optimal basis for developing the attitudes and skills necessary for academic achievement and getting ahead in the mainstream society. On the other hand, the kinds of mental and behavioral norms valued by the dominant culture and its institutions were not necessarily useful in helping minority individuals participate effectively in their community life. The patterns of cognitive skills and affective dispositions that would enable an individual to function effectively in a given situation are relative to the person's social, cultural, and intellectual contexts. Demands of people's way of life determine their styles of social interaction and thinking, which in turn influence their ways of learning. Thus, different cultures encourage the performance of certain tasks and the development of related talents and abilities to be fostered in their members. Goodwin Watson of Teachers College and Frank Riessman, author of *The Culturally Deprived Child,* noted that minority children could be helped to attain much greater academic achievement if educators understood the culture of these children (Riessman, 1962). Further, teachers and other members of the mainstream culture may learn something from the so-called deprived children. A central point in this view is that rather than attempting to proselytize these children into the middle-class culture, the schools should respect their culture and values and try to meet the special needs of poor and ethnic minority children.

As intense debates over the soundness of the cultural deprivation perspective continued, the term *culturally deprived* was modified to *culturally disadvantaged,* which eventually took the current form of *culturally different* in an attempt to erase ethnocentric and racist connotations. Teachers were reminded that cultural factors affected the teaching-learning processes, and various other specialists were encouraged to convey a more positive image of minority cultures through revising instructional methods and materials. But unfortunately, many of these attempts were based on rather general views about the relationship between culture and education without specific information about it or strategies for educating the culturally different. The disputes about whether the poor had a distinct culture of their own or whether they "suffered" the same sort of cultural deprivation as the children of ethnic groups complicated the issues regarding the educational needs of minority children. Even today, there is a serious and conspicuous absence of knowledge regarding how varying cultural variables affect the teaching-learning processes and the cognitive and affective development of children. This indeed is a consequence of educators' inability or unwillingness to understand the dynamic relationship between culture and education.

More specific educational implications of the notion of cultural deprivation and its implicit assumptions about minority cultures will be discussed in greater detail in Chapters 6 and 7. One important point should be made here. The central issue in the cultural deprivation debate is not about whether poor and minority children should learn the ways of the dominant culture to the exclusion of their own cultural norms, nor is it about the desirability of allowing these children to keep their own ways without learning the mainstream culture. The American school and society should be concerned with helping all children regardless of race, ethnicity, and gender to function effectively in a wide range of sociocultural and intellectual environments and divergent contexts without doing violence to the worth of their own culture and self-esteem. To accomplish this, it is not enough to be generally aware that cultures influence how children learn and grow. We must have specific knowledge about the varied ways of thinking, believing, learning, and communicating and how they impinge upon what schools and other institutions do. Cross-cultural research studies need to be conducted to develop concrete instructional strategies and curricular materials to assist our children, particularly those who come from lower socioeconomic classes and minority cultures, in developing social and intellectual skills that will allow them to deal successfully with a myriad of life concerns.

Minority Languages in the Classroom

Standard English v. Black Dialect

One manifestation of the social pathology perspective is the way in which the dominant group views the use of such nonstandard English as Black Dialect (also called Black English or Ebonics). Even today, most school administrators and teachers regard standard English as the only "correct" form of English. Consequently, they treat the linguistic patterns of black children "as a structureless, unexpressive, 'incorrect' version of what arrogant cultural elites are pleased to call standard English" (Valentine, 1971, p. 138). Hence, these children are labeled as nonverbal or verbally deficient, and their use of nonstandard English is viewed as a serious barrier to their cognitive development and classroom success. But systematic studies (Dillard, 1972; Keddie, 1973; Harber & Bryan, 1976) indicate that the so-called errors actually conform to discernible grammatical rules, different from those of the standard language but not less systematic (Labov, 1972). Moreover, "there is simply no evidence that certain formal characteristics interfere with the learning of anything except other formal characteristics" (Horner & Gussow, 1985, p. 157). The Black Dialect appears to be a language pattern more closely associated with the black lower middle class than the middle class. Studies suggest that higher academic performance is more positively correlated with higher social class; thus, the lower academic achievement by poor black children may be a function of social class rather than language (Schacter, 1979).

According to professor Jane W. Torrey (1970), a psychologist, statements such as "We at Jane house," "Jane makin' me a cow," and "It look like you don't brush your teeth" follow the rules of Black English consistently. Using these rules, the words *is* and *are* can be deleted in many contexts, the possessive *s* is optional, and the third person singular or present tense verb has no distributive *s* ending. The dialect is no less systematic in its rules and structure or more ambiguous in its expression than standard English. This implies that Black English is a legitimate linguistic form both structurally and functionally. Hence, we ought not to regard it as a "corrupt" version of the "right," or standard English. This is not to suggest that children from black or any other ethnic communities should not be taught to use standard English, but it does mean that the standard form should be taught as a second language in addition to their own linguistic pattern. In other words:

> The teaching of standard English should not have the purpose of "stamping out" the native dialect. Standard English would be a second language, or rather, a second dialect, to be available alongside the native one for special purposes such as school and contact with the standard-community. (Torrey, 1970, p. 254)

The perspective on teaching standard English to ethnic minority children is particularly important when we consider the fact that "youngsters learn the content of their ethnic cultures through their parent's dialect" and that it also "serves the youngsters in the formation of their perceptions, attitudes, and values about their physical and human environment" (Banks, 1981, p. 164). For this reason, the dominant group's view of Black English is likely to have a significant impact on how black children see themselves and their culture.

It is a handicap for a French-speaking child if he has to do all of his schoolwork in English. It is also a disadvantage for an English-speaking child to function in a French-speaking school. Similarly, just as it is a handicap for black children to be able to speak only their own dialect in the "standard-speaking" community, it is equally disadvantageous for them to speak only standard English on the streets of Harlem. Again, as Kochman (1985) points out, "black social workers, news reporters, and others find that knowledge of black dialect is an invaluable asset in communicating with indigenous community people, a factor that puts white workers in these and other professions at a clear disadvantage" (p. 230). This suggests that "education for culturally different children should not attempt to destroy functionally viable processes of the subculture minority cultures. . . . The goal of such education should be to produce a bicultural [multicultural] child who is capable of functioning both in his subculture and in the mainstream" (Baratz & Baratz, 1970, pp. 42–43).

The most pernicious effect of assimilating all minority children into a single linguistic, behavioral, and value orientation toward the dominant culture is that these children learn to regard themselves and their ethnic community as bad, ugly, and inferior. When the linguistic forms that they have learned spontaneously and that have served them so well are associated with a low-status, rejected culture, children become alienated from the teacher and his or her culture as well as from their own ethnic heritage. This then becomes a basis of hostility toward and rejection of the whole educational process and the mainstream culture as racist and culturally imperialistic. Mitchell-Kernan (1985) suggests that in recent years, the use of the Black Dialect has taken on a special symbolic value; that is,

> differences in language use are seen as adaptions to the circumstances of pariah status. They are also viewed as reflecting a culture history linked to Africa as well as Western Europe. . . . The use of Black English is beginning to symbolize a spirit of liberation in the black community, and the separatist function of Black English has become more explicit. (p. 209)

As we have already seen in the preceding analysis of the assumptions of compensatory education, these educational measures were insensitive to the unique and meaningful ethnic traits minority children bring to the classroom setting. The school defined educability only in terms of the children's ability to perform within an alien (dominant) culture. Hence, the school was unable (or unwilling) to use the children's distinct cultural patterns as the means for teaching them new skills and additional cultural styles.

We should not regard ethnic minorities as worthy of our respect only to the extent that we can "melt" them into the mainstream culture. We must see their culturally based characteristics, such as their use of language, as legitimate and functional patterns worthy of respect and growth. To achieve this goal, the schools should offer a curriculum "which is not only immediately functional within the student's present life experience but also preparatory toward developing skills that are necessary for future use. For example, developing elaborate style in the native dialect would have the effect of creating a use of language that has the same functional capacity as standard dialect, yet would not tamper with the student's identification with and self-realization through his native dialect" (Kochman, 1985, pp. 252–253). For this to happen, the school personnel involved in teaching culturally different children as well as all of middle-class America must free themselves from their narrow "Anglo ethnocentric bag" (p. 254).

It would be unrealistic to expect to change the attitude of school administrators and teachers toward minority cultures without also reforming the whole educational, social, and economic system of America. Educationally, this means that "the academic world in general must broaden its cultural base beyond those subjects, methods, and media that have been traditional in schools and universities, or they will continue to discriminate against the 'other' cultures and languages of the nation" (Torrey, 1970, p. 259). Cultural pluralism based on multicultural education is, then, essential as a broader cultural foundation of American education. Finally, it should be pointed out that in criticizing the assumptions underlying compensatory education, no attempt is made to suggest that minority groups need not acquire those skills and attitudes that the dominant society requires for socioeconomic success. Rather, we should see that the unexamined assumptions of compensatory education, namely, the deficit view, may have defeated the very purposes for which the Great Society programs were initiated.

Today, we cannot ignore the fact that ethnic minorities seek to achieve higher social and economic status by "making it" in the mainstream society. And to "make it" they must learn those cognitive and social skills, behaviors, and attitudes that the dominant society regards as necessary for economic, social, and political success. Granting that some individuals may wish to remain in their own ethnic enclave permanently, most members of minority cultures should become multicultural so that they can function optimally both in the dominant and in their own cultures.

Bilingual Education

Bilingual education involves more than teaching schoolchildren in two languages, for it is closely bound up with the issues related to educational equality, assimilation of minority children, and the development and maintenance of the ethnic identity of the culturally different young people in our society. Indeed, these matters are intimately connected with the concerns discussed in the preceding section. Although there are many different types of bilingual education programs, they can be grouped into the following general categories: (1) transitional programs, (2) immersion programs, (3) submersion programs, (4) programs for English as a second language (ESL), and (5) bilingual/bicultural programs.

In transitional programs, children's native or primary languages and the English language are used as a means of helping them learn English. The immersion approach involves teaching the new (English) language to non-English-speaking (NES) and limited-English-speaking (LES) children by a teacher who is proficient in the learners' primary language, but only English is used by the teacher. In transitional as well as immersion programs, children are usually moved into regular English-speaking classes as soon as they acquire sufficient command of the English language to do their academic work. Accordingly, maintaining a learner's primary language is not an objective of either approach. Unlike the immersion approach, in submersion programs NES and LES children are placed directly in all English-speaking classes without special help. Figuratively speaking, submersion classes may be called the "sink or swim" type programs. The submersion experiences cannot be called bilingual, in the strict sense of the term, because neither the children nor their teacher use more than one language. However, some contend that this is the most rapid and effective way to help children master English. As one may infer, the primary purpose of the transitional, immersion, and submersion approaches is not only to teach English to NES and LES children but also to help them learn the norms of the dominant culture so that they can function effectively in the mainstream society. Hence, critics accuse these programs of assimilating language minority children into the dominant group without promoting the development of pride in their own ethnic heritage.

Unlike the programs just described, teaching English as a second language involves placing NES and LES children in all-English-speaking classes, but they are assigned to separate classes or tutors who are trained to teach English as a second language (ESL). Although most ESL instructors are prepared to use special methods and techniques in their work, they may or may not have proficiency in a language other than English. ESL programs are usually used for transitional purposes, but they may also be used to teach English while maintaining the primary languages of NES and LES children. Finally, bilingual/bicultural programs, otherwise known as maintenance programs, are based on the belief that linguistically and culturally different children have distinctive educational needs, for they must live in bilingual and bicultural environments. To linguistically different children, maintaining their primary languages and developing pride in their cultural heritages are thought to be as important as mastering the English language in becoming productive and responsible citizens. Bilingual/bicultural programs teach English as well as studies in ethnic heritages, and at the same time promote maintenance of the native languages of NES and LES children.

Implementation of bilingual/bicultural programs and the immersion programs have had problems and will continue to encounter serious difficulties because few bilingual teachers can conduct these classes effectively. Even in teaching English as a second language there appears to be a shortage of qualified personnel. Ironically, the submersion and even the immersion approaches may encounter problems in large metropolitan areas where the majority of children in many classes are from linguistic and cultural minority groups. Hence, in cities such as Los Angeles, New York, and Chicago the language in which the children are to be immersed or submerged could be a language other than English.

Controversies About Bilingual Education   Bilingual education has been one of the most controversial issues in American education because its purposes have deep ideological roots. In the late 1960s to about 1970, when the controversy first took hold, many viewed bilingual education as a means of assimilating minority children into the dominant culture. They argued that the sooner these children became an integral part of the mainstream society the more likely they would be to attain socioeconomic success. Advocates of this perspective supported transitional, immersion, or submersion programs. Others were convinced that bilingual education should help minority children develop positive self-images by maintaining their primary language and perpetuating their unique cultural patterns while teaching English so they could function in the larger society. Thus, bilingual education needed to be also bicultural. These opposing views were held (and are still held) not only by educators and legislators but also by members of minority groups themselves. The divisions in the opinions regarding the primary purpose of bilingual education have been directly related to the conflicting findings of program evaluation studies. Moreover, these disputes added to the public's negative perception of bilingual education and non-English-speaking groups and may have fueled the impetus for the so-called English Only or English as the Official Language movements in 37 states in recent years ("English Only," 1987).

Prior to the passage of the Bilingual Education Act of 1968, a congressional hearing on bilingual education was held in 1967. The hearing focused on meeting the unique educational needs of Hispanic children who had either no or limited command of the English language. At the time, not much was known about the cause-effect relationship between Hispanic children's negative self-image, their school failure, and the use of English rather than Spanish as the language of instruction. Yet witnesses at the hearing argued that Spanish-English bilingual education would enable Hispanic young people to achieve higher self-esteem and academic success (Ravitch, 1983, p. 272). Whether facts or assumptions, the beliefs that bilingual/bicultural education (including the use of Black English) would improve the self-concept of linguistically different children and that their positive self-concept would help them do well in school were and still are widely accepted by many educators. They are persuaded that a significant connection exists between the maintenance of minority children's primary language, their sense of ethnic identity, and their academic performance. In spite of the testimony given at the 1967 hearing, the intent of the Bilingual Education Act of 1968 was to provide the resources for transitional rather than "maintenance" programs to poor and non- or limited-English-speaking children.

In 1974, a suit was brought against the San Francisco Board of Education before the United States Supreme Court on behalf of 1,800 Chinese children. In this class action suit, known as *Lau v. Nichols,* the plaintiffs argued that the San Francisco Board of Education had failed to meet the educational needs of the non-English-speaking Chinese children by not providing programs specifically designed for them. They further held that the board therefore violated Title VI of the Civil Rights Act of 1964 as well as the Equal Protection Clause of the Fourteenth Amendment. In response to these charges, the school board insisted that all children received equal education and that children's ability to understand the English language was the responsibility of their families rather than the school district. In deciding for the plaintiffs, the Supreme Court upheld the 1970 guideline of the Office of Civil Rights, which required that a school district must provide appropriate instructional programs to children with limited proficiency in the English language.

Although the Lau decision did not mandate bilingual education programs, it required school districts to develop and offer special language programs for NES and LES children. The Supreme Court opinion did not favor either the transitional or the maintenance programs. However, the "Lau remedies" formulated by then Commissioner of Education Terrell Bell and a special task force unequivocally recommended the teaching of English or the primary language as well as the cultural heritages of non-English-speaking children. Throughout the 1970s and into the early 1980s the federal government attempted to clarify, redefine, and reshape the purpose and the future direction of bilingual education without much success. The Department of Education's own skepticism about the effectiveness of bilingual programs as well as opposition from various citizens' groups and professional organizations in education may have contributed significantly to the federal government's inability to set a clear direction for bilingual education. For example, in 1985 the Reagan administration wanted to eliminate a measure that allowed the bulk of funding for bilingual education to be used for programs using students' native languages. This proposal was based on the belief that local schools should be given more flexibility in selecting instructional methods, such as those emphasizing English. However, bilingual educators insisted that more funds be given to the methods using students' native languages because these approaches were believed to be more effective. This long-standing disagreement was not resolved until March 1988, when the administration agreed to guarantee the present level of funding for bilingual education. A compromise agreement "to increase from 4 percent to 25 percent the portion of federal bilingual-education that can go to alternative, English-based programs" ("House-Senate Conferees," 1988, p. 16) was also reached at this time.

The disparate views regarding the purposes of bilingual education are closely tied to attitudes and beliefs about whether ethnic minority children should be assimilated into the mainstream culture or be allowed to maintain and develop their own culture while learning the dominant norms. These ideological elements have influenced not only what type of bilingual programs have been considered worthwhile but also the results of program evaluations. Reports have presented conflicting evidence of the programs' effectiveness. A 1977 report of the American Institute of Research (AIR) indicated that the academic performance of participants in the bilingual/bicultural programs did not improve consistently as a result of their involvement in them (American Institute of Research, 1977). Nor did participants learn English better in bilingual classrooms as compared to regular classes. But these findings were disputed by bilingual educators.

Reports on effectiveness of bilingual education programs continue to be mixed. Willig (1985) indicated that "participation in bilingual education programs consistently produced small to moderate differences favoring bilingual education for tests of reading, language skills, mathematics, and total achievement when the tests were in English, and for reading, language, mathematics, writing, social studies, listening comprehension, and attitudes toward school or self when tests were in other languages" (p. 269). In another study, Genesee (1985) points out that many children who speak nonstandard English and/or are from lower socioeconomic classes showed normal levels of first language development in immersion programs. Moreover, "contrary to some expectations, these types of students [ethnic minority students with below-average levels of academic ability] have been found to demonstrate the same rate and level of development in English and in academic domains as comparable groups of students attending regular English schools" (p. 557). He goes on to suggest that the two-way bilingual/immersion programs are truly bilingual programs in which both language/cultural groups or students and their teachers are integrated into the teaching-learning processes (p. 559). Today, some educators enthusiastically support the effectiveness of the two-way immersion approach ("Language Acquisition," 1987), but others caution against the prolonged use of native-language instruction, because the child is kept from the mainstream classroom and placed in a remedial program ("Language Acquisition," 1987). In a similar vein, a 1987 report issued by the Program Evaluation and Methodology Division of the U.S. General Accounting Office held that the native-language methods have failed to show superiority over other methods and that no sound research basis exists for the use of native languages as an effective bilingual education method.

As was the case with the evaluation of Project Head Start, wide variations in the types of programs offered, their purposes, and the quality of instruction are responsible for the conflicting assessments of bilingual education programs. Moreover, because of the ideological nature of the programs it is not likely that we will have clear consensus about either the efficacy or the desirability of bilingual education in any form. Learning to use two or more languages in any society is not merely an intellectual activity, because "languages often represent different social networks and associated value systems, and the choice of language can come to symbolize an individual's identification with either system" (Hakuta, 1986, p. 233). In a society that views the use of a minority language or a nonstandard English language as "strange," children are not apt to be motivated to learn or maintain anything other than standard English. It is for this reason that "bilingualism will be most stable when there are social norms that govern differential use of the two languages depending on the situation" (p. 233). This implies that significant changes in the attitudes of the larger society toward minority languages are essential for successful bilingual/bicultural education. But as opponents of bilingual education might ask, Is this type of education necessary in our society at all? Would it not be better for poor and ethnic minority young people to become assimilated into the dominant society as soon as possible for their socioeconomic success? Or as the proponents of the English Only movement might argue, Would bilingual/bicultural education not threaten the well-being of our society by encouraging separatism; isn't the use of a common language at the base of national unity?

As has been pointed out earlier, one out of every three schoolchildren will be from an ethnic, racial, or linguistic minority by the year 2000. More specifically, between 1978 and 1982 the number of non- or limited-English-speaking elementary and junior high school children increased from 3.8 million to 4.5 million ("When Children," 1986). When we consider the fact that the growth in the population of these children is not likely to decrease dramatically in the near future, the policy and programmatic decisions made at the local, state, and national levels are going to profoundly impact schooling in the United States. Insofar as these linguistically different children are members of this nation, the extent to which their special needs are or are not served will affect the future of the larger society. As Levine and Havighurst (1984) admonish:

> Regardless of whether one believes that bilingual education in the United States has been more or less effective or ineffective, it is clear that bilingual programs for linguistic minority students from economically disadvantaged families will have to do more than simply provide transitional or continuing instruction in the native language if it is to improve their achievement substantially in English and other subjects. (p. 474)

Regardless of our own perspectives on bilingual education, the reality for culturally different young people is that they must live in environments with at least two different linguistic and cultural norms, those of their own ethnic group and those of the dominant society. For them to lead a fulfilled life and preserve their personal dignity, they need not only linguistic, social, and cognitive skills but also the respect and the acceptance that should be accorded to diversities of all sorts in a democratic society. Although the relationships between diversity and democracy will be explored further in the next chapter, for now it is enough to say that the development of positive attitudes toward different cultures can be promoted not only through teaching language but also by developing the critical ways in which we understand and analyze our own culture and its underlying values.

In 1908, President Theodore Roosevelt demanded the deportation of immigrants who failed to learn English five years after their arrival on American shores, and the State of Iowa prohibited the use of languages other than English in gatherings of three or more people. In the United States today, there are still a significant number of individuals who are convinced that English is an endangered language needing legal protection. When asked why he supported Proposition 63, a legislative proposal to make English the official language of California, former U.S. Senator S. I. Hayakawa gave the following response:

> The whole idea is that there are so many so-called bilingual encroachments upon the use of English, even in official quarters, that we felt it was necessary to protect the English language. ("Is English," 1986, p. E6)

Implicit in this "protect English" or English Only movement is the belief that use of a common language is a necessary and sufficient condition for national unity. Although it is erroneous, many societies subscribe to this notion. This is not to suggest that a common language is unimportant in unifying a nation, along with such other elements as people's sense of historical continuity, a common purpose, individual uniqueness, and so on; sharing a language can become the foundation of a nation's unity. However, when "protecting English" is used as a central argument against bilingual education and bilingualism it often becomes a latent expression of hostility against ethnic and linguistic minority groups or immigrants as a whole. As Larmouth (1987) reminds us, educators must recognize that "the very concepts which unify a nation can divide it, if they are perceived by a disenfranchised minority . . . who feel themselves to be apart from the dominant population . . . and see themselves excluded from any realistic opportunity for advancement" (pp. 54–55). He goes on to suggest that if we were to adopt a constitutional amendment to make English our official language, we would increase

> a risk of disenfranchising a significant number of people, perhaps sufficiently to give rise to the very disunity that we fear. Though it may seem paradoxical, the best strategy would seem to be to continue to support a full range of opportunities for participation in the social and economic opportunities of the dominant culture, including opportunities to learn English, without disenfranchising or threatening ethnocultural minorities and their languages. Furthermore, since it seems clear that minority lan-

guages pose no threat to national unity in the United States, there is little basis for opposition to efforts to recover or maintain them. (p. 55)

Intelligence, IQ, and Culture

Because an extensive discussion of the cultural influences on the nature and the uses of IQ tests in the psychoeducational assessment of the learner will be included in Chapter 6, only a brief discussion of the conceptual relationships between intelligence, IQ, and culture will be given in this section. As one may suspect, the compensatory education programs of the 1970s were founded on the assumption that poor minority children could be helped to develop their cognitive and social skills by compensating for their environmental (sensory and cultural) deprivation. Hence, IQ gains were used as an important criterion in evaluating the effectiveness of Project Head Start. But Arthur Jensen's challenge that environmental conditions can do very little to boost children's IQ scores revived the old controversy regarding the heritability of intelligence (Jensen, 1969). Nature v. nurture disputes between the advocates of the heritability of intelligence and the environmentalists still go on. But is intelligence the same as IQ? Does a gain in one's IQ score imply a growth in intelligence?

As many psychologists and anthropologists have pointed out, intelligence is not a single unitary power a person has. Rather, it represents a complex of abilities that enable a person to recognize and solve problems. As Sternberg (1982) notes, "a social context (be it a classroom, a tribe, a family, a profession, or whatever) sets up a variety of problems, and intelligence consists in large part of the ability to solve these problems [of life]" (p. 17). This suggests that intelligence varies in quantity and quality. It involves much more than the kinds of skills or abilities measured by a paper-and-pencil or performance test. IQ is an index of a narrow set of abilities measured by a standardized test. Thus, the IQ score represents the child's standing in relation to other children of the same age who took the same test, that is, the norm group. In addition to certain special factors peculiar to a particular test, IQ tests in general measure the kinds of cognitive skills necessary to do academic work as well as the general intelligence factor called g. It is this g factor that Arthur Jensen (1981) believes to be highly heritable. In his words, "If what we are mainly interested in is not just a particular IQ score, but the general mental ability that a person manifests over an extended period, the genetic part of the variance of that ability in the population is considerably greater than the environmental part" (p. 108). He notes that blacks as a group score 10 to 15 points lower than whites on IQ tests.

The environmentalists attribute the lower IQ score of blacks to the *cultural loading* of IQ tests. In other words, the items in the tests favor the white middle-class population. But Jensen (1981) insists that "neither black nor white psychologists could pick out such [culturally loaded] items any better than chance" and that "bias can only be detected by objective statistical techniques applied to actual data" (p. 130). This leads him to the conclusion that "in all, educational inequalities of one kind or another probably account for at most 20 percent of IQ variance" (p. 184). What Jensen does not seem to recognize is the fact that tests, whether verbal or performance, are cultural artifacts themselves and that doing well on such instruments requires a whole set of skills and attitudes that are closely tied to the culture in which the tests were made and administered. It is probably for this reason that people in other cultures who do some very smart things in solving their life problems are often considered not intelligent because they perform poorly on standardized IQ tests in the West.

As we have already seen, the evaluation results of Project Head Start are very mixed at best. But even if evidence did support the view that Head Start children were able to maintain significant IQ gains throughout their elementary school days, it would be erroneous to conclude that their intelligence has increased significantly. For poor minority children, or for that matter for any children, a growth in their ability to solve life problems—that is, intelligence—requires the development of many more kinds of cognitive and affective as well as sociocultural skills than can be measured by standardized tests of g (Gardner, 1985). Notwithstanding the usefulness of IQ tests in certain limited areas, educators need to be cautious about classifying students in terms of such global indicators as IQ scores, thereby prejudging their "true" intelligence. Furthermore, learning about and relating to other cultures are skills at least as important as learning to function in one's own culture, for we live in a society with diverse races, cultures, religions, and socioeconomic and political perspectives.

In this chapter, we have examined the ways in which the dominant culture and its deficit model of viewing other cultures have affected the process of schooling, its policies and practices in the United States from the 17th century to the 1970s. Our nation has gone through many varied approaches in dealing with minority groups. In the 1960s and the 1970s, many individuals, groups, and agencies seriously attempted to eradicate prejudice, discrimination, and inequality in our society. As a result of these efforts, we are perhaps more sensitive to matters concerning human rights, equality, and freedom for all individuals regardless of race, culture, religion, gender, or age. On the other hand, the very nature of disputes regarding such issues as cultural deprivation, compensatory education, bilingualism and bilingual education, and the English Only movement strongly suggests that the age-old perspective of viewing schooling as Americanization rooted in the deficit view continues to persist in many subtle ways. Several interpretations of an ideology, cultural pluralism, and their educational implications will be discussed in the following chapter, for these perspectives are said to be the basis for establishing cultural democracy and multicultural education in America.

CASE STUDIES

In reading the following case studies, keep in mind these discussion questions pertaining to educational reform: Have some aspects of American culture and its institutions changed as a result of the educational reform measures in the post-*Sputnik* era (after 1957)? If education and schooling reflect the culture of the society in which they occur, did some aspects of American culture contribute to the fact that educational reform movements in the late 1950s into the 1960s were less effective than educators might have expected? If there were such aspects, do they still exist in our society today? And how might they affect the current movements for reforms in education and teacher education?

"ACTING WHITE"

In their attempt to understand why so many black teenagers do poorly in school, Sigithia Fordham of the University of the District of Columbia and John Ogbu of Berkeley interviewed 33 eleventh graders at "Capital" High Schools in Washington, D.C. According to Fordham and Ogbu, black adolescent culture defines itself partly by highlighting differences between itself and the majority culture. While it approves certain paths to upward mobility—like entertainment and professional sports—it defines success in school as "white."

Although Capital High School is 99% black . . . students need to reassure one another constantly of group identity and group loyalty. They do this partly by avoiding a wide range of activities that they scorn as "acting white." These include: Speaking standard English; listening to white radio stations; going to the opera or ballet; spending time in the library studying; getting good grades in school; going to the Smithsonian; going to a Rolling Stones concert; going camping, hiking or mountain climbing; having cocktails or a cocktail party; having a party with no music; listening to classical music; being on time; reading or writing poetry.

Students at Capital High, who do get good grades, camouflage success in order to fit in. . . . Even these successful students limit their academic efforts in order to keep their friends.

In integrated schools . . . some ambitious black students face an even more difficult situation: they distance themselves from black classmates when they work hard, speak standard English, and sign up for honors classes, but at the same time many whites still question their intelligence and deny them full membership in the academic elite. Success in school isolates them from all groups.

Source: Excerpted and adapted from Featherstone, Helen, "The Burden of 'Acting White'," *Harvard Education Letter,* Vol. III, No. 6, p. 6. Copyright © 1987 by the President and Fellows of Harvard College.

QUESTIONS

1. What sociocultural and educational factors may have contributed to the development of this kind of black adolescent culture? In what ways are the norms of this adolescent culture different from those of white middle- and lower-class youth cultures?
2. What implications does conformity to the norms of this black adolescent culture have for black youth in the larger society?
3. If you had the power to do anything you wish, what would you do to provide educational equality for these black adolescents? What role should the school play in helping these young people become fulfilled, productive, and contributing members of their ethnic community as well as the larger society?
4. In what ways is the dominant culture responsible for developing black adolescent culture? What could the dominant society do to help each minority youth become the best that he or she can be?
5. Is bilingual/bicultural education possible at Capital High? Specifically, what would you do if you were the principal? As a teacher at Capital High, what would you do to promote cultural understanding as well as academic excellence?

• • •

BILINGUAL "PROBLEM"

"I foresee many problems if you don't make English the official language" of the United States, Barbara Bush, the wife of the Vice President, told the National Press Club.

The one "problem" she cited was bilingual education.

Forty languages are spoken by students in Washington, D.C., schools, Mrs. Bush said. "Wouldn't it be terrible if you had to teach them in all those languages? How can each child have [that] privilege?"

Besides the "practical" difficulties of native-language instruction, children need English to succeed, she said in response to the questions following a prepared speech on literacy.

"Foreign languages are very important," Mrs. Bush said in an interview. "But English first!" She added that she was "appalled" on learning recently that the nation has no official language.

Since 1981, a proposed Constitutional amendment to give English that status has languished in the Congress.

Source: Reprinted with permission from *Education Week* Volume 6, Number 4 (October 1, 1986).

The following data regarding using English only and using other languages are based on 1,618 telephone interviews conducted by CBS News from June 19 through 23, 1986 ("Is English," 1986):

	Use Other Languages	Use Only English
Total	36%	60%
White	32	64
Black	44	50
Hispanic	63	34
Northeast	39	58
Midwest	36	60
South	34	60
West	33	65

QUESTIONS

1. If you were president of the National Association of Bilingual Education, which in 1983 recognized Mrs. Bush for her work on literacy, how would you respond to her statements about English as the national language and the "problems" connected with bilingual education?
2. If you were going to have a long discussion with Mrs. Bush about the goals and aims of schooling in America, what kinds of questions would you ask her? What would you like to tell her about what American schools ought and ought not to do?
3. What kinds of exchanges would you like to have with Mrs. Bush about the education of the culturally different?
4. How would you interpret the CBS News data? If you were asked to describe the United States on the basis of the data, what description would you give?
5. Assuming that the constitutional amendment were passed and English was designated as the official (or national) language, what implications might there be for everyday life, employment opportunities, schooling, economy, and so on?

REFERENCES

Administration for Children and Families (ACF). (1995). *Administration of Children, Youth and Families: Head Start* (On Line). Available World Wide Web: http://www.act.dhhs.gov//ACFPrograms/HeadStart/hdst.txt

American Institute of Research. (1977). *Evaluation of the impact of the ESEA Title VII Spanish/English bilingual education program.* Palo Alto, CA: Author.

Banks, J. A. (1981). *Multiethnic education: Theory and practice.* Boston: Allyn and Bacon.

Baratz, S. S., & Baratz, J. C. (1970). Early childhood intervention: The social science base of institutional racism. *Harvard Educational Review, 40*(1), 29–50.

Bernstein, B. B. (1985). A critique of the concept of compensatory education. In C. B. Cazden, V. P. John, & D. Hymes (Eds.), *Functions of language in the classroom* (pp. 135–151). Prospect Heights, IL: Waveland Press.

Berkson, I. B. (1969). *Theories of Americanization.* New York: Arno Press and the *New York Times.*

Bloom, B. S. (1976). *Human characteristics and school learning.* New York: McGraw-Hill. Bloom discusses how environmental intervention can overcome learning differences among culturally deprived children.

Bloom, B. S., Davis, A., & Hess, R. (1965). *Compensatory education for cultural deprivation.* New York: Holt, Rinehart & Winston. See this volume for a discussion of the concept of cultural deprivation and its relationship to cognitive growth and school success.

Bronfenbrenner, U. (1974). *Is early intervention effective? A report on longitudinal evaluations of preschool programs.* (DHEW-OHD-74-25). Washington, DC: U.S. Department of Health, Education and Welfare.

The burden of "acting white." (1987). *Education Letter, 3*(6), 6.

Carlson, R. A. (1975). *The quest for conformity: Americanization through education.* New York: John Wiley & Sons.

Caruso, D. R., & Detterman, K. K. (1981). Intelligence research and social policy. *Phi Delta Kappan, 63*(3), 183–187.

Castaneda, A. (1974). The educational needs of Mexican Americans. In A. Castaneda, R. L. James, & W. Robbins (Eds.), *The needs of minority groups* (p. 15). Lincoln: Professional Educators Publications.

Conant, J. B. (1959). *The American high school today.* New York: McGraw-Hill.

Cremin, L. A. (1961). *The transformation of the school.* New York: Knopf.

Cremin, L. A. (1977). *Traditions of American education.* New York: Basic Books.

Cubberly, E. P. (1909). *Changing conceptions of education.* Boston: Houghton Mifflin.

"Cultural Differences in the Classroom." (1988). *Education Letter, 4*(2), 1–4.

Dillard, J. L. (1972). *Black English.* New York: Random House.

"English only" measures spark rancorous debates. (1987, June 17). *Education Week,* 1, 14–15.

FitzGerald, F. (1979). *America revised.* Boston: Little, Brown & Co.

Gardner, H. (1985). *Frames of mind: The theory of multiple intelligences.* New York: Basic Books.

Genesee, F. (1985). Second language learning through immersion: A review of U.S. programs. *Review of Educational Research, 55*(4), 557.

Glazer, N., & Ueda, R. (1983). *Ethnic groups history textbooks.* Washington, DC: Ethics and Public Policy Center.

Gordon, M. M. (1964). *Assimilation in American life.* New York: Oxford University Press.

Hakuta, K. (1986). *Mirror of language: The debate on bilingualism.* New York: Basic Books.

Harber, J. R., & Bryan, D. N. (1976). Black English and the teaching of reading. *Review of Educational Research, 46,* 420.

Horner, V. M., & Gussow, J. D. (1985). John and Mary: A pilot study in linguistic ecology. In C. B. Cazden, V. P. John, & D. Hymes (Eds.), *Functions of language in the classroom* (pp. 155–194). Prospect Heights, IL: Waveland Press.

House-Senate conferees agree to loosen bilingual rules. (1988, March 16). *Education Week*, 1, 16–17.

Illiteracy in America [Special issue]. (1970). *Harvard Educational Review*, 40(1). See this issue for several articles on the Project Head Start evaluation.

Is English the only language for government? (1986, October 26). *New York Times*, p. E6.

Jensen, A. R. (1969). How much can we boost IQ and scholastic achievement. *Harvard Educational Review*, 39(4), 1–123.

Jensen, A. R. (1981). *Straight talk about mental tests*. New York: Free Press.

Kane, M. B. (1970). *Minorities in textbooks*. Chicago: Quadrangle Books.

Keddie, N. (Ed.). (1973). *The myth of cultural deprivation*. Baltimore: Penguin Books.

Kochman, T. (1985). Black American speech events and a language program for the classroom. In C. B. Cazden, V. P. John, & D. Hymes (Eds.), *Functions of language in the classroom* (pp. 211–266). Prospect Heights, IL: Waveland Press.

Labov, W. (1972). The logic of nonstandard English. In P. P. Giglioli (Ed.), *Language and social context* (pp. 179–215). Baltimore: Penguin Books.

Language acquisition theory revolutionizing instruction. (1987, April 1). *Education Week*, 30–37.

Larmouth, D. W. (1987). Does linguistic heterogeneity erode national unity? In W. S. Vanhorne & T. V. Tonnesen (Eds.), *Ethnicity and language* (pp. 37–57). Milwaukee: University of Wisconsin Institute on Race and Ethnicity.

Levine, D. U., & Havighurst, R. J. (1984). *Society and education*. Boston: Allyn and Bacon.

Levine, D. U., & Havighurst, R. J. (1989). Society and education (3rd ed.). Boston: Allyn and Bacon.

Mayo-Smith, R. (1904). *Emigration and immigration*. New York: Scribner.

Mitchell-Kernan, C. (1985). On the status of Black English for native speakers: An assessment of attitudes and values. In C. B. Cazden, V. P. John, & D. Hymes (Eds.), *Functions of language in the classroom* (pp. 195–211). Prospect Heights, IL: Waveland Press.

Ornstein, A. C. (1978). *Education and social inquiry*. Itasca, IL: F. E. Peacock.

Pulliam, J. D. (1987). *History of education in America*. Upper Saddle River, NJ: Merrill/Prentice Hall.

Ravitch, D. (1983). *The troubled crusade*. New York: Basic Books.

Riessman, F. (1962). *The culturally deprived child*. New York: Harper & Row.

Rockefeller Brothers Foundation. (1958). *The pursuit of excellence*. New York: Doubleday.

Schacter, F. F. (1979). *Everyday mothers talk to toddlers: Early intervention*. New York: Academic Press.

Schweinhart, L. J., & Weikart, D. P. (1977). Research report: Can preschool education make a lasting difference? *Bulletin of the High Scope Foundation*, 4, 231.

Sternberg, R. J. (Ed.). (1982). *Handbook of human intelligence*. London: Cambridge University Press.

Torrey, J. W. (1970). Illiteracy in the ghetto. *Harvard Educational Review*, 40(2), 253–259.

U.S. General Accounting Office. (1987). *Bilingual education: A new look at the research evidence* (GAO/PEMD-87-12BR). Washington, DC: Author.

U.S. Department of Health and Human Services. (1984). *The Head Start synthesis, evaluation, and utilization project* (HSSEU-HHS-84). Washington, DC: C.S.R. For a brief summary of this report, see *Education Weekly,* September 23, 1983.

Valentine, C. A. (1971). Deficit, difference, and bi-cultural models of Afro-American behavior. *Harvard Educational Review,* 41(2), 137–157.

When children speak little English how effective is bilingual education? (1986). *Education Letter,* 2(6), 1–4.

Willig, A. C. (1985). A meta-analysis of selected studies on the effectiveness of bilingual education. *Review of Educational Research,* 55(3), 269–317.

Zangwill, I. (1909). *The melting pot.* New York: Macmillan.

Zigler, E., & Muenchow, S. (1992). *Head Start: The inside story of America's most successful educational experiment.* New York: Basic Books.

4

Cultural Pluralism, Democracy, and Multicultural Education: 1970s–1990s

In this chapter, we will critically examine several different conceptions of cultural pluralism and their connection with democracy and multicultural education as these views were debated in the 1970s through the 1990s. More specifically, our discussion will focus on (1) setting concerns for cultural pluralism within the contexts of educational reforms of the time, (2) comparing several different views of cultural pluralism and multicultural education, (3) analyzing the relationship between democracy and cultural pluralism, (4) formulating broader conceptions of cultural pluralism and multicultural education, and (5) exploring some possible implications of multicultural education for special education, sexism, ageism, and global, or international, education.

CULTURAL PLURALISM AND THE AMERICAN SCHOOL

The Context of Reform

A plethora of major educational reform proposals appeared in the 1980s and 1990s, and they had implications, sometimes by omission, concerning education in a culturally diverse society. To better understand what occurred in schools during this period, it is important to understand the context of reform in which education was set.

As a result of the publication of *A Nation at Risk* in 1983 by the National Commission on Excellence in Education, the American public's attention turned once again to the alleged failure of the American school to produce competent young people. The report was followed by more than 30 evaluations of public education in the United States. America was going through another educational soul-searching experience similar to the one it underwent in the post-*Sputnik* era. In the late 1950s, educational reforms were spurred by America's desire to surpass the USSR in the aerospace race. But in 1983, the impetus for educational reforms came from this nation's aspiration to outstrip other nations in economic competition. Not surprisingly, most of the educational reform proposals stemming from *A Nation at Risk* and other studies recommended additional work in English, science, mathematics, and foreign languages.

In 1989 the nation's governors and the president met in Charlottesville, Virginia, for an education summit. At this meeting, a process for establishing national goals in education was put into place. In 1990 the president and the governors announced their commitment to a set of *National Education Goals*. In 1991, President Bush released *America 2000: An Educational Strategy,* which included the six goals that had been agreed to at the governors' conference. These goals stated that by the year 2000:

1. All children in America will start school ready to learn.
2. The high school graduation rate will increase to at least 90%.
3. American students will leave grades four, eight, and twelve having demonstrated competence in challenging subject matter including English, mathematics, science, history, and geography;[1] and every school in America will ensure that all students learn to use their minds well, so they may be prepared for responsible citizenship, further learning, and productive employment in our modern economy.
4. U.S. students will be first in the world in science and mathematics achievement.
5. Every adult American will be literate and will possess the knowledge and skills necessary to compete in a global economy and to exercise the rights and responsibilities of citizenship.
6. Every school in America will be free of drugs and violence and will offer a disciplined environment conducive to learning.

---

[1]Although the governors claimed that they had not meant this list of subject matter to be exhaustive or exclusive, professional groups representing areas that were not included in the list protested. By 1994 Goal 3 was amended to include English, mathematics, science, foreign languages, civics and government, economics, arts, history, and geography.

The Clinton administration later recommended two additional goals, which passed Congress in 1994. These were:

1. The nation's teaching force will have access to programs for the continued improvement of their professional skills and opportunity to acquire the knowledge and skills needed to instruct and prepare all American students for the next century.
2. Every school and home will engage in partnerships that will increase parental involvement and participation in promoting the social, emotional, and academic growth of children.

In 1991, the National Goals Panel was established to oversee and report on progress toward achieving these goals, including the development of federally sanctioned and funded standards that would establish baseline expectations for what students should know and be able to do by the time they leave fourth, eighth, and twelfth grades. At the same time, many state governments began to initiate reform efforts that generally included the establishment of standards in core subjects and a reexamination of ways to assess whether or not those expectations have been met.

In addition, such major works on education as Mortimer J. Adler's *The Paideia Proposal: An Educational Manifesto* (1982), Allan Bloom's *The Closing of the American Mind* (1987), Henry Giroux's *Theory and Resistance in Education* (1983), John Goodlad's *A Place Called School: Prospects for the Future* (1984), and E. D. Hirsch, Jr.'s *Cultural Literacy: What Every American Needs to Know* (1987), as well as numerous articles and position papers on education, have appeared in the last 15 years. Each reform proposal has a set of unique elements rooted in its own social, historical, and ideological basis. Hence, the proposals do not fall into neat and clear-cut groups. But for our purpose of examining the contexts of reform, the following categories will be used: (1) schooling as back-to-the-basics, (2) schooling as back-to-the-classics, (3) schooling as life enrichment, and (4) schooling as liberation and empowerment. These expressions are introduced as convenient "handles" with which to discuss divergent reform recommendations. Clearly, they do not describe individual proposals in any exhaustive sense. The word *schooling* is deliberately used because the reforms do not address informal education; instead, they are specifically related to improving the American school.

Schooling as Back-to-the-Basics

Individuals who advance this reform proposal may be called conservatives, or perhaps ultraconservatives, who place the weakening of American economic strength, the rise of social problems, and the decline in morality at the doorstep of the American school. They believe that assuring U.S. economic well-being and returning to an idealized past are directly related to restoring discipline, accountability, traditional American values, and prayer and religious instruction in the schools. At the same time, they demand that the school move away from teaching evolutionism and so-called secular humanism, which emphasizes relativistic ethics.

A back-to-the-basics curriculum would consist of teaching basic skills in English, mathematics, and the sciences. Advocates are also convinced that parents should participate actively in making decisions about school policies and curricula. This means the school should be controlled by the community. Although these conservatives are concerned with preserving religious pluralism, they hold that minority groups should be mainstreamed into the dominant culture. Rev. Jerry Falwell's Moral Majority (now disbanded) and other religious fundamentalist groups as well as individuals such as Phyllis Schlafly (1989) and Paul Viz (1989) represent this perspective.

Schooling as Back-to-the-Classics

This perspective is reminiscent of the 16th- and 17th-century Renaissance and of classical humanism, which is based on the belief that the highest form of human wisdom is contained in the classical works of Western civilization. Mortimer J. Adler (1982), E. D. Hirsch, Jr. (1987), and Allan Bloom (1987) advocate this contemporary version of classicism: The school's primary function is to produce intellectual leadership, and there should be a return to teaching the liberal arts, including the study of Western classics. Accordingly, institutions of higher learning should not be concerned with vocational education, which may be reserved for the less bright. For someone like Bloom, the downfall of American education is directly connected with the neglect of Western philosophy, history, and literature at the expense of rampant relativism in knowledge and morality. He finds that these intellectual failings have led to social chaos and moral decay in American society. In addition to resuming study of the classics, schools should eliminate the teaching of cultural relativism and sexual and racial revolutions. Because Bloom is convinced that not all schools can accomplish these changes, he relies on about two dozen elite schools to undertake the job of restoring educational excellence.

As a classicist, Adler agrees with Bloom and Hirsch in the eternal value of the Western classics in leading a good life. But he also recognizes that individuals should not only become good citizens but must also be able to make a living. This means all students must learn to think critically, communicate effectively, fulfill civic duties, and gain a broad understanding of the history, philosophy, and literature of Western civilization through Socratic dialogue. He is convinced that all schools should have a common core curriculum regardless of learners' future academic or occupational aspirations.

Schooling as Life Enrichment

Although there are major differences in their proposals, both Ernest Boyer (1983) and John Goodlad (1983) contend that schools should not try to do everything for everyone or prepare the young for social roles. What schools can do is enrich the lives of their students by enabling them to (1) achieve mastery of the basic skills and deeper intellectual development, (2) obtain an understanding and appreciation of their cultural heritages, (3) acquire the necessary knowledge and skills for their future career, and (4) cultivate their sense of citizenship. Both Boyer and Goodlad agree that the traditional three-track system—academic, vocational, and general education—should be abolished and that all young people be given a core of common learning (general education) that includes English, history, mathematics, science, civics, and computer literacy. Although Goodlad considers the autonomy of individual schools in constructing their own curriculum as a centerpiece in improving the American school, he concurs with Boyer in insisting that individual families and the larger community become partners with the school.

Schooling as Liberation and Empowerment

The best-known proponents of this view are Stanley Aronowitz and Henry Giroux, whose views will be discussed in greater detail under "Critical Theory" in Chapter 5. Aronowitz and Giroux's writings are not considered reform proposals in the usual sense. However, some of their basic tenets are worth repeating because their perspective suggests a change that is radically different from other proposed reform measures.

Aronowitz and Giroux's view of educational reform derives from their view of what goes on in our schools today. According to Giroux (1988b), schools do not meet the needs of all students democratically. Instead, they serve to legitimate the dominant culture by "sanctioning the voices of white, middle-class students, while simultaneously disconfirming or ignoring the voices of students from subordinate groups, whether they be black, working class, Hispanic, or other minority groups" (p. 179). In this way, ethnic minorities, women, and working-class people become marginalized and oppressed individuals whose experiences and histories are considered no longer legitimate (p. 181).

Truly democratic schools should liberate the oppressed women and minorities by listening to their voices and allowing them to struggle with power relations in the school to change the conditions in which they live. Accordingly, young people should be helped to acquire critical knowledge about how the larger society functions and become concerned with social justice and political action (Giroux, 1988b, p. 180). Students should be taught to think critically, detect hidden assumptions, see the implications of various views, and argue persuasively. Hence, teachers should not be mere transmitters of information or technicians who teach the "how to"; they should function as intellectuals (1988a) who understand how the structure of the dominant society works and the ways in which it affects the lives of all minorities. They must learn to raise questions about the assumptions underlying various teaching strategies, research methods, and educational theories so that students can be helped to become critical, creative, and imaginative thinkers. In short, democratic schools should become agents of social transformation through which both teachers and students are liberated and empowered to shape their own future.

Demands for Pluralism

The debates about academic excellence and school improvement that were embedded in most of the calls for reform often overwhelmed concerns about equity and pluralism. Nonetheless, throughout this period there continued to be concern for and debate about the response of schools to the demands of a pluralistic nation. In the 1970s the often emotionally charged debates regarding the effectiveness of compensatory education programs and their underlying assumptions about minority cultures in the United States reflected deeper, disquieting concerns regarding the extent to which freedom, dignity, and human rights were assured for minority groups. These concerns were expressed in the form of demands for the establishment of a culturally pluralistic society and for multicultural education. In the early 1970s, many more educational and economic opportunities were open to poor and ethnic minorities than even a decade earlier. Even so, minority groups were convinced that, like the melting pot ideal, neither the governmental measures nor educational "reforms" in the area of ethnic studies had a significant impact on the attitude of the dominant group. To the members of minority cultures, Americanism as Anglo-conformity still persisted, because "'the model American minority' is made from a strictly majority point of view. [For example] Japanese-Americans are good because they conform—they don't make waves—they work hard and are quiet and docile. As in a colonial situation, there tends to be one set of prescriptions for those in power and another for the subject people [minority culture]" (Kitano, 1969, p. 146). In other words, the attitude of Anglo-superiority still prevailed in the country and the granting of full civil rights to all was not yet a reality.

The quest for cultural pluralism through a search for freedom, equality, and identity was fervently expressed by Marie Evans (1970) in *I Am a Black Woman,* in which she asks the black community to build black schools, black children, black minds, black love, black impregnability, and a strong black nation. Similarly, young Asian Americans were "challenging the monocultural idea of the majority society which, in their eyes, caused imperialism abroad and various manifestations of racial inequality at home" (Hata, 1973, p. 129). By seeking to establish a culturally pluralistic society, minority cultures were challenging the moral validity of the white system of domination. This challenge and the demand for sociocultural reforms in America were expressed in the following words of Vincent Harding, director of the Institute of the Black World, an independent research center belonging to the Martin Luther King, Jr., Memorial Center in Atlanta:

> Pluralism as a next, but not ultimate, stage must be wrested from the white nationalist system of today. A new order must come to birth within the mothering belly of the old, with all the dangerous tensions involved. Release cannot come without hard, persistent, organized struggle. . . . But unless that release comes, and unless new humane systems of life and growth are developed, the identity of no man will be secured and we shall be fated to wander with Black Everyman in the sewers . . . of the Western world. (1973, p. 113)

These cries for cultural pluralism were echoed by Eugene Sekaquaptewa, Education Programs Administrator for the Hopi tribe Indian Agency in Keams Canyon, Arizona.

> The fact cannot be overemphasized that over a hundred American Indian cultures and languages form the foundation for Indian communities; therefore, the right of the Indian community or any other ethnic community to exist, to participate in, and to maintain its role in America must be the ultimate objective of all programs designed to initiate change in American education. (1973, p. 36)

Yet another proponent of cultural pluralism was Manuel H. Guerra, who was awarded the Presidential Citation and a bronze medal for his bilingual and bicultural studies concerning Mexican-American children. He concurred with Sekaquaptewa:

> Until very recently, the monolingual and monocultural approach to the problems of the Indian, Chicano, and Puerto Rican at most have been good intentions with bad results, and more often a rude imposition of undemocratic concepts and practices. . . . Cultural pluralism in education is recognition of the facts and the truth about people in society in America. . . . It is precisely this view of America that has not predominated in our classrooms, textbooks and mass media. (1973, pp. 30–31)

In the 1970s, the demands for cultural pluralism and multicultural education also came from members of the mainstream culture. As we will see later, in response to demands for cultural pluralism and multicultural education, the board of directors of the American Association of Colleges for Teacher Education (AACTE) endorsed an official statement on multicultural education in October 1972. By 1977, the National Council on Accreditation of

Teacher Education (NCATE) required compliance with a new set of standards on multicultural education as a part of its accreditation of teacher education programs.

The promotion of cultural pluralism and multicultural education in the schools and in teacher education probably reached a peak between the late 1970s and the early 1980s, when a flood of publications and workshops on cultural pluralism and multicultural education appeared. As a result of the concentrated efforts of various professional organizations, state departments of education, and accreditation and governmental agencies, many public schools, colleges, and universities attempted to incorporate multicultural education components into their curricula. School and university personnel appeared to have become more sensitive to the need to address the special educational needs of the culturally different. The scope of multicultural education, however, continued to remain restricted to the concerns for ethnicity and educational equality for minority groups.

The push toward multicultural education was still alive in the mid-1980s, but very few substantive gains were made in this area. On the contrary, supporters of cultural pluralism and multicultural education sensed that the movement was waning, overwhelmed, perhaps, by the increasing emphasis on establishing standards and demanding excellence. By June 1987, for example, 37 states had made attempts to pass varying forms of English Only legislation ("English Only," 1987), and federal funds for bilingual education and Head Start programs had been reduced substantially. In 1994, California passed Proposition 187, which made illegal immigrants ineligible for social services, including public school education at all levels. The reported decrease in the number of minority public school teachers as a result of teacher competency testing reinforced the belief that the implementation of affirmative action and other civil rights-related provisions had lost ground since the beginning of the Reagan administration. In the area of minority enrollment, ethnic minority groups, excepting Asian Americans, gained very modestly. For example, in 1988, 1,081,000 blacks were enrolled in 3,200 institutions of higher education as compared to 1,054,000 in 1976 ("1986 Minority Enrollment," 1988).

In *The Closing of the American Mind*, Allan Bloom (1987) argued that the emphasis on cultural diversity and ethnicity may lead to a decay of American individualism (pp. 192–193). By the 1990s Bloom's concern was echoed by others. Arthur Schlesinger (1992) captured the feeling of many Americans when he argued that an emphasis on cultural diversity threatened to undermine national unity.

> The new ethnic gospel rejects the unifying vision of individuals from all nations melted into a new race. Its underlying philosophy is that America is not a nation of individuals at all but a nation of groups, that ethnicity is the defining experience for most Americans, that ethnic ties are perma-

nent and indelible, and that division into ethnic communities establishes
the basic structure of American society and the basic meaning of American
history. (p. 16)

Attacks on multicultural education appeared in the popular press (see, for
example, Gray, 1991). These attacks were often based on a very narrow definition of multicultural education as "ethnic studies." Arthur Schlesinger asked
"at what point does it [multiculturalism] pass over into an ethnocentrism of its
own? The very word, instead of referring to all cultures, has come to refer
only to non-Western, nonwhite cultures" (1992, p. 74).

While this was not an accurate portrayal of what most advocates of multicultural education were arguing for, it resonated with a good many Americans' fears that our traditions and culture were being diminished in the face
of changing demographics and power arrangements. The work of Bloom and
Schlesinger became best-sellers, while efforts to limit immigration and enforce
English-only legislation increased during the 1990s. The rise of political con-
servatism and religious fundamentalism exacerbated the pluralists' uneasy
feeling that America might be returning to an era of ethnocentric Anglo-conformity. What all this suggests is that the future of cultural pluralism and multicultural education remains an open question.

Cultural Pluralism in America

One of the problems with cultural pluralism in America is that the term is
often used ambiguously; as Tesconi (1984) observes, it "possesses a descriptive
meaning, which portrays an empirical state of affairs, and a prescriptive
meaning, carrying ideological connotations and suggesting a particular forging of social and educational policy" (p. 88). In other words, sometimes *cultural pluralism* is used simply to describe the fact that cultural diversity exists
in our society. But at other times, it refers to an ideological perspective that
stands for a set of interrelated ideas or ideals that characterize a social group.
As is the case with all ideologies, cultural pluralism contains ideals, slogans,
and directions and strategies for social, political, and educational actions; it
also includes some statements about the nature of reality and values as well as
the arguments in support of their validity.

Beyond Tolerance

The demand for cultural pluralism in America is based partly on the belief
that it is intrinsic to democracy. Yet its proponents have not always clearly
articulated the meaning of cultural pluralism; its social, political, and educational implications; or its alleged connections with democracy. Clearly, the
kind of cultural pluralism believed to be consistent with democracy is much
more than the separate and independent existence of disparate ethnic groups

without any contact between institutions or individuals. Rather, it is an ideal that seeks to establish and encourage not only cultural diversity but also a basis of unity from which America can become a cohesive society enriched by shared, widely divergent ethnic experiences. Hence, cultural pluralism is based on the belief in equality of opportunity for all people, respect for human dignity, and the conviction that no single pattern of living is good for everyone. In this context, the traditional notion of tolerance for different cultural patterns is said to be patronizing, for it suggests an attitude in which the dominant group regards human dignity as a grant bestowed by "me" on "you" or by "you" on "me" (Hazard & Stent, 1973, p. 15).

Cultural pluralism, then, must include the belief that in the coexistence of people with diverse cultural backgrounds, to be different is not to be inferior. Although this pluralistic view necessitates the acceptance of the intrinsic worth of all human beings as unique individuals, it does not require that one's "native" cultural pattern must never change. On the contrary, the individual life, or the culture of a group or a nation, may be enriched by preserving and sharing different sociocultural patterns. The possibility of changing one's lifestyle by interacting with other ethnic groups, based on mutual interest, should not be restricted. For example, one can belong to and participate in the activities of racially or ethnically mixed community groups, Asian-American groups, or Mexican-American groups, and at the same time develop a unique lifestyle that incorporates various aspects of these groups.

In a somewhat similar vein, Horace N. Kallen (1949), a Harvard-educated philosopher and an American Jew, earlier asserted that ethnic groups should develop a positive self-image and a pride in their respective group's cultural heritage and communal values, but still function as partially integrated political and economic entities in American society. He was convinced that America would be richer as a result of cultural diversity, for he was not persuaded that the value systems the immigrants brought to this country were inimical to American democracy. Kallen believed that democracy involves the interaction of semi-independent, autonomous groups and communities on important issues of life experience. To him, a culturally pluralistic society was a natural state, because human beings have differing needs that are so deeply rooted in their nature that they cannot be eliminated and should not be deliberately suppressed. Accordingly, he conceived of America as consisting of a number of nationalities comprising a single nation, a "federation of nationalities."

> The American way is the way of orchestration. As in an orchestra, the different instruments, each with its own characteristic timbre and theme, contribute distinct and recognizable parts to the composition, so in the life and culture of a nation, the different regional, ethnic, occupational, religious, and other communities compound their different activities to make up the national spirit. (p. 117)

Thus, the American national spirit was to be a union of the different. The spirit was to be sustained by equality of different ethnic groups and the inter-actions (transactions) among the "different but equal" without domination by any single group.

Another advocate of cultural pluralism, Isaac B. Berkson, supervisor of schools and extension activities of the Bureau of Jewish Education and a stu-dent of John Dewey, joined in disavowing Anglo-conformity and the melting pot ideal as inconsistent with American democracy. Like Dewey, Berkson and Kallen believed that a democratic society has the obligation to provide equal opportunities for "the perfection and conservation of differences" in every individual (Berkson, 1969, p. 55). But because Berkson saw self-determina-tion as the quintessence of democracy, he criticized Kallen's federation of nationalities for being too restrictive in allowing minorities to leave their eth-nic enclave if they so desired. He argued that Kallen's model would lead to freedom of association for the various cultural groups, but not enough free-dom of contact for the individual. For example, Kallen encouraged different ethnic groups to have joint activities but discouraged ethnically mixed mar-riages.

Unlike Kallen, Berkson was more concerned with the integrity of ethnic groups within the larger society. His primary concern was with reducing, if not eliminating, societal forces that would pressure a minority to either dis-solve or perpetuate itself. If an individual member of an ethnic community decides to leave the group and join the dominant group, such a decision should be accepted as proper and legitimate. (This view is also known as the community model.) Both Kallen and Berkson adhered to the desirability of preserving ethnic communities, but the latter argued for greater flexibility and opportunities for choice. Kallen envisioned ethnic communities as "reser-voir(s) of some specific tradition and excellence which one or another of its sons may lift into the powers and perspectives of the larger national life, mak-ing it stronger and richer" (1949, pp. 117–118).

The New Pluralism

From the mid-1960s and into the mid-1970s there was a resurgence of cul-tural pluralism, but with a different thrust. As Broudy (1981) points out, the "new pluralism" came out of attempts to translate the civil rights and Great Society legislation into educational and economic programs. Although the new pluralists held, as did Kallen, that the different in our society should be unified into a cohesive democratic nation, their arguments were heavily skewed in favor of allowing minority cultures, as different but equal groups, to participate in the various activities of the country on their own terms. Fur-ther, the social institutions, particularly our schools, were asked to "take into account the linguistic and other cultural differences that children of minority groups bring to the classroom, and that the schools refrain from imposing the majority culture both in its language and ethos on these children" (Broudy, 1981, p. 232).

Advocates of the new pluralism insisted that participatory democracy is fundamentally pluralistic and that it entails the acceptance of the intrinsic worth of all human beings and their unique individuality. Cultural differences between groups should be viewed as differences, not deficits. As already indicated in Chapter 2, Stephen and Joan Baratz echoed the same sentiment when they noted that many social science research studies with minority groups "have been postulated on an idealized norm of 'American behavior' against which all behavior is measured. This norm is defined operationally in terms of the way the white-middle-class American is supposed to behave" (Baratz & Baratz, 1970, p. 31). They go on to point out that acceptance of such a norm in place of the legitimate values of minority groups leads to the belief that to be different from white is to be inferior. Thus, "differences in behavior are interpreted as genetic pathology or as the alleged pathology of the environment" (p. 32).

The view that a difference is not a deficit is useful in highlighting the unwarranted assumptions underlying the deficit model of viewing other cultures. However, as discussed earlier, when interpreted literally it leads to an extreme form of cultural relativism that considers all human actions and practices equally adaptive and effective. This kind of cultural relativism results in cultural separatism, or what Broudy (1981) calls *cultural atomism.* Broudy goes on to say that the advocates of the new pluralism do not agree on how far toward such separatism they wish to go (p. 232). Even James Banks (1981), who has written widely in support of cultural pluralism and multicultural education, warns that the cultural pluralism argument can be carried to the extreme to justify racism, cultural genocide, and other cultural practices.

Although it is not clear what Banks means by "the cultural pluralism argument," it is clear that building a cohesive democratic society cannot follow from an argument that (1) all cultures are equally functional, (2) there can be no objective standards with which to judge other cultures, and (3) therefore all cultural groups should be permitted to practice their own ways regardless of the consequences to the larger society. This, of course, is not what the pluralists are advocating. Yet educators often view cultural pluralism and multicultural education as representing an extreme cultural relativist view that would allow anything and everything. It is not unusual to find that multicultural education is understood as being concerned exclusively with preserving and extending minority ethnic patterns. The fact that different cultures have different norms does not necessarily imply that values ought to be relative or that there cannot be some objective way of justifying value judgments. As Pratte (1979) cautions:

> While it is true that the same action or thing is judged differently in different cultures, it is a major and unwarranted jump from the description of existing relativism to the claim that no objectively valid rational way of justifying basic ethical or value judgments exists. (p. 51)

In point of fact, those who value cultural diversity and support cultural pluralism do not view religious bigotry and racial discrimination as practiced by certain groups in America as mere cultural differences; rather, they judge them to be unethical and undemocratic.

The central problem of cultural pluralism is how minority groups can maintain enough separation from the dominant culture to perpetuate and develop their own ethnic traditions without, at the same time, interfering with the execution of their responsibilities to the American society. That is, how can cultural diversity and unity be maintained simultaneously, particularly when conflicts arise between the dominant society and its subunits? One suggested solution is that a

> value conflict, where it exists, is to be fought out in the arena of the ballot box and public opinion, but the goal is to keep such conflict at a minimum by emphasizing the areas of flexibility, permitted alternatives, and free choice in American life and by refraining from imposing one's own collective will as standards of enforced behavior for other groups. (Gordon, 1964, p. 159)

Value conflicts between groups should be resolved according to majority rule, but society should avoid such conflicts as much as possible by giving the groups many alternatives from which to choose their own courses of action. For example, one can choose to learn the dominant language and behavior patterns and work outside of one's ethnic group, or one can choose to remain in the ethnic enclave and carry on a trade that would serve primarily the members of that community. A constantly recurring theme of cultural pluralism is the belief that no single group should impose its own pattern as the idealized norm for every other group.

To some, cultural pluralism as a social ideal to preserve each ethnic group's cultural distinctiveness within the context of American citizenship involves contradictory social practices. To maintain one's unique cultural traits, a person must maintain the most meaningful personal relationships with his or her group. But if an individual is to achieve social, political, and economic status in the larger society, he or she must also participate in the processes of the dominant culture. Whether these practices are contradictory to each other or not is quite debatable.

Generally speaking, two phenomena have taken place among ethnic minority groups in the United States since the 1970s. First, in large metropolitan areas such as Los Angeles, San Francisco, San Diego, Seattle, Chicago, New York, Detroit, Atlanta, Dallas, Houston, and Washington, D.C., masses of new immigrants maintain their cultural patterns by associating only with members of their own ethnic groups at the primary, or face-to-face, level. Their contact with the dominant society remains at the secondary level. Only in institutions such as schools, hospitals, and workplaces do they have significant interaction with members of the dominant culture. Second, many well-educated minority group members have shed much of their cultural distinctiveness. Yet they too interact only minimally with other minority groups or with the dominant society.

Cultural Pluralism or an Open Society?

Albeit there are continuing calls for cultural pluralism in our society, there are some who argue that America is approaching a so-called open society, rather than a culturally pluralistic society (Green, 1966, p. 25). Whereas a pluralistic society encourages cultural differences, an open society regards cultural differences as no longer relevant in determining the worth or merit of individuals. Hence, America as an open society should emphasize individual equality and national unity rather than cultural diversity, so that each member of any given minority group can form his or her identity as a citizen of the country rather than as a member of a subculture.

Although America may be approaching a state wherein an individual's position and merit are evaluated in terms of competence and achievement, it is little help to tell nonwhite minority youth that their identity should be achieved in terms of their status as citizens of this country. These young people find that their status as Americans is still affected by their color and ethnic backgrounds. At the same time, they discover that they belong to neither the dominant white culture nor the culture of their parents, and consequently they see themselves as dislocated and alienated. This condition is common among today's younger generation of minority cultures, whose self-image is not intimately tied to their legal citizenship in the United States. Children of ethnic groups must be helped to develop pride in their own racial and cultural heritage and to achieve their identity as unique and intrinsically worthwhile human beings by rejecting the belief that to be different is to be inferior. This kind of positive self-image and cultural integrity needs to be developed not only in the children of poor ethnic minorities but also in the children whose parents occupy middle-class and upper- middle-class socioeconomic statuses. The so-called identity crisis is no less severe among these children.

In a culturally diverse society such as the United States, it is not enough to propose that an individual be evaluated according to merit and competence. We must also regard cultural diversity as an asset to be developed, for even a person with full civil rights cannot escape from the racial and ethnic backgrounds that inexorably govern one's view of oneself. The identity crisis experienced by most minority children cannot be resolved unless special efforts are made to develop a pride about the Mexican, Asian, or African parts of the labels *Mexican American, Asian-American,* and *African-American.* For culturally different and economically poor children, developing a positive self-image is hard to achieve without persistent attempts by the mainstream to appreciate the worth of other cultures. The fundamental assumptions underlying the dominant norms must also be critically examined. As Giroux (1983) cogently puts it:

> Culture as a political phenomenon refers to the power of specific meanings, message systems, and social practices in order to "lay the psychological and moral foundations for the economic and political system they control." Within the dominant culture, meaning is universalized and the historically contingent nature of social reality appears as self-evident and fixed. (p. 196)

Implicitly or explicitly, those who advocate cultural pluralism or multiculturalism in the United States do not seek to maintain cultural diversity alone, for there needs to be a basis for national unity. However, the pluralists argue that this unity should not be founded on establishing one linguistic, ethical, or behavioral pattern as the only idealized norm for all individuals. The unity should be based on the belief that all human beings are to be regarded as ends in themselves so that no person can be exploited by other individuals or institutions. The question of whether cultural pluralism is or is not achievable in this country hinges on the meaning of cultural pluralism in the context of American democracy. Neither Kallen's federation of nationalities nor Berkson's community model is wholly acceptable. The former is likely to result in insular pluralism in which minority groups perpetuate themselves in their own ethnic communities with minimal participation in the mainstream society of which they are an important part. Berkson's community model and the open society concept are also unsatisfactory, for they minimize the dominant culture's pressure on minority individuals to assimilate into the dominant culture by divesting themselves of their heritages. These two perspectives do not pay sufficient attention to the critical role ethnicity plays in the development of self-identity among minority people.

Cultural Pluralism: A Definition

Cultural pluralism as an ideology consonant with the principles of participatory democracy goes beyond mere cultural relativism, in which all and any cultural practices are viewed as equally functional and hence permissible. Cultural pluralism is an ideal that seeks to encourage cultural diversity and establish a basis of unity so that America can become a cohesive society whose culture is enriched by sharing widely divergent ethnic experiences. Cultural pluralism is a state

> of equal coexistence in a mutually supportive relationship within the boundaries or framework of one nation of people of diverse cultures with

> significantly different patterns of belief, behavior, color, and in many cases
> with different languages. To achieve cultural pluralism there must be
> unity with diversity. Each person must be aware of and secure in his own
> identity and be willing to extend to others the same respect and rights that
> he expects and enjoys. (Hazard & Stent, 1973, p. 14)

Cultural boundaries must be seen as "porous, dynamic, and interactive,
rather than the fixed property of particular ethnic groups" (Gates, 1992).

The ideology of cultural pluralism is founded on the belief that diversity
is enriching. Human life becomes much more interesting, stimulating, and
even exciting when there are many varied ways of thinking, feeling, expressing, acting, and viewing the world. Perhaps more importantly, given the
range in the kinds and complexity of human needs and wants, the more
alternative problem-solving approaches there are the more we are likely to
find solutions that enable us to live our lives in an increasingly effective way.
Cultural differences as alternative ways of dealing with essentially similar
human problems and needs present us with a wide variety of options from
which we can learn to grow. Green (1966) asserts that no one person's or
group's way of life is so rich that it may not be further enriched by contact
with other points of view.

> The conviction is that diversity is enriching because no man has a monop-
> oly on the truth about the good life. There are many ways. Diversity is fur-
> ther valued because it provides any society with a richer pool of leadership
> from which to draw in times of crisis. (p. 10)

The worth of one's culture is not based solely on the fact that it is ours; rather,
a culture is worthy because its patterns and norms have enabled us to achieve
our purposes.

The belief in the enriching nature of cultural diversity suggests that it is
the responsibility of the dominant group to actively promote the right of
minority cultures to exist and develop in their own way and to examine critically the assumptions underlying the dominant norms. As a democratic ideology, cultural pluralism implies that minority groups become actively committed to and deeply involved in the affairs that affect the growth and well-being
of the larger society.

> Cultural pluralism is characterized by a commitment to the worth of cul-
> tural diversity and factions promoting an agenda of politics, but goes
> beyond the promotion of the values of cultural subgroups to the forming
> of a public as the result of a recognition of a problematic situation having
> direct and indirect consequences. (Pratte, 1979, p. 151)

In the broadest sense, cultural pluralism's fundamental tenets should apply to
the relationships between dominant society and ethnic minority groups as
well as groups characterized by differences in gender, age, socioeconomic status, and other mental or physical exceptionalities.

Cultural Pluralism and Democracy

The preceding discussion implied a close connection between cultural pluralism and democracy. But is there a sound basis for arguing that cultural pluralism is indeed intrinsic to American democracy? The fundamental principles of democracy as articulated in the Declaration of Independence and the Constitution of the United States clearly indicate that the founders of this country believed that each person is to be treated as an end. As John L. Childs (1951), a noted philosopher of education and a student of John Dewey, pointed out, "Democracy is an attempt to embody in our social relationships the principle which regards each individual as possessing intrinsic worth or dignity" (p. 441). It is for this reason that exploitation of any individual or group violates a democratic maxim. Institutions in our society must be made to serve the individual, not vice versa.

To regard each individual as an end is to affirm the belief that there is an "intrinsic connection between the prospects of democracy and belief in the potentialities of human nature—for its own sake" (Dewey, 1939a, p. 127). In building democracy we must begin with the faith that all people have the capacity to develop and exercise their own intelligence in shaping their own future (Dewey, 1957, p. 49). It is not that these capacities are already formed and ready to be unfolded, but if given the opportunity individuals can grow socially, emotionally, and intellectually so that they can not only decide what is good for them but also find the most effective means of attaining it. Hence, democracy "denotes a state of affairs in which the interest of each in his work is uncoerced and intelligent: based upon its congeniality to his own aptitudes" (Dewey, 1961, p. 316). Consequently, freedom of all kinds is essential to democracy, and "the cause of democratic freedom is the cause of the fullest possible realization of human potentialities" (Dewey, 1957, p. 129).

A democratic society is necessarily pluralistic (culturally, politically, intellectually, and socially), because it is founded on a belief in the intrinsic worth of individuals and their unique capacities to become intelligent human beings. In this sense, the unique qualities of individuals or groups become assets rather than hindrances. Accordingly, "there is no physical acid which has the corrosive power possessed by intolerance directed against persons because they belong to a group that bears a certain name" (Dewey, 1939a, p. 137). In a more revolutionary vein, Freire (1984) points out:

> They [the oppressed or minorities] are treated as individual cases, as marginal men who deviate from the general configuration of a "good, organized, and just" society. The oppressed are regarded as the pathology of the healthy society, which must therefore adjust these "incompetent and lazy" folk to its own patterns by changing their mentality. These marginals need to be "integrated," "incorporated" into the healthy society that they have "forsaken." (p. 102)

For Freire, the oppressed minorities of all sorts are not "marginals," that is, people living "outside" society. They have always lived "inside" the socio-cultural structure that made them "being for others" because they did not conform to the norms of the dominant culture. Hence, they were not treated as ends in themselves but rather as means to someone else's end—that is, objects of exploitation and oppression. The solution, Freire concludes, is not to completely absorb or assimilate minorities into the dominant social structure but to transform that structure so that they are "being for themselves." From Dewey's perspective, this means that a society must provide equality of opportunity that will enable individuals to develop their capacities to the fullest. Hence, "all individuals are entitled to equality of treatment by law and in its administration. Each one is affected equally in quality if not in quantity by the institutions under which he lives and has an equal right to express his judgment" (1939b, p. 403). Thomas Jefferson's insistence that a system of education be open to all youth as a necessity for democracy reflects this equal opportunity principle.

The demand of ethnic minorities to preserve and develop their own cultural patterns stems from the firm belief in the democratic principle, which regards uniqueness of individuals and equal opportunity for their development as intrinsically good. However, democracy requires not only an emphasis on personal needs and interests and on various points of shared interest, but also a recognition of mutual interest as a means of social control. A democratic society should encourage not only free interactions among individuals and groups but also changes in social habits, that is, continuous readjustments as a result of meeting new situations in a wide variety of personal interactions. It is essential for the members of a democratic society to recognize that the needs of others are as important to those people as their own are to them. This recognition is a necessary prerequisite for effective handling of conflicts among individuals and groups.

In a truly democratic society, no single group rules over others because of the implicit faith in the human capacity for intelligent behavior. Democracy requires a method of resolving conflicts by inquiry, discussion, and persuasion rather than by violence. Hence, the kind of education that cultivates reflective thinking and conflict resolution through discussion and persuasion is essential for realizing cultural pluralism.

CULTURAL PLURALISM AND MULTICULTURAL EDUCATION

In the early 1970s, many educators and minority groups became increasingly vocal in pointing out that schooling in America was ethnocentric and mono-cultural. Because genuine democracy was believed to be necessarily connected with cultural pluralism and multicultural education, these educators and minority groups argued that the American school was undemocratic. That is, our schools failed to provide equal educational opportunity to poor and minority children. Not surprisingly, minority groups and concerned educators demanded that our schools provide multicultural education by becoming more sensitive to the unique cultural norms, language patterns, cognitive and learning styles, and communication styles of the ethnic and socioeconomic minority groups.

The mounting interest in and concern for cultural pluralism in education was given a boost when the Board of Directors of the American Association of Colleges for Teacher Education (AACTE) officially sanctioned the cause in its "Not One Model American" statement of October 1972. The fact that AACTE was (and still is) one of the largest and most influential organizations involved in teacher preparation suggested the seriousness and urgency with which American educators viewed the problem of making the schools a major means of achieving cultural pluralism in our society. The following excerpts from the adopted statement summarize AACTE's key concerns:

> Education for cultural pluralism includes four major thrusts: (1) the teaching of values which support cultural diversity and individual uniqueness; (2) the encouragement of the qualitative expansion of existing ethnic cultures and their incorporation into the mainstream of American socio-economic and political life; (3) the support of explorations in alternative and emerging life styles; and (4) the encouragement of multiculturalism, multilingualism, and multidialectism. (AACTE, 1972)

In addition to the action taken by the AACTE Board of Directors, numerous conferences and workshops promoted multicultural education in our public schools and universities with teacher education programs. Of these efforts, the inclusion of a standard on multicultural education into the accreditation standards of the National Council for Accreditation of Teacher Education (NCATE) in 1977 had important consequences. Although the degree to which the multicultural education components have genuinely permeated the curricula of the colleges and universities for teacher education is not known, these institutions did attempt to infuse studies of minority cultures and the role of cultural factors into the teaching-learning processes.

According to NCATE (1977), multicultural education was to be seen as "preparation for the social, political, economic realities that individuals experience in culturally diverse and complex human encounters. These realities have both national and international dimensions" (p. 4). By 1984, NCATE had completely redesigned its structure and accreditation policies and procedures. In its new standards, multicultural education as a separate category of standards was deleted. Instead, the term *culturally different* was included in various standards. Such concepts as *global perspective* and *exceptionalities* were also added to enlarge the meaning of multicultural education. By 1994, the NCATE standards included the expectation that evidence of attention to cultural diversity would be found throughout the standards.

In spite of the attempt to broaden the multicultural concept, many educators persisted in viewing it only as a strategy for dealing with the educational concerns of minority children. Still others thought multicultural education was synonymous with ethnic studies. Unfortunately, these misconceptions about multicultural education have led many school and college personnel to insist that multicultural education components were unnecessary in their programs because their institutions either did not have many minority students or were located in ethnically homogeneous areas. In short, many educators consider multicultural education merely an add-on set of strategies for addressing the issues related to the education of minority students. Such a narrow and distorted conception of multicultural education may contribute to the rise of resentment among teachers and teacher educators stemming from the belief that the state and national accreditation standards on multicultural education should be made applicable only to urban and other institutions with substantial minority enrollments. Indeed, a broader conception is necessary if multicultural education is to serve as a means of making our schools more democratic in a culturally, racially, and socioeconomically diverse society.

Approaches to Multicultural Education

As described above, by the 1990s the neoconservatives' argument that multicultural education failed to serve the common good of the nation had begun to permeate the national consciousness. Multicultural education, argued opponents such as Schlesinger (1992), D'Souza (1991), and Ravitch (1990), was an attempt on the part of special interests to fragment the curriculum and to serve their own ends. However, as Banks (1994) points out, the opponents to multicultural education were, themselves, representing a special interest:

> A clever tactic of the neoconservative scholars is to define their own interests as universal and in the public good and the interests of women and people of color as *special interests* that are particularistic (Ravitch, 1990). When a dominant elite describes its interests as the same as the public interests, it marginalizes the experiences of structurally excluded groups, such as women and people of color. (p. 22)

The confusion of meanings of multicultural education may result from the multiple meanings used both in the field and in classrooms where multicultural education is implemented. In her study of the literature on multicultural education, bilingual education, education for pluralism, and ethnic studies in the United States, Gibson (1984) found four major approaches or views of multicultural education. They are (1) education of the culturally different, or benevolent multiculturalism; (2) education about cultural differences, or cultural understanding; (3) education for cultural pluralism; and (4) bicultural education (p. 95). Gibson presents *multicultural education as the normal human experience* as a broader and more adequate approach because education is viewed as a cultural process (pp. 111–113). More recently, Sleeter and Grant (1987) examined 17 articles and 11 books dealing with the same topics. They found (1) teaching the culturally different, (2) human relations, (3) single group studies, and (4) multicultural education to be the four principal approaches. Following an examination of the four approaches, *education that is multicultural and social reconstructionism* is presented as a more sound approach to multicultural education. Although the categories used by Sleeter and Grant appear to be substantially different from those given by Gibson, the key concepts and assumptions related to the various approaches discussed by Sleeter and Grant and Gibson are essentially the same. For the sake of brevity, only findings will be discussed as a basis for suggesting a broader and more adequate view of multicultural education.

According to Gibson (1984), the primary purpose of *education of the culturally different,* or *benevolent multiculturalism,* is to provide equal educational opportunities for culturally different children. Implicit in this approach is the notion that educational equality will lead to parity of power between the dominant and minority groups. This approach is based on the premise that students from certain ethnic minority groups continue to fail academically because of the unique learning difficulties experienced by these young people. The advocates of benevolent multiculturalism argue that these learning difficulties stem from the discrepancies between the cultural norms of the students and our schools, which are dominated by the mainstream values (pp. 95–96). However, they not only reject compensatory education as a solution, but they also deny that cultural, social, or genetic deficits are causally responsible for these students' school failure. For Gibson, the first approach has two shortcomings. One is that no empirical evidence supports the view "that cultural differences are the cause of minority groups' failure in mainstream schools" and that multicultural education is indeed a viable solution to school failure (p. 97). The second weakness is the unwarranted belief that implementing multicultural education will lead to parity of power. Moreover, many may find this approach patronizing and paternalistic, for benevolent multiculturalism seems to imply that although minority groups are given help, little contribution to the dominant group is expected from them (p. 98).

The second approach, *education about cultural differences,* or *cultural understanding,* differs from the first in that "its focus is education about cultural differences rather than education for the so-called culturally different" (Gibson, 1984, p. 98). Hence, its primary goal is to educate the young to recognize the value of cultural diversity, to understand and respect other cultures, and to accept the right of others to be different. In addition, education for cultural understanding will enrich the lives of all students; decrease racism, prejudice, and discrimination; and increase social justice (pp. 98–99). Notwithstanding the worthiness of the expected outcomes of this approach, Gibson argues that it is doubtful that programmatic changes within the established schools alone can bring about radical changes in the existing social order (pp. 101–102). Because the nature of belief systems, values, and institutions in any given society is influenced by socioeconomic, political, and technological factors, a set of curricular offerings related to cultural understanding alone is not likely to bring about a new social order. Another shortcoming of the cultural understanding approach is that the emphasis on cultural differences to the exclusion of similarities may lead to unintended stereotyping of culturally different groups (pp. 100–101). In other words, all Chicanos, all Asians, or all blacks may be thought of as having the same beliefs, values, and behavioral norms. In a society that is already ethnocentric, emphasizing the differences may reinforce ethnocentrism.

As compared to the first two approaches, *education for cultural pluralism* appears to be broader in scope. Its purpose is to "preserve and extend cultural pluralism in America" (Gibson, 1984, p. 102). The impetus for this approach comes from ethnic minority groups' rejection of assimilationism or the melting pot ideal and promotion of cultural diversity, which is essential for the survival of minority groups. Underlying the education for cultural pluralism approach is the presumption that through its school programs ethnic minorities will be able to increase power of cultural pluralism. The third approach may be regarded as "a strategy for the extension of ethnic groups' socio-political interests" (pp. 103–105). One of the difficulties connected with education for cultural pluralism is that although many have a rather general understanding of cultural pluralism, neither the fundamental tenets nor their ideological or philosophical bases are clearly and systematically articulated. Further, any number of educational strategies may be consonant with the ideals of cultural pluralism, but we do not yet have a definitive body of data to indicate that a particular educational approach may be more effective than others. An ironic aspect of the third approach is that whereas other forms of multicultural education emphasize the importance of a person's ability to function across cultural boundaries, "education for cultural pluralism seeks to create and preserve boundaries between groups" (p. 107). This is probably unavoidable, because the distinctive identity of an ethnic group cannot be preserved without establishing and maintaining boundaries between groups.

The fourth approach, *bicultural education,* is almost always associated with bilingual education, primarily because language reflects the culture in which it is used. A primary purpose of bicultural education is to develop children's language competencies in their primary, or native, language and in the language of the mainstream society. But more fundamental than this is helping children to function effectively in two cultures, their own and that of the dominant group. In the case of children from the mainstream society, they would benefit from learning to operate in a second culture. Accordingly, "bicultural education programs are seen as the avenue for providing instruction in two cultures" (Gibson, 1984, p. 108). Like the education for cultural pluralism approach, bicultural education, too, gets its impetus from the need to reject the melting pot ideal so that ethnic groups can maintain their distinctive identities and develop their linguistic, social, and intellectual competencies to function in the larger society.

From Gibson's perspective, the bicultural education approach tends to equate culture with language or ethnic group, thereby "overemphasizing ethnic identity, running the risk of preventing students from choosing to emphasize other identities" (p. 109). The advocates of this fourth approach see bicultural education as a panacea for all social and educational ills. In a society that is as culturally, racially, and socioeconomically diverse as the United States, it is not enough that the young be able to operate in two cultural settings; rather, they should be able to live and work effectively in many different sociocultural contexts. In this sense, bicultural education is limited in its purpose.

The Need for a Broader View

The four approaches to multicultural education we have just discussed overlap in their purposes, instructional strategies, and materials. In reviewing the four different conceptions of multicultural education, we find that all of them regard the best way of dealing with the learners' cultural differences as offering special programs within the established school system. The needs for promoting cultural understanding, fostering respect for cultural differences, and cultivating the belief in the worth of cultural diversity are viewed as "a response to ethnic groups' pressure for a fairer representation in . . . American history and society" (Gibson, 1984, p. 111). As Gibson cogently notes, multicultural education can be seen as a minority strategy for minority students rather than a majority group program for minorities (p. 111).

When we consider the shortcomings of the four approaches, it is not surprising that multicultural education is frequently viewed as something for minority groups only. Nor should we wonder why student members of the mainstream culture feel left out of a supposedly important part of American education. Finally, from the early 1970s to the present, multicultural education has almost always been associated with schooling. This erroneous equating of schooling with education inclines us to minimize the enormous impact our families, churches, industry, mass media, and other institutions outside of the school have on the development of the young. Further, as Gibson (1984) warns, if we attempt to change people's fundamental attitudes toward others and increase social justice by merely changing our schools, we are likely to disregard the larger sociopolitical and economic context of formal education (p. 113).

In spite of the conceptual weaknesses of the four approaches, some benefits are likely to accrue from implementing multicultural education programs connected with any one of the approaches. However, a broader conception of multicultural education is needed if we are to avoid the tendency of equating culture with ethnicity and multicultural education with special school programs for ethnic minorities. A broader perspective will provide a basis for gaining a more realistic and comprehensive understanding of the educative process and its relationship to schooling. Such an understanding may enhance our ability to develop strategies and programs to make our schools genuinely multicultural for all.

MULTICULTURAL EDUCATION: A BROADER VIEW

Private and Operating Cultures

In formulating a broader conception of multicultural education, we need to review the relationship between education and culture. As Dewey (1961) pointed out, education is "the process of forming fundamental dispositions, intellectual and emotional, toward nature and fellow men" (p. 328). The specific fundamental dispositions toward nature and fellow human beings that need to be formed are culture bound. As already pointed out in Chapter 2, there is no getting away from the fact that education is a cultural process. From the society's perspective, education is the process of transmitting its culture to the young. For the young, education becomes the process of learning societal norms. More specifically, because cultural diversity exists to some degree in every society, "the process of learning a society's culture, or macroculture . . . is one of learning a number of different or partially different micro-cultures and their sub-cultural variants, and how to discern the situations in which they are appropriate and the kinds of others to whom to attribute them" (Goodenough, 1976, p. 5).

A person's ability to function effectively in a socioculturally diverse society depends on the individual's specific knowledge about other subcultures and the skills needed to function appropriately in varying cultural contexts. Hence, learning to understand other cultures and to interact effectively with their members should be an integral part of the educational goal in any society. Multicultural education then should be defined as "the process whereby a person develops competencies in multiple systems of standards for perceiving, evaluating, believing, and doing" (Gibson, 1984, p. 112). Multicultural education should not be seen only as "an educational encounter with unjust, exclusive, and exclusionary educational policies, programs, and practices" (Garcia, 1982, p. 8), because it should promote cross-cultural competencies in all students regardless of their ethnic and racial backgrounds, gender, age, or other exceptionalities.

For a person to be competent in multiple cultural settings, the individual should not only have knowledge about disparate cultures. We all have several different positions (identities) in the dominant culture and the particular ethnic group to which we belong, so it is important that we should also be able to make intelligent decisions about the most appropriate modes of thinking, acting, and communicating in any given situation. It is for this reason that critical and reflective thinking must play a key role in multicultural education. The following brief discussion of Goodenough's (1963) notions of private and operating culture will help clarify the conceptual basis of the broader view of multicultural education discussed here.

Private Culture

As every society has a culture, so may we speak of each person as having his or her own private culture, which includes the generalized view of the culture of the individual's own community, that is, public culture, as well as the awareness of several distinct cultures of other individuals (Goodenough, 1963, pp. 261, 264). This cultural awareness within a person's private culture represents the individual's perceptions of how other human beings have organized their experiences based on the standards by which others perceive, predict, judge, and act. It is through our knowledge of the private cultures of our associates that we learn to accomplish those goals that are best achieved through working together. Hence, a person's private culture may include knowledge of several language patterns, norms of conduct and valuation, and procedures for getting things done (Goodenough, 1963, pp. 260–261). Depending on the nature of one's purpose and its context, the individual often moves from one set of cultural norms to another. For example, when we go from our classroom to a Hispanic community center, our spoken language, communication style, and etiquette change to fit the new situation. Such a change is possible only if certain aspects of the Hispanic culture are part of the repertoire of our private culture.

Operating Culture

In interacting with others in various social and cultural contexts, a person shifts from one culture to another within his or her repertoire, but tends to use the cultures in which he or she is already proficient. "The particular other culture he selects is . . . his operating culture" (Goodenough, 1963, p. 261). Most individuals have several or more operating cultures, but they tend to use only one or two of them. As individuals become more skilled in using a limited number of operating cultures, they tend to use them as guides to their behavior in all contexts. Consequently, in unfamiliar situations these individuals tend to be clumsy and awkward. Their behaviors are often inflexible and maladaptive because their operating cultures are inappropriate for the new situations. For example, individuals who operate only in terms of the middle-class culture may not be able to interact effectively with those who are in lower socioeconomic minority groups. Similarly, people whose lives are confined to the central city environment are not likely to be competent in interacting with suburbanites. The inability of many of our teachers to relate effectively with culturally or socioeconomically different children may be attributable to the fact that teachers as a group are monocultural in their experience and education. Only when individuals increase the repertoires of their private and operating cultures and make use of them can they function proficiently in culturally divergent situations.

If a person operates rigidly in terms of a single culture, (e.g., using standard English only in a multiethnic and multilingual community), that person will be less effective in accomplishing his or her purposes. This suggests that the greater a person's breadth of cultural competencies and the more flexible he or she is in shifting from one appropriate cultural context to another, the more successful that person will be in achieving desired outcomes. As Goodenough (1963) points out, an increase in interethnic contacts is educationally important because such an increase enlarges "the number of other cultures in the private [and operating] cultures of the individuals [from which they can select]" (p. 262).

Typically, a person uses only a limited number of cultural orientations. If the dominant culture views other cultural patterns as deficits, the number of alternative cultural orientations that an individual could use would be limited to those the mainstream culture regards as legitimate. Minority children, for example, may be pressured, implicitly or explicitly, to reject their own language and use only standard English. Rejection of their language pattern as a low-status form reinforces the negative image minority children have of their own culture and personal identity. One problem of the deficit view for minorities of all kinds is that the more one conforms exclusively to the dominant (the "right") norm, the more one crushes self-esteem and pride in one's own identity. The deficit view not only robs richness from both the dominant and minority cultures but also increases alienation and sociopsychological conflicts.

Changes in Private and Operating Cultures

A fundamental purpose of multicultural education is to modify the ways in which individuals see themselves and others so that they can function in a progressively more effective way in an increasingly complex world. Changes in a person's perceptions of and attitude toward other people and their culture may properly be seen as the results of changes in the individual's private and operating cultures. According to Goodenough (1963), changes in private culture occur through the adding or refining of the existing organization of experiences (pp. 272–274). In other words, a person's private culture may be changed by acquiring completely new experiences or restructuring the organization of past experiences. For example, learning a new foreign language enlarges one's cultural repertoire, and intense personal encounters with ethnic minorities may modify the individual's pattern of interaction with minority students. "Whatever form change takes, its results represent additions to one's private culture, not replacement within it" (p. 272).

The impetus for changes in private culture comes from a person's desire to seek a more effective way of dealing with new situations that he or she could not handle successfully within the existing private culture. But the quest for alternative approaches to problem solving may not arise if the individual is ethnocentric and views all differences as deficits. Thus, whereas some immigrants become engrossed in learning the ways of their new country, others choose to live in the confines of their ethnic community. Similarly, some members of the mainstream culture are deeply interested in learning about other cultures at home and abroad because they are concerned about becoming more successful in their work. On the other hand, there are those who have no desire to expand their private culture because they are convinced that only their cultural norms are valid. An operating culture may also be changed by acquiring new experiences or refining or reorganizing certain aspects of one's private culture. But a change in the person's identification with a particular group can also lead to a change in the individual's operating culture.

Syncretism

There is yet another way in which changes in an operating culture may occur. A person may change his or her operating culture through syncretistic incorporation of elements from a different culture into the private culture (Goodenough, 1963, p. 275). That is, ethnic minorities may develop distinctive ways of interacting with other people by maintaining certain aspects of their own ethnic norms and integrating them with mainstream standards. For example, an Asian-American girl may discard her unquestioning obedience to elders and become more self-assertive while retaining that part of Asian culture that requires her to be responsive to the needs and expectations of others. This is tantamount to saying that in a culturally pluralistic and democratic society, ethnic minorities should preserve and extend their culture through the syncretic process. Here, the notion of "preservation and extension" should not be seen as a reactionary, "back-to-the-blanket" move. Rather, "Syncretism is the reconciliation of both two or more cultural systems or elements, with the modification of both" (Burger, 1966, p. 103). This concept is not the same as the "melting" of distinctive cultures into one allegedly superior one. Syncretism refers to the development of a new and unique culture and a new personal identity by interweaving different cultural elements. The syncretic process is important to the members of both minority and dominant cultures, for everyone's private and operating cultures can always be expanded for effective handling of disparate contingencies in life.

Multicultural Education: A Redefinition

What we learn about other cultures is not classified neatly into different cultural pigeonholes in our mind so that the right pattern is pulled out of an appropriate category when a situation calls for a particular way of acting. Our knowledge of and experiences in other cultures become integrated into the complex terrains of our private and operating cultures. Hence, acting appropriately in different situations or having multicultural competencies requires not only knowledge of divergent patterns but also an ability to evaluate the situation. Equally important is the ability to formulate available options in relation to one's goals and then to critically choose the option that will help achieve the present objective as a means to accomplishing future goals. Thus, multicultural education should be seen as the process by which each individual can learn to live in a progressively effective and enriching way by increasing the individual's cultural repertoire and reconciling divergent patterns so that a new and unique approach to life may emerge. This should indeed be a central goal of lifelong learning.

This view of multicultural education implies the centrality of our ability to think critically and reflectively about our own ways and those of others in selecting and developing the most appropriate means of achieving our many varied purposes (Bennett, 1995, p. 33). This approach to multicultural education is what James Banks (1994) calls the *transformative approach* to multicultural education and what Jack Mezirow (1984) calls *perspective transformation*. According to Mezirow, this is the process of becoming aware of the ways in which existing sociocultural and psychological assumptions, processes, and patterns have inhibited the development of one's potentialities (pp. 124–125).

> It is the learning process by which [individuals] come to recognize their culturally induced dependency roles and relationships and the reasons for them and take action to overcome them. (p. 124)

Mezirow (1984) explains that this process of perspective transformation could occur as the result of a sudden insight into the cultural and psychological assumptions and patterns that have limited our role and development or "by a series of transitions which permit one to revise specific assumptions about oneself and others until the very structure of assumptions become transformed" (pp. 125–126). By exposing the deficit assumptions underlying the prevailing views of ethnic minorities, women, or the aged, a person may begin to redefine his or her own role and self-identity in the larger society. Through this kind of experience, the person's experiences and thinking can become more inclusive, discriminating, and integrating as well as becoming "sufficiently permeable to allow one an access to other perspectives" (p. 127). The perspective transformation process should be an essential characteristic of multicultural education. Clearly, increasing the number of cultural orientations in one's repertoire through culturally diverse experiences is a prerequisite to such a process.

Conflicts in interest and values are bound to arise in a society with many diverse cultural elements. We are constantly in a position of having to interact with individuals who do not share our own system of norms and beliefs. Thus, we cannot depend on our own cultural ways to gain a reliable reading of what others are going to do next or how we will deal effectively with our own life problems. In a culturally diverse society, all of its members need to modify some of their ways by going beyond their own culture. To do this, we need to understand the dominant as well as minority cultures in terms of their points of agreements, disagreements, and conflicts with our own norms so that there may emerge new and unique cultural patterns consonant with the fundamental ideals of participatory democracy. But we cannot normally go beyond our own culture without "first exposing its major hidden axioms, and unstated assumptions concerning what life is about—how it is lived, viewed and analyzed, talked about, described and changed" (Hall, 1976, p. 195). Helping learners to "construe experience in a way in which they may more clearly understand the reasons for their problems and understand the options open to them" through a critical understanding of their own culture and those of others "so that they may assume responsibility for decision making is the essence of multicultural education" (Mezirow, 1984, p. 135). For members of minority groups, the key question should not be about the extent to which they should or should not assimilate the dominant norms. Rather, the critical concern should be about what one must know and be able to do to function most effectively in life.

The Aims of Multicultural Education

The specific aims of multicultural education just described are (1) the cultivation of an attitude of respect for and appreciation of the worth of cultural diversity, (2) the promotion of the belief in the intrinsic worth of each person and an abiding interest in the well-being of the larger society, (3) the development of multicultural competencies to function effectively in culturally varied settings, and (4) the facilitation of educational equity for all regardless of ethnicity, race, gender, age, or other exceptionalities.

Developing an appreciation of cultural diversity as enriching rather than harmful to individuals or the national unity is the first aim of multicultural education. As pointed out in Chapter 1, culture represents a system of practices that enable a group of people to deal successfully with needs and problems arising out of their environment and interpersonal or intergroup relationships. In this sense, having many different cultures in our society is tantamount to having a wide range of tested alternative problem-solving approaches. Cultural diversity is enriching because we can become progressively effective and efficient in dealing with our problems by learning from other cultural patterns. Appreciating different cultures, which should be viewed as pools of collective experiences, knowledge, wisdom, and the vision of other people, can make our own lives richer. Hence, other cultures are worthy of our respect. This implies that no one culture represents the best and the only right way of coping with human needs and problems. There cannot be a single cultural perspective from which the world and human encounters must always be seen.

Members of ethnic minority groups in this country may indeed have to or should learn to behave according to the dominant norms. But their own cultural patterns should not be judged as either inferior or deficits to be eliminated. Put differently, educators should not ban the student's voice "by a distorted legitimation of the standard language [dominant norms]," but they should help the young appreciate the "value of mastering the standard dominant language [culture] of the wider society" (Freire & Macedo, 1987, p. 152). In this way, we may begin to treat other cultures with the same sense of respect and appreciation we show toward our own.

The belief in the worth of cultural diversity is also based on the assumption that each person's identity is rooted in the culture to which he or she belongs. Hence, if we are to respect other cultures, we must also respect their members. Similarly, if we demean other people's cultures, we not only impugn their legitimacy, we also denigrate the dignity of other human beings. By affirming the worth of cultural diversity we are attesting to the positive value of individuals with varied cultural heritages and perspectives.

Belief in the intrinsic worth of each person and an abiding interest in the well-being of the larger society comprise the second aim of multicultural education. In a democratic society, each person should be treated as an end or as having intrinsic worth. Democratic institutions must serve the individual in becoming the best that he or she can be. Accordingly, rather than exploiting others we should be willing to extend to others the same respect and rights that we expect and enjoy ourselves. As our actions have direct or indirect bearing on others, other people's conduct also influences our lives. Members of a democratic and pluralistic society must then have a deep and enduring interest in the affairs of the larger society. In so doing, freedoms of all sorts are possible insofar as our deeds do not violate the rights of others or harm the health and growth of the larger society.

There is indeed a symbiotic relationship between the social collective and its members. Our recognition of this inextricable relationship between individuals and society and our commitment to the belief in the intrinsic worth of each person constitutes the fundamental principles to which all members of a free society should subscribe. Extolling cultural diversity without such a basis for social control and unity may lead to an extreme form of cultural relativism and separatism. If we insist that all values are completely relative to the cultures in which they are found and if we reject the possibility of having any objective criteria of evaluating cultures, then all cultures may be considered as equally good and functional. Under such relativism, all things are permissible. Further, if individuals identify themselves exclusively in terms of their membership in a particular ethnic group, their sense of loyalty to and concern for the larger society may diminish to the minimal level. There is little doubt that such a phenomenon would fragment the larger society and undermine its unity.

Allan Bloom, author of *The Closing of the American Mind,* suggests that ethnic minority groups' insistence on preserving their culture may weaken our belief in God and the country that has helped to unify the American people (1987, p. 192). Bloom goes on to say that "the blessing given the whole notion of cultural diversity in the United States by the culture movement has contributed to the intensification and legitimation of group politics, along with a corresponding decay of belief that the individual rights enunciated in the Declaration of Independence are anything more than rhetoric" (p. 193). He argues that the emphasis on cultural diversity and ethnicity or "roots" is a "manifestation of the concern with particularity" (p. 192). For Bloom, this concern with particularity (ethnicity) is superficial because it fails to deal with the real differences among human beings, which he insists are based on the "differences in fundamental beliefs about good and evil, about what is highest, about God. Differences of dress or food are either of no interest or are secondary expressions of deeper beliefs" (p. 192). What Bloom is suggesting is that the fundamental beliefs that unite a society of people are universals or perhaps absolutes that go beyond the routine concerns of daily life.

Bloom's apprehension regarding the possible effects of preoccupation with cultural diversity is reasonable and even appropriate. However, the argument is marred by his failure to recognize the fact that the specific contents of the fundamental beliefs about "good and evil, about what is highest, about God" are determined by the cultures in which they are found. Bloom holds that what we wear and what we eat are either of no interest or are secondary expressions of deeper beliefs. But he does not recognize that these deeper beliefs are reflections of each culture's unique worldview. Even more questionable is Bloom's tacit assumption that the beliefs about "good and evil, about what is highest, about God" as found in the allegedly superior Western culture are cultural universals and absolutes.

As Aronowitz and Giroux (1988) point out, Bloom considers ethnic or racially based cultures as the anti-intellectual elements that threaten the "moral authority of the state," because he sees the foundation of the Western ethic as its capacity to "transcend the immediate circumstances of daily life in order to reach the good life" (p. 174). If Bloom had his way, he would have this society return perhaps to the Puritan era, in which cultural diversity was seen as harmful to the national unity. This unity was to have come from everyone conforming to the allegedly superior Anglo-norms in language, behavior, government, morality, and religion. Yet what the Puritan perspective accomplished was to reinforce the ethnocentric attitude of the dominant group and intensify the sense of alienation and discrimination experienced by ethnic and racial minority groups.

The third aim of multicultural education deals with multicultural competencies. We live in a world in which individuals and groups constantly influence each other. For example, an agricultural disaster in the midwestern states would affect the food processing industry, the trucking industry, the supermarkets, and the pocketbooks of every family in the country. Such a chain of consequences would eventually lower the sales and production of automobiles, appliances, and other durable goods as well as the rate of national employment. Similarly, prolonged bitter warfare between two major oil-producing countries could and would have a calamitous impact on the technology and politico-economic conditions of almost every nation in the world. In a world where human beings not only affect each other but also are interdependent, we cannot always resolve difficulties by relying exclusively on our own devices. Social, political, and economic realities of our time demand that we learn to work with each other, for no one person or group or nation is capable of solving complex human problems singlehandedly. As Banks (1994) argues, the ability to see issues, themes, and problems from diverse perspectives and points of view is crucial to the success of democracy (p. 26). Specific knowledge about the ways in which people in other cultures think, behave, communicate, and interpret the world is imperative for establishing an effective working relationship. Respecting other cultures as we do our own and critically understanding our own culture are equally important requisites in intercultural cooperation.

Educational equity, the fourth aim, is based on the conviction that each person be treated as an end and helped to become the best he or she can be in terms of capacities and envisioned possibilities. As Gollnick and Chinn (1986) advocate, "in a country that champions equal rights and the opportunity for an individual to improve his or her conditions, we must be concerned with helping all students reach their full potential" (p. 27). Accordingly, "educational and vocational options should not be limited by sex, age, ethnicity, native language, religion, socio-economic level, or exceptionality" (p. vii). Providing educational equity is then a necessary condition for aiding all learners to realize their fullest potential.

Broadly speaking, educational equity has two key elements. One is providing equal access to educational opportunities so that each person can participate in the desired programs to develop his or her interests and capacities. This goal would require all sorts of academic advising, career counseling, and other appropriate support services to help learners find the most effective means of becoming self-fulfilling and socially productive individuals. The second aspect of educational equity is the facilitation of conditions under which students can maximize their learning outcome. Clearly, all learners share certain common traits and needs. But they also possess those special characteristics and conditions that are unique to each person.

The idiosyncratic characteristics and conditions may be culture, race, gender, or age. Accordingly, educators need to have specific knowledge about the ways in which social, cultural, and even biological factors affect the teaching-learning processes. Developing instructional strategies based on such knowledge is imperative in multicultural education, for every learner has his or her own exceptionalities or hurdles to overcome and distinctive capacities to develop in achieving personal goals. Additionally, using curricular materials that contain balanced and representative accounts of the experiences and contributions of ethnic groups, women, and other minorities in the history of this nation and the world is indispensable in multicultural education.

Sexism, Ageism, and Exceptionality

The primary purpose of the following discussion is not to examine the specific issues and problems related to sexism, ageism, and discrimination against exceptional learners in education. Rather, it is to suggest a perspective that may be useful in developing concrete measures for providing egalitarian respect, treatment, and education to all learners. This perspective, which will be called the multicultural perspective, rests on the premises that (1) women, the elderly, and exceptional learners constitute distinct subcultural groups in the mainstream society and (2) the fundamental concepts and principles of the suggested view of multicultural education are applicable to these groups. More specifically, women, the elderly, and exceptional learners should be accorded the same kind of equality of opportunity, freedom, justice, and respect to which ethnic and racial minority groups are entitled.

The multicultural perspective rejects the belief that all deviations from the norms of the dominant society or group are deficits or pathological conditions rather than differences. From the deficit perspective, minority groups are either excluded from participating in the activities of the dominant group

or thought to require special compensatory measures to remedy their pathological conditions. By rejecting the deficit view, educators should encourage
all learners to examine the society's racist, sexist, or otherwise discriminatory
expectations.

> Learners [regardless of their sex, age, or exceptionality] must conse-
> quently be led to an understanding of the reasons imbedded in these
> internalized cultural myths and concomitant feelings which account for
> their felt needs and wants as well as the way they see themselves and their
> relations. Having gained this understanding, learners must be given access
> to alternative meaning perspectives for interpreting this reality. (Mezirow,
> 1984, p. 133)

Sexism

In spite of the strides made in attempting to eliminate sexism from our society, ample evidence suggests that men and women are not equally treated in
this country. More often than not, women are considered inferior to men.
The consequences of sex discrimination in our society appear in the forms of
higher prestige and wages attached to the so-called men's occupations as compared to the stereotypic feminine jobs. But more fundamentally, a primary
source of sexism is the fact that although our culture assigns different sex
roles to men and women, "the dominant male culture is used as an arbitrary
yardstick of success and both cultures are evaluated in terms of the modal
achievement of one [male]" (Lee & Gropper, 1974, p. 382). Unless men and
women encounter some experience that casts a cloud of doubt over the legitimacy of their culturally assigned sex roles, they will continue to work toward
fulfilling the established gender roles and positions.

Culturally assigned sex roles are derived from generalized stereotypic
characterization of different genders as groups. Hence, the range of developmental opportunities and options available to those who seek their future
outside of the culturally determined gender expectations is severely
restricted. From the multicultural perspective, educators should encourage
learners to critically examine and expose the hidden assumptions underlying
the sex-role culture "as a way of helping them avoid prescribed role traps
[and] teachers can derive similar educational leverage from society's sexist
expectations" (Lee & Gropper, 1974, p. 390). The purpose of promoting such
critical reflection about students' sex roles is to help them develop competencies to function effectively in our multicultural world. The appropriateness of
specific competencies then is to be determined by one's capacities, envisioned
possibilities, and the setting in which the individual must live and work.

In recent years, many plans have been proposed to make our schools
gender-free by eliminating sex or gender bias; in a democratic society, they
affirm, gender should be taken as completely irrelevant in determining peo-

ple's roles, status, or social organization. Concurring with this ideal, Barbara Houston (1985) also suggests that the so-called gender-free strategies are likely "(1) to create a context which continues to favor the dominant group, and (2) [undermine] certain efforts which may be needed to realize equalization of educational opportunities" (p. 365). Houston cogently points out that there are three possible meanings of the expression *gender-free* (pp. 359–360). In the first sense, gender-free education refers to the attempts to disregard gender by eliminating all gender-related differentiations. An example of such an attempt is the elimination of activities such as wrestling and other contact sports in which gender differences in achievements are due to certain biological differences between the sexes. In the second sense, gender-free education means that gender is not taken into account in any aspect of education. Gender-related standards for admissions are not used; special programs are not offered. The elimination of gender bias from education is the third meaning of gender-free education.

According to Houston (1985), research findings do not support the belief that these gender-free strategies lead to greater participation by women either in sports or in teacher-student interactions. On the contrary, such efforts "had the effect of bringing about a greater loss of educational opportunities for girls" (p. 361). This unexpected consequence of gender-free strategies is attributable to the fact that in a male-dominated society, the patterns of male conduct, speech, and interpersonal relationship are used as the norms by which females are judged. Hence, even though the teacher may ignore gender, the students do not disregard gender-related roles. In other words, "gender may be excluded as an official criterion, but it continues to function as an unofficial factor" (p. 363).

As a basis for formulating strategies for making our schools nonsexist, Martin (1981) and Houston (1985) suggest that we take the *gender-sensitive* perspective, which recommends that attention be paid to gender when such action can prevent sex discrimination and advance sex equality. What this means is that gender interactions should be carefully monitored to equalize opportunities for both sexes. The gender-sensitive perspective differs from the gender-free approach in that the former "allows one to recognize that at different times and in different circumstances one might be required to adopt opposing policies in order to eliminate gender bias" (Houston, 1985, p. 368). In consonance with the multicultural perspective, the gender-sensitive perspective also encourages constant and critical analysis of the meaning and significance attached to gender.

Ageism

There are at least two major reasons for studying ageism and its educational implications as an important aspect of multicultural education. One is that the

aged as a group constitute another minority group that frequently encounters discrimination. The other is that, unlike racism or sexism, those who discriminate against the aged will necessarily have to confront their own membership in this minority group. Here, we should keep in mind that the term
minority is not merely a numerical concept but also that it involves the notion
of "having power of control." Consequently, even if the number of aged surpasses the number of younger individuals in our society, the aged as a group
may continue to occupy minority status, for the group is not likely to have
power of control. Like racism and sexism, ageism stems from the deficit view
that stereotypes elders as unproductive; outmoded in thinking, attitude, and
behavior; and outdated in their views of the world and morality. The aged
are also depicted as tired, less capable, forgetful, slow in thinking, and sickly.
As children are often described in terms of their inabilities, the aged are also
characterized by their disabilities. As Butler (1978) explains, ageism as the
"new American bigotry" is the "stereotyping of and discrimination against
people because they are old. Ageism allows younger generations to see older
people as different from [and inferior to] themselves; thus, they subtly cease
to identify with their elders as human beings" (p. 12).

As is the case with individual members of ethnic minority and gender
groups, elderly individuals have their own unique values, beliefs, lifestyles,
communication and cognitive styles, and problem-solving approaches.
These patterns have special meanings and significance for the elderly
because they have served them well. Yet, because of the pervasive deficit
view of the aged in this society, the elderly often live out their lives by conforming to their culturally assigned roles. They frequently become with-
drawn, sickly, unproductive, and less capable. Thus, the aged become victims of the culturally ascribed deficit view. It goes without saying that the
process of aging is absolutely not escapable. There can be no compensatory
programs to bring back youth. We cannot restore youthful physical traits in
the aged to have them redefine their role and identity. Ideally, both the
individual and the society can benefit enormously by helping the aged to
become self-fulfilling, productive, and contributing human beings. But if we
are to accomplish this end, we need to change (1) the deficit view of the
aged and (2) the way in which the aged see themselves so that they may be
empowered.

One way to eliminate the deficit view is to demythologize what Sorgman
and Sorensen (1984) call the *theory of disengagement*, which refers to "a process
whereby the aged person and the society cooperate in a process of mutual
withdrawal from each other" (p. 120). The acceptance of the theory of disengagement leads to a misconception of the aging process, because it implies
that the elderly withdraw from interpersonal relationships and participation
in social affairs as a result of aging. Though this view is contrary to the known
fact that "those who are 'joiners' in earlier years will also be social minded as

they age, neither the media nor the books portray this aspect of the aged" (p. 121). Further, the theory implicitly assumes that the process of disengagement is a natural process of aging. Sorgman and Sorensen point out that although some elderly may become socially inactive, the theory reflects our society's indifference toward them. The fact that the media almost never portray the elderly in situations in which they are sought out or involved in social affairs or participating in a decision-making process reveals our society's lack of serious interest in providing meaningful alternatives for this increasingly large group of people.

An in-depth study of ageism, its hidden assumptions, key concepts, and history, as well as a balanced view of the elderly's needs and their roles by the younger generations and the aged themselves, should give a basis for understanding the culture of the aged. As increased interethnic contacts are important in understanding other cultures, more frequent interaction between the aged and younger people in different situations should have a positive effect in modifying our attitudes. These efforts may also help us avoid the deficit view so that the culture of the aged can be seen in terms of how well it serves the elderly in dealing with their own unique needs and problems. Rather than being bound by their culturally ascribed role and image of themselves, the aged need to seek a new identity and options in their lives by developing multicultural competencies. To begin this search for new meaning, the aged must, as Mezirow (1984) suggests, learn to explore critically the reasons for their problems and understand the options available to them so that they may assume responsibility for decision making (p. 135). Multicultural education for the young and the aged equally necessitates an increased cultural repertoire and critical thinking in choosing the cultural patterns most appropriate in achieving one's ends in view.

Exceptionality

Exceptional learners, whether disabled or gifted, may suffer alienation from the mainstream society because they are viewed in terms of the extent to which they deviate from the standards of "normal" people. Yet learners with disabilities tend to experience much more severe discrimination and rejection than the gifted. Gollnick and Chinn (1986) point out that the rejection of the gifted is most likely to come from "a lack of understanding or jealousy rather than from the stigma that may relate to certain handicapping conditions" (p. 260). Like ethnic minorities, women, and the aged, those with disabilities are seen through a deficit model so that they are accepted to the extent to which they conform to the idealized norms of the nondisabled. Thus, for example, the patterns of behavior, interpersonal relationships, and communication and cognitive styles of the hearing and visually impaired are evaluated according to the norms of hearing and sighted people.

A harmful consequence of the deficit view is that ethnic minority children who do some very smart things in coping with their life problems are often classified as mentally disabled, because they do not deal with their world using the ways of the mainstream culture. In a very real sense, persons with disabilities may be called "the unexpected minority" (Glideman & Roth, 1980). There is yet another way in which learners with disabilities are similar to ethnic minorities. As the mainstream society's images of minority groups are derived from distorted and unbalanced portrayals of these groups, our views of disabilities are influenced by negative descriptions of the group. The media rarely show people with disabilities occupying leadership or prestigious positions or making other notable contributions to the society. They are often seen as marginal individuals who are tolerated only to the extent that they fit into stereotypic and culturally assigned roles and statuses.

As has been suggested earlier, every person has to cope with certain contingencies if he or she is to achieve optimal learning. In some instances these contingencies are affective, cognitive, social, or physical in nature, but we need not see them as deficits or pathological conditions that must be eradicated. Groups of individuals with various kinds of disabilities have certain cultural patterns that arise out of their unique needs and circumstances. As the mainstream culture serves its members well most of the time, so do the cultures of those with disabilities. Yet, as Reagan (1985) points out, "the deaf [handicapped or disabled] community has had a more difficult time overcoming inferiority stereotyping by the majority culture than other minority groups, since deaf [handicapped] people are viewed as medical pathology" (p. 277).

There is no justifiable reason to insist that people with disabilities must conform only to the norms of the mainstream society, for they too live in a culturally diverse world requiring multicultural competencies. Quite the contrary, there is every reason to reconceptualize the education of the handicapped so that they may be able to function effectively in socially and culturally diverse environments. Again Reagan (1985) persuasively argues that "the need for the deaf child to learn to cope with and function in both the hearing and deaf cultures would make a bicultural—as well as bilingual—approach especially desirable" (p. 276). Here he is speaking not only about the education of the deaf but also of disabled or handicapped learners as a whole. To provide bicultural or, rather, multicultural education to the handicapped, we need not only reeducate the teachers but also have them rethink the ways in which they view the handicapped. "To do otherwise, however, would be to allow an essentially imperialistic approach to the education of a sizable minority group in the United States to continue unabated" (p. 277).

In this chapter, we have examined the conceptual similarities shared by cultural pluralism, democracy, and multicultural education. Our discussion of several different approaches to multicultural education revealed the need to define it more broadly so that culture may not be exclusively connected with ethnicity or ethnic minorities in the United States. It is critical that multicultural education is understood to include an in-depth study of other cultures and how cultural factors affect education as well as the provision of educational equity to all individuals regardless of ethnicity, race, sex, or age. In sum, the fundamental principles of multicultural education should be applicable to all groups and individuals.

CASE STUDY

CURRICULA FOR MULTICULTURAL TEACHER EDUCATION

The following curricula from a small liberal arts college gives one approach to multicultural teacher education. This college is located in a small town in the upper midwest. The town population is socially, culturally, and racially homogeneous.

All students enrolling at the college are required to have at least one course that includes the study of non-European and non-North American culture and civilization as a part of their general studies requirement.

All of the courses related to aspects of multicultural education available in the college have been identified by the Teacher Education Committee. These courses are classified into the following five areas that make up the cognitive component for the human relations requirements: (1) identifying ethnic diversity, (2) identifying religious diversity, (3) identifying cultural diversity, (4) identifying economic diversity, and (5) understanding human behavior.

Students may choose from among the courses to meet each of the five cognitive components.

Professional Studies All students must take a minimum of five courses offered by the education department in order to be recommended for certification. These include: (1) Educational Psychology, (2) Principles of Secondary Education, (3) Special Methods in the major field, (4) Historical and Contemporary Issues in Education, and (5) Student Teaching and related experiences.

Students are also required to take a noncredit course in drugs and alcohol as well as course work and experiences for meeting the human relations requirement. Other education courses offered include Guidance and Counseling in Schools, Independent Research, and The Exceptional Child.

In the course Historical and Contemporary Issues in Education, the issues of cultural pluralism, racism, sexism, and parity of power are presented and discussed. Skills for values clarification and basic human interaction are covered in the Educational Psychology course.

Students can choose to participate in the Chicago urban education program for one semester. This program seeks to provide the student teacher with illustrations–including firsthand experience–of the learning problems peculiar to the urban situation. Students observe and student teach in metropolitan area schools. They are also exposed to various approaches to learning, including Montessori, Gestalt, and open classrooms. Placements of those interested in bilingual education, learning disabilities, or special education can be arranged.

Students may also choose one of the three offerings of the Department of Education during the January interim. Perspectives on Teaching is an off-campus program designed to provide practical experiences and insights into different facets of education. Other January interim offerings in education include Education for the Deaf: Communication Training and Field Experience.

The Human Relations Components   Before a student can be recommended for certification, he or she must present evidence of the completion of eight human relations units to the Department of Education. Four of these units must reflect cognitive learning that has increased knowledge and intellectual understanding of (1) contributions and lifestyles of people, and (2) the facts and causes of prejudice and discrimination and ways to create learning environments conducive to students' self-esteem. The other four units must relate to personal encounters that have led toward attitudinal change, respect, and appreciation of others; or they must have provided experience in handling human reactions—including the student's—to real-life situations.

Within each of these broad classifications the committee, in helping prepare students to teach in a multicultural society, designed these specific subareas:

Cognitive:
Identifying Ethnic Diversity; Identifying Religious Diversity; Identifying Cultural Diversity (including sex roles); and Identifying Economic Diversity

Experiential:
Living Within an Ethnically Diverse Setting; Living With Religious Diversity; Living With Cultural Diversity (including sex roles); and Living With Economic Diversity

Students are required to keep records of how they are meeting both the cognitive and experiential areas of the human relations requirements. These are reviewed by the teacher education faculty for approval. Following student teaching, students must write a brief personal essay that indicates how they feel they can fit into a multicultural society.

QUESTIONS

1. To what extent does this program reflect the broader view of multicultural education suggested in this chapter?

2. Some argue that if our multicultural education includes studies of all sorts of diversity, we drift away from the original intent. That is, we pay little or no attention to the special needs of the ethnic groups in our own community. What is your reaction to this view?

3. All teacher education students enrolled in the program described here have to take courses dealing with non-European and non-North American culture and civilization as well as the courses dealing with guidance and counseling, exceptional children, and historical and contemporary issues in education. Yet even through these courses students may be able to bypass an in-depth study of and experiences in dealing with inequities in the social, economic, political, and educational experiences of minorities in the United States. What provisions would you introduce to ensure that such components are not bypassed by anyone in the program?

4. Given the small size of the town and the college as well as the homogeneous nature of the town and college population, what would you do to help students acquire the experiential components of the program?

5. Would you delete or augment any aspects of the program to improve it? Would you modify other program elements or means of organization? What rationale would you have for making such changes?

6. What would you do to prepare the faculty and staff to implement this or any other type of multicultural education by infusing it into the entire college or university program?

REFERENCES

Adler, M. J. (1982). *The Paideia proposal: An educational manifesto.* New York: Macmillan.

American Association of Colleges for Teacher Education. (1972). *AACTE bulletin: Not one model American.* Washington, DC: Author.

Aronowitz, S., & Giroux, H. A. (1988). Schooling, culture and literacy in the age of broken dreams: A review of Bloom and Hirsch. *Harvard Educational Review, 58*(2), 172–194.

Banks, J. A. (1981). Cultural pluralism and the schools. In J. M. Rich (Ed.), *Innovations in education* (pp. 226–230). Boston: Allyn & Bacon.

Banks, J. A. (1994). *An introduction to multicultural education.* Boston: Allyn & Bacon.

Bennett, C. I. (1995). *Comprehensive multicultural education: Theory and practice*. Boston: Allyn & Bacon.

Baratz, S. S., & Baratz, J. C. (1970). Early childhood intervention: The social science base of institutional racism. *Harvard Educational Review, 40*(1), 29–50.

Berkson, I. B. (1969). *Theories of Americanization*. New York: Arno Press.

Bloom, A. (1987). *The closing of the American mind*. New York: Simon & Schuster.

Boyer, E. L. (1983). *High school*. New York: Harper & Row.

Broudy, H. S. (1981). Cultural pluralism: New wine in old bottles. In J. M. Rich (Ed.), *Innovations in education* (pp. 230–233). Boston: Allyn & Bacon.

Burger, H. (1966). Syncretism, an acculturative accelerator. *Human Organization, 25,* 103.

Butler, R. N. (1978). Ageism: Another form of bigotry. In M. M. Seltzer, S. L. Corbett, and R. C. Atchley (Eds.), *Social problems of aging* (p. 12). Belmont, CA: Wadsworth.

Childs, J. L. (1951). The educational philosophy of John Dewey. In P. A. Schilpp (Ed.), *The philosophy of John Dewey* (pp. 419–443). New York: Tudor.

Dewey, J. (1939a). *Freedom and culture*. New York: Capricorn Books.

Dewey, J. (1939b). The modes of societal life. In J. Ratner (Ed.), *Intelligence in the modern world* (pp. 365–404). New York: Random House.

Dewey, J. (1957). *Reconstruction in philosophy*. Boston: Beacon Press.

Dewey, J. (1961). *Democracy and education*. New York: Macmillan.

"English only" measures spark rancorous debates. (1987, June 17). *Education Week,* pp. 1, 14–15.

D'Souza, D. (1991). *Illiberal education: The politics of race and sex on campus*. New York: Free Press.

Evans, M. (1970). *I am a black woman*. New York: Morrow.

Freire, P. (1984). Pedagogy of the oppressed. In S. B. Merriam (Ed.), *Selected readings on philosophy and adult education* (pp. 103–112). Malabar, FL: Robert Krieger.

Freire, P., & Macedo, D. (1987). *Literacy: Reading the word and world*. South Hadley, MA: Bergin & Garvey.

Garcia, R. L. (1982). *Teaching in a pluralistic society*. New York: Harper & Row.

Gates, H. L. (1992). *Loose canons: Notes on the culture wars*. New York: Oxford University Press, xii.

Gibson, M. A. (1984). Approaches to multicultural education. *Anthropology and Education Quarterly, 14,* 94–114.

Giroux, H. A. (1983). *Theory and resistance in education*. Malabar, FL: Robert Krieger.

Giroux, H. A. (1988a). *Teachers as intellectuals*. Granby, MA: Bergin & Garvey.

Giroux, H. A. (1988b). *Schooling and the struggle for public life: Critical pedagogy in the modern age*. Minneapolis: University of Minnesota Press.

Glideman, J., & Roth, W. (1980). *The unexpected minority—Handicapped children in America*. New York: Harcourt Brace Jovanovich.

Gollnick, D. M., & Chinn, P. C. (1986). *Multicultural education* (2nd ed.). Upper Saddle River, NJ: Merrill/Prentice Hall.

Goodenough, W. H. (1963). *Cooperation in change*. New York: Russell Sage Foundation.

Goodenough, W. H. (1976). Multiculturalism as the normal human experience. *Anthropology and Education Quarterly, 7*(4), 4–7.

Goodlad, J. J. (1984). *A place called school*. New York: McGraw-Hill.

Gordon, M. M. (1964). *Assimilation in American life*. New York: Oxford University Press.

Gray, P. (1991). Whose America? *Time*, July 8, 1991, 12–20.

Green, T. (1966). *Education and pluralism: Ideal and reality*. Twenty-sixth A. J. Richard Street Lecture at Syracuse University School of Education, Syracuse, NY.

Guerra, M. H. (1973). Bilingual and bicultural education. In W. R. Hazard, M. D. Stent, & H. N. Rivling (Eds.), *Cultural pluralism in education: A mandate for change* (pp. 27–33). Upper Saddle River, NJ: Prentice Hall.

Hall, E. T. (1976). *Beyond culture*. Garden City, NY: Anchor Press/Doubleday.

Harding, V. (1973). Black reflections on the cultural ramifications of identity. In W. R. Hazard, M. D. Stent, & H. N. Rivling (Eds.), *Cultural pluralism in educa-tion: A mandate for change* (pp. 103–113). Upper Saddle River, NJ: Prentice Hall.

Hata, D. (1973). Asian Americans and education for cultural pluralism. In W. R. Hazard, M. D. Stent, & H. N. Rivling (Eds.), *Cultural pluralism in education: A mandate for change* (pp. 123–130). Upper Saddle River, NJ: Prentice Hall.

Hazard, W. R., & Stent, M. D. (1973). Cultural pluralism and schooling: Some preliminary observations. In W. R. Hazard, M. D. Stent, & H. N. Rivling (Eds.), *Cultural pluralism in education: A mandate for change* (pp. 13–25). Upper Saddle River, NJ: Prentice Hall.

Hirsch, E. D. (1987). *Cultural literacy: What every American needs to know*. Boston: Houghton Mifflin.

Houston, B. (1985). Gender freedom and the subtleties of sexist education. *Educational Theory, 35*(4), 359–370.

Kallen, H. N. (1949). *The education of free men*. New York: Farrar and Straus.

Kitano, H. H. L. (1969). *Japanese Americans*. Upper Saddle River, NJ: Prentice Hall.

Lee, P. C., & Gropper, N. B. (1974). Sex-role culture and educational practice. *Harvard Educational Review, 44*(3), 276–411.

Martin, J. R. (1981). The ideal of the educated person. *Educational Theory, 31*(2), 97–110.

Mezirow, J. (1984). A critical theory of adult learning and education. In S. B. Merriam (Ed.), *Selected writings on philosophy and adult education* (pp. 123–140). Malabar, FL: Robert Krieger.

National Council for the Accreditation of Teacher Education. (1977). *Standards for the accreditation of teacher education*. Washington, DC: Author.

1986 minority enrollment at 3,200 institutions of higher education. (1988, July 6). *The Chronicle of Higher Education*, p. A20.

Pratte, R. (1979). *Pluralism in education*. Springfield, IL: Charles Thomas.

Ravitch, D. (1990). Diversity and democracy: Multicultural education in America. *American Educator, 14*, 16–20, 46–48.

Reagan, T. (1985). The deaf as a linguistic minority: Educational considerations. *Harvard Educational Review, 55*(3), 265–277.

Schlesinger, A. M., Jr. (1992). *The disuniting of America: Reflections on a multicultural society*. New York: W. W. Norton & Co.

Schlafly, P. (1989). Education, the family and traditional values. In H. Holtz, I. Marcus, J. Dougherty, J. Michaels, & R. Peduzzi (Eds.), *Education and the American dream* (pp. 21–29). South Hadley, MA: Bergin & Garvey.

Sekaquaptewa, E. (1973). Community as a product of education for cultural pluralism: Conformal education vs. mutual respect. In W. R. Hazard, M. D. Stent, & H. N.

Rivling (Eds.), *Cultural pluralism in education: A mandate for change* (pp. 35–38). Upper Saddle River, NJ: Prentice-Hall.

Sleeter, C. E., & Grant, C. A. (1987). An analysis of multicultural education in the United States. *Harvard Educational Review, 57*(4), 421–444.

Sleeter, C. E., & Grant, C. A. (1988). *Making choices for multicultural education: Five approaches to race, class and gender.* Upper Saddle River, NJ: Merrill/Prentice Hall.

Sorgman, M. I., & Sorensen, M. (1984). Ageism: A course of study. *Theory into Practice, 23*(2), 119–122.

Tesconi, C. A. (1984). Multicultural education: A valued but problematic ideal. *Theory into Practice, 23*(2), 86–89.

Viz, P. C. (1989). Religion in school textbooks. In H. Holtz, I. Marcus, J. Dougherty, J. Michaels, & R. Peduzzi (Eds.), *Education and the American dream* (pp. 80–87). South Hadley, MA: Bergin & Garvey.

PART THREE

Culture, Schooling, and Educational Development

5

Culture and the Role of Schooling

An understanding of the school-culture relationship is important in developing a theoretical perspective from which to assess and interpret the respective roles of school and society in a situation where educational reforms are needed. In this chapter we will discuss the relationship between schooling and culture by examining four major items about the role of schooling. Our inability or unwillingness to examine the relationship between school and society usually leads to the erroneous belief that the school is solely to blame for the socioeconomic lags and moral ills of American society. This exaggerated notion about the educational system's capacity as an agent of social change may in turn result in blaming the teachers and schools for practically every adversity in our society. Disappointments in and frustrations about our schools are the usual consequences of taking an oversimplified approach to educational reform.

As we have seen in preceding chapters, an intimate relationship exists between schools and sociocultural conditions of the larger society in which they function. The school is a major institution through which the young learn both explicit and implicit cultural norms. Notwithstanding the inextricable connection between culture and schooling, past attempts at major educational reforms in the United States have been focused primarily on organizational and curricular changes. For example, the United States attempted to overtake the USSR in the aerospace race through educational reforms in the late 1950s. But these measures were largely concerned with placing greater emphasis on such academic subject matters as the sciences, mathematics, and foreign languages rather than on the so-called life adjustment process.

No more than a decade later American education was charged as inhumane because it was allegedly preoccupied with only the intellectual growth of the learners. Again, schools and teachers were accused of killing children's love for learning with oppressive and punitive practices. The remedy for this sorry state of American education was to have come from humanistic, or confluent, education, which claimed to nurture the learner's heart as well as the mind. In practice, this approach emphasized developing skills to deal with one's feelings and interpersonal relations. Similar to those of the post-*Sputnik* era, most of the reform measures proposed since the mid-1980s also have sought to improve American education by having students devote more time to studying the liberal arts.

There is little evidence to suggest that the educational reforms tried out since the late 1950s have had a lasting impact on the quality of American education or on the socioeconomic or moral conditions of this society. Indeed, whatever impact the reform programs had were short-lived and superficial. The reformers simply failed to understand that the school is only one of a multitude of institutions in our society and that no amount of tinkering with any single institution could bring about fundamental social, economic, or moral changes. On the contrary, without major social changes, educational reforms are bound to have minimal impact in our lives because the school as a specialized social institution reflects the culture of the larger society. As an illustration, our production-consumption oriented worldview inclines us to see education as a type of industrial production. Hence, we speak of packaging and marketing educational programs and holding our schools accountable to the consumers of educational products.

SCHOOLS AS A SOCIAL AND CULTURAL SYSTEM

School as a Social System

A system is anything that can be divided into smaller parts or subsystems. Natural systems include our own bodies, plants, forests, and the surroundings in which we live. Artificial systems are products of human invention—for example, computers, television sets, automobiles, and various types of institutions. An educational system, a school district, or a school is a type of artificial system consisting of many parts. These parts are related to each other organizationally, functionally, and in their purposes and goals. Further, a school district is in a community, a larger system, or suprasystem, for which it carries on assigned functions. For example, the school board, the central administrative office, the support service units, the resource centers, the individual schools, and the staff and faculty are some of the major subsystems of the school district. Each of these subsystems (for example, an elementary school) may be considered a system with many subsystems of its own. For a school system to function productively, all of its parts must be able to effectively and efficiently discharge their assigned roles.

School as a Cultural System

Unlike a crowd or an informal group, in which behavior is random, a social institution such as a school functions within an organized pattern of system parts designed to accomplish its goals and purposes according to a set of operational policies and procedures (Weber, 1947; Katz, 1971). The powers and responsibilities of the subsystems reside in the appropriate offices rather than the individuals who occupy them (Weber, 1947, pp. 56–57). In general, a system's goals, policies, and rules of operation reflect the broader social and cultural norms of the suprasystem. Additional patterns of behavior, interpersonal relationships, and idiosyncratic language evolve within individual systems. Hence, each social system possesses its own unique culture, consisting of a complex of norms for assigning meanings and significance to objects, events, and human behavior. For example, a school district or a school has a set of specific purposes and goals, an organization, and a body of policies and governing procedures. Further, each district or school has its own "lingo," rules concerning the conduct of its members, and such unique "rites of passage" as initiation, induction, and commencement ceremonies. Whereas some of these norms are explicitly stated, others are implicitly required. Accordingly, all schools have written rules regarding attendance, academic standards, curricular requirements, and other areas of school operation. Schools also have certain unwritten rules, or mores, regulating the behavior of faculty, students, and staff.

Finally, school is not only a social or a cultural system; it is also an action system. Human action is understood as a response to the patterns of the meaning and orientations individuals develop through experience (Parsons, 1961). What this means is that a person moving from one system to another needs to learn a new culture if he or she is to function effectively.

CULTURAL TRANSMISSION AND THE ROLE OF SCHOOLING

Every society makes deliberate attempts to transmit its culture to the young. In this way, they may become full-fledged and contributing members of the society. Culture includes those beliefs, values, and attitudes that a society considers fundamental to its survival and perpetuation. Hence, education is necessarily a deliberate and value-laden (moral) enterprise (Durkheim, 1961). As pointed out in Chapter 2, the educative process can be carried on with or without schools. Schools are specialized social institutions specifically designed to transmit the culture of the larger society to the young. This implies that the cultural norms of a society are the primary sources from which schools derive their goals and that each society has its own particular view of the role of schooling.

In a society such as the United States, where the schools are governed and supported by local communities, the unique values and needs of those communities have direct bearing on the development of specific school goals. For instance, the educational goals of a school district in a politically and religiously conservative agricultural community must not only be consonant with the broad cultural norms of the larger society but must also conform to local demands. More specifically, the district may include agriculture-related subject matters in the curriculum to meet the community's special needs. In accordance with the community's religious and moral perspectives, the district may require school prayer and the teaching of creationism while restricting other activities viewed as liberal. However, the district's responsiveness to the special needs and expectations of the local community may conflict with the role of the school as envisioned by the larger society. Such conflict becomes much more severe if the larger society expects its schools to work toward perpetuating the established culture and also serve as an agent of social change. *Dare the School Build a New Social Order?* by George S. Counts (1932) and the writings of John Dewey, John Childs, Harold Rugg, and William Heard Kilpatrick represent early arguments for making the American school and its teachers agents of social reform.

Disputes regarding the proper role of schooling often are attributable to the fact that cultural transmission as the school's primary goal is usually stated in very broad terms. Hence, there is no consensus about the relative importance of different cultural norms or the order in which such norms are to be transmitted to the young. But even if different interest groups and individuals agree about a school district's general educational goals, many disparate views regarding how such general goals are to be translated into concrete school policies, operational procedures, curriculum and a myriad of other school activities are likely. Such recent court cases as *Pico v. Board of Education* (1980) over book banning, *Wallace v. Jaffree* (1985) concerning silent prayer in schools, and *Lubbock Civil Liberties Union v. Lubbock Independent School District* (1983) on religious gatherings on school premises are only a few examples of attempts to resolve conflicts between disparate conceptions of the role of schooling through legal means. Further, these cases also demonstrate how conflicting beliefs about school activities stem from the divergent ways in which our educators, communities, and other special interest groups interpret the broadly conceived role of the American school.

THE ROLE OF SCHOOLING

If there are disagreements about how schools should translate transmission of culture into specific instructional objectives, policies, and programs, there are even more disparate views regarding the nature of the role of schooling. The following sections will examine four perspectives: (1) structural/functionalist, (2) critical, (3) interpretivist, and (4) postmodern.

The Structural/Functionalist Perspective

According to the structural/functionalist theory (henceforth called the functionalist theory), society is a living organism with many interrelated parts. The life of a society as an organism depends on how well each part performs its distinctive role in relation to the workings of other parts. As one type of institution responsible for the socialization of the young, the school's object "is to arouse and to develop in the child a number of physical, intellectual and moral states which are demanded of him by both the political society as a whole and the special milieu for which he is specifically destined" (Durkheim, 1985a, p. 22). To borrow Talcott Parsons's (1985) words, socialization is "the development in individuals of the commitments and capacities which are essential prerequisites of their future role-performance" (p. 180). The commitments consist of the implementation of the broad *values* of society; the performance of a specific type of role within the *structure* of society. Thus, a society cannot survive unless its members possess and perpetuate a set of common physical skills, intellectual knowledge, and ethical values (Durkheim, 1985a, p. 21). The acquisition of these skills, knowledge, and values by the young is too important to be left to chance. Although there are many agents of socialization, according to Emile Durkheim (1985b), schools are primarily responsible for systematically organizing the welter of divergent beliefs, knowledge, and skills to "set off what is essential and vital; and play down the trivial and the secondary" (p. 29).

For Durkheim and Parsons, members of a society need to have a set of common beliefs, knowledge, and values for social unity and cohesion. But they are equally persuaded that the school should provide different and more highly specialized knowledge and skills to certain people, for every society requires that its members have different roles (Durkheim, 1985a, p. 21; Parsons, 1985, pp. 180–182). For example, not everyone in our society can or should become engineers or historians, because our society has diverse needs and problems that require different competencies at varying levels. Further, although both the family and the school socialize the young through transmission of culture, the school has a set of very distinctive roles. According to Parsons (1985), schooling enables the child to emotionally separate from the family and learn to internalize a set of cultural values and norms that are

PART 3: CULTURE, SCHOOLING, AND EDUCATIONAL DEVELOPMENT

broader than those learned from the family alone (p. 191). Through schooling children learn to function in the larger society as adults. They also learn that people can be grouped according to such criteria as age, sex, interest, and level of competencies and be rewarded differently according to actual achievements. In a very real sense, the school is a microcosm of the larger society. As such, the school *reproduces* and perpetuates the established social, cultural, economic, and political structures and norms. As we will see later, other theories of the role of schooling criticize the functionalist perspective. For this reason, it is useful to examine the functionalist view more closely.

Robert Dreeben (1968), a leading contemporary functionalist, argues that the social experiences available to children in schools are uniquely suited for preparing their transition from life in the family to occupation and life in the larger society. More specifically, children are more likely to learn the fundamental social norms of independence, achievement, universalism, and specificity in school than from their family life (pp. 65–76). "The nature of experiences available in [the family] could not provide conditions appropriate for acquiring those capacities that enable people to participate competently in the public realm" (p. 65). But in school, pupils learn to belong to and interact with different groups wherein their social positions are based on personal accomplishments as judged according to objective criteria.

Independence

In school, children learn to accept the need to do certain tasks on their own and the legitimate right of others to expect such independent behavior at various times. *Independence* means more than "doing things alone"; it includes such notions as self-reliance, accepting responsibility for one's actions, "acting self-sufficiently, and handling tasks with which under different circumstances, one can rightfully expect the help of others" (Dreeben, 1968, p. 66). Classroom characteristics such as the number of other children and teacher expectations of pupil behavior demand that the young become independent. Dreeben points out that whereas parents expect their children to act independently in certain situations, teachers are much more consistent in requiring their students to behave independently in doing academic work. Various occupations and institutions in the larger society require their members to self-initiate activities to accomplish their assigned tasks and to accept personal responsibility for their own actions. Clearly, schools are much more systematic than families in providing conditions for the development of independent attitudes in the young.

Achievement

Another important societal norm taught in school is *achievement*. In our society, independently attained achievements of individuals are prized highly.

However, Dreeben (1968) warns, independence and achievement should be distinguished from each other, because "achievement criteria can apply to activities performed collectively" (p. 71). In developing achievement motivation, there is little doubt that the family's child-rearing practices are influential. But schools provide even more significant conditions for cultivating the achievement-oriented attitude in children. After all, children's positions in school are determined by their personal accomplishments.

Most of what goes on in school is organized in such a way that achievements in curricular and extracurricular activities play a key role in determining the young people's status both in and out of the school environment. In most instances, achievement alternatives are given so that those who do not perform well in one field can do well in another. One student may excel in academic activities but perform poorly in sports; an outstanding athlete may do less than mediocre work in academic programs. These young people must learn to deal with both achievement and failure. For example, an individual may be an honor student to one group but just an egghead to another. Similarly, a star quarterback may be seen as nothing more than a jock to those who are not football fans. And what of the youngster whose talents do not fit neatly into any of the school-sanctioned achievement areas? In many ways, schools do provide a greater variety of opportunities for young people to experience achievement than does the family. But it may also be less effective in helping pupils to protect their self-esteem in coping with failure.

Universalism and Specificity

Universalism refers to a way in which a person is placed in a particular group according to a set of standards or common characteristics he or she shares with other members of that group. For example, a student may be considered a member of an honor society because he or she shares such common traits as having an outstanding academic record and recognized leadership qualities. On the other hand, *specificity* stands for treating an individual in a group as a unique case because he or she possesses certain traits that differ from those shared by other group members. However, a person is treated "particularistically" if given an exceptional treatment even though he or she does not possess special traits as compared with the rest of the group (Dreeben, 1968, p. 75).

To illustrate, universalism requires that all students in one class be treated equally, for example, not allowing anyone to make up an examination. But the norm of specificity makes it possible to permit one student to make up a missed examination because of illness on the day of the test. However, if another student is allowed to make up the test because he or she says flattering things about the instructor's teaching, then that student is treated particularistically. In other words, particularistic treatment of the student is unfair to the rest of the class. Universalism involves categorizing individuals according to common characteristics and equal treatment of everyone in the group. Specificity permits certain exceptions to be made, but only on legitimate grounds. By accepting categorization, children can learn to deal with other individuals in terms of their positions rather than according to their personal identity. In the larger society, powers and privileges accompany certain social positions. Young people need to understand that individuals exhibit certain behaviors when acting in an official capacity and that this behavior stems from the positions they occupy rather than their personal rights or privileges. Through the norms of universalism and specificity children learn to deal with the criteria of equal treatment or what is fair and what is unfair.

School and Society

From the functionalist perspective, "the family, as a social setting with its characteristic social arrangements, lacks the resources and the competence to effect the psychological transition" from life in the family to life in the larger and industrial society (Dreeben, 1968, p. 85). The school is especially well suited for transmitting the four norms of the society because its organizational structure and the behavioral patterns of the school personnel enable the young to have the kinds of experiences not available in other institutions. More specifically, because classrooms are organized according to age or ability, students are able to compare their own successes and failures in learning the norms of independence, achievement, universalism, and specificity with those of their peers. Schooling is effective in socializing the young because its structural organization, the school personnel's behavioral patterns, and its values reflect those of the larger society.

As Parsons (1985) points out, the school serves not only as an agent of socialization but also as a principal instrument of allocating roles in the society. Hence, those who can come close to the society's shared norms in their work and behavior are likely to be rewarded with higher socioeconomic status than those unable or unwilling to do so (p. 191). He goes on to suggest that there is a general and tacit consensus in our society that individuals should be rewarded differentially for different levels of achievement as long as there has been fair and equal access to opportunity. As might be expected, the school incorporates the ways in which the society rewards its successful members into its operational policies and procedures by placing "value *both* on initial equality and on differential achievement" (p. 191).

In industrial societies, the positions requiring complex knowledge and skills lead to greater rewards than those roles that demand simpler and more routine competencies. Because a primary function of the school is to transmit knowledge, develop special skills, and cultivate attitudes that are consonant with societal norms, the amount of reward (monetary reward and/or status) a person receives depends on the individual's ability in these areas and on the level of schooling. Given the nature of the school-society relationship, there are bound to be significant differences among individuals of different socioeconomic classes. For example, more doctors and lawyers occupy the upper classes than the lower classes. The functionalist sees class differences as not due to an inherent superiority of any particular group; rather, they are rooted in the merits of the individual. An individual's success at the highly complex skills of law and medicine is rewarded amply by society and, thus, he or she earns a high socioeconomic status. This means that the issues concerning equal access to educational, economic, and political opportunities for all people become key concerns in an allegedly meritocratic society such as the United States.

Functionalists would approach educational reform in at least two major ways. The first approach is to understand the conditions under which young people can acquire the competencies and attitudes necessary to do better in school so that appropriate conditions could be provided for the poor to succeed in school. This strategy is consistent with the functionalist view that higher academic accomplishments in school lead to higher-paying positions. The compensatory education programs that began in the early 1970s are good examples of such an approach. The second way to accomplish educational reform is to improve our schools by making instruction more effective. Two assumptions underlie this approach. One is the belief that improved teaching leads to academic success, which in turn will result in socioeconomic success. The other is the premise that the school's primary function is to expand students' knowledge and improve their cognitive skills. In the United States, outcomes of the compensatory education programs begun in the 1970s and other school reform measures during the past three decades suggest that these efforts did help certain individuals to move out of lower socioeconomic classes. But no sufficient evidence indicates that educational and economic equality has been assured for all or that significant changes have occurred in the class structure. Further, the validity of the view that success in school is causally related to socioeconomic success remains to be demonstrated.

The Hidden Curriculum

The school as an agent of socialization and role allocation has an "official" curriculum with a set of explicitly stated goals and objectives. These goals and objectives relate to what knowledge and skills ought to be imparted and attitudes developed. The school promotes the learners' motivation for academic success and their desire to practice the norms and values of the larger society for the established systems of rewards. In addition to the formal curriculum, the school also has an informal set of practices with which the learners are socialized. The expression *hidden curriculum* refers to the school's indirect means of helping young people learn the norms and values of their society. For example, our schools reinforce punctuality, assertiveness, self-involvement, and competitiveness by rewarding such acts as turning in assignments on time, expressing one's own opinions, participating in a classroom project, and asking for extra homework for a higher grade. The hidden curriculum has also been referred to as the *lived* curriculum, emphasizing that these informal set of practices define the day-to-day experiences of students and often assume a greater importance than the formal, subject matter curriculum.

The hidden curriculum occupies a key position in the functionalist view of schooling, for it is through this informal curriculum that young people learn to adapt themselves to the existing societal values and norms. The ability of the young to work and behave accordingly plays a pivotal role in determining their future social status and economic rewards. But this also means that similar rewards will not be given to individuals whose values and behavioral patterns deviate from the norms sanctioned by the larger society. For this reason, success in school is often correlated with socioeconomic success, and school failure is frequently viewed as causally responsible for poverty.

The use of the hidden curriculum is not exclusively connected with the functionalist perspective. Regardless of our theoretical perspectives, what children learn is affected by the overall school climate, the administrative styles of the school staff, the nature of the teacher-pupil relationship, and the teaching approaches being used to reinforce or discourage. However, the functionalists are accused of holding an erroneous belief that schools impart the same set of attitudes, values, and norms to all children through the use of the hidden curriculum. Critics point out that instructors apply the hidden curriculum differently according to students' social class status. For example, upper-class children are more likely to be taught such qualities as self-control, leadership, and creativity. Lower-class children tend to be instructed to respect authority, comply with instructions, and conform to the dominant norms.

The Technological View of Schooling

There are those who argue that the functionalist view of schooling also embodies what has been called an *instrumentalist* or technological perspective, which views schooling as a form of technology that can be treated as essentially similar to the process of industrial production. Industrial production begins with a predetermined set of product specifications, which then are assembled according to a specified sequence so that the desired product can be manufactured with consistent quality. This process requires a system of quality control mechanisms that evaluates each unit of the production sequence. The degree of cost efficiency with which each unit can perform its assigned functions then becomes a basis for accountability. An industry is held accountable in terms of (1) how closely the products match the initial set of product specifications and (2) whether or not the value of the products or outcomes is equivalent to or greater than the resources invested in the production.

When schooling is seen as a form of technology, a learning objective is divided into specific instructional components. These components are then organized according to a predetermined sequence. As students master each component they move up to the next level until they reach the desired learning objectives. This process necessarily involves translating learning objectives in observable and measurable behavioral terms. In general, teachers are held accountable on the basis of how well their students have mastered the learning objectives. Hence, frequent and consistent testing is necessary to monitor each learner's progress toward a specific goal. Although the ways in which this process of industrial production is applied to education and schooling vary, the basic principles remain the same. An emphasis on competency-based instruction, quality control, minimum competency testing, accountability, and cost efficiency reflect the influence of the technological perspective in education.

A fundamental shortcoming of the technological view of schooling is that not all worthwhile educational goals can be behaviorally defined in any exhaustive sense. By putting so much emphasis on what is quantifiable and measurable, we are likely to neglect such important educational goals as creativity, imagination, and appreciation. The technological approach to schooling is not just a matter of doing the same thing more efficiently, because it necessarily demands predetermined goals and tighter and precise control of learning conditions, the learner, and the quantifiable outcomes. If we are serious about making the American school a place where our children can re-create rather than inherit democracy, then it behooves all of us to scrutinize how technology is used and where the concept of technology is to be applied.

Questions About the Functionalist/Reproductive Theory

As we have seen, the functionalists view the role of schooling as the process of transmitting the established sociocultural, economic, and political norms so that the young can become productive and contributing members of the society. Hence, the school enables the society to perpetuate itself by reproducing its existing patterns. But should the primary role of schooling be limited to such a reproductive function alone? If we adopt the functionalist perspective, would the school not become a major force in perpetuating the status quo that makes the rich richer and the poor poorer? How can the school assure equal and fair access to educational and economic opportunities to all citizens if it is seen as a primary agent of reproducing the established social order? What can the school do to eliminate or minimize the socioeconomic inequities among different classes of people? Can the school perform special functions to isolate those who belong to lower socioeconomic classes? How should we determine the proper role of schooling? These are some of the questions that need to be asked about the strengths and weaknesses of the functionalist theory. In many ways, the critical, postmodern, and interpretivist theories, which we are about to discuss, are responses to these and other fundamental questions about the proper role of schooling.

Critical Perspectives

Marxist and Neo-Marxist Conflict Theories

According to the advocates of Marxist and neo-Marxist conflict theories, schools in a capitalistic society do not reproduce the established social system to fulfill the expanding educational needs of increasingly complex positions in modern society. Nor does the school aid individuals to select high-status positions with greater rewards through better education. Quite the contrary, the school functions to serve the interest of the dominant, the powerful, and the wealthy by perpetuating socioeconomic inequities. According to Marxists, who represent a major segment of the conflict theorist group, the private owners of the means of production maintain their domination of the working class by controlling the process of allocating roles, social status, and rewards. Struggles among the classes are bound to ensue as working-class people become aware of their low status and seek to gain a greater share of the available wealth. For Marxists, the socioeconomic inequities in a capitalistic society cannot be eliminated unless the private ownership of the means of production is wrested away from the dominant group by the working class.

Seen from this perspective, schools in a capitalistic society play a central role in enabling the dominant class to maintain the class structure by controlling the kinds of knowledge, skills, and attitudes available to people of different classes. Hence, children of the powerful are educated to self-direct and control others, and working-class youth are taught to conform to the norms of the workplace as prescribed by the dominant group. Educational inequalities are then responsible for maintaining social inequities and the class structure. As two contemporary Marxists, Samuel Bowles and Herbert Gintis (1977), explain:

> The social relations of the educational process ordinarily mirror the social relations of the work roles into which most students are likely to move. Differences in rules, expected modes of behavior and opportunities for choice are most glaring when we compare levels of schooling. Note the

wide range of choice over curriculum, life style, and allocation of time afforded to college students, compared with the obedience and respect for authority expected in high school. (p. 142)

Further, the class differences in school are perpetuated through "the capacity of the upper class to control the basic principles of school finance, pupil evaluation and educational objectives" (p. 142).

Bowles and Gintis go on to argue that differences in intellectual abilities and achievements have very little to do with what status a person is to occupy. They insist that empirical evidence simply does not show that differences in individual IQ scores are significant factors in allocating individuals to different roles in the class structure (pp. 215–225). Because values, personality traits, and class-linked roles are the primary determinants of one's social class, the principle of rewarding academic excellence and the use of cognitive abilities in educational promotion are employed as a way to legitimize the role of schooling as a means of making the society more egalitarian. As Apple and Weis (1983) point out, schools "foster the belief that the major institutions of our society are equally responsive to race, class, and sex," but available data show that "in almost every social arena from health care to anti-inflation policy, the top twenty percent of the population benefit much more than the bottom eighty percent" (pp. 5–6). Schools as agencies of legitimation reflect the social relationship of production as well as "the differences [inequities] in the social class composition of the student bodies" (Bowles, 1977, pp. 142, 149). But schools not only legitimize the socioeconomic system of the capitalistic society, they legitimize their own existence as well (Apple & Weis, 1983, p. 6). This being the case, educational equality cannot be achieved by simply changing the school system. Only by exposing "the unequal nature of our school system and destroy[ing] the illusion of unimpeded mobility through education" can we hope to serve the cause of educational equality (Bowles, 1977, p. 149).

While neo-Marxists agree that schools in a capitalistic society reproduce and perpetuate social hierarchical classes, they argue that the socioeconomic class structure is not the result of each individual's sole or even primary desire to maximize their rewards. That is, the privileged upper class controls the lower class through the means of noneconomic domination because the student is taught *status culture* rather than the social relations of production, that is, the roles of owners, managers, and workers of industry.

Drawing from Max Weber's view, Randall Collins (1985) holds that the basic units of society are *status groups,* associations whose members share common cultures, styles of language, conversational topics, manners, opinions and values, and preferences of all sorts as well as a sense of status equality based on participation in a common culture (p. 71). Collins explains that each status group distinguishes itself from others in terms of such "moral evaluation" as *honor, taste, breeding, cultivation, property,* and so on. Individuals derive their sense of identity from participation in such cultural groups. From this perspective, the primary role of schooling is to teach status cultures rather than to transmit technical skills and knowledge. In the words of Collins (1985), "schools primarily teach vocabulary and inflection, style of dress, aesthetic tastes, values and manners. The emphasis on sociability and athletics found in many schools is not extraneous but may be at the core of the status culture propagated by the schools" (p. 73). Being schooled is an indication of membership in a particular status group rather than a mark for technical knowledge, skills, or achievements. "Educational requirements may thus reflect the interests of whichever groups have power to set them" (p. 70). Hence, schooling is used to identify and help "insiders" to stay in their status culture and discourage "outsiders" from entering a more prestigious status group. This means that the status group system that controls schooling also controls workplaces, and constant struggles for wealth, power, and prestige are carried out through status groups or classes.

There is no disputing the fact that there has been a profound increase in the educational requirements for employment throughout the last century. But there is no consensus regarding the explanation of this fact. For example, the functionalists interpret the increased educational requirements as a consequence of ever-increasing demands for complex knowledge and technological skills for new and better-paying positions. They see a direct connection between more schooling and greater socioeconomic rewards. However, neo-Marxists regard the same increase in educational requirements for employment as the result of three conditions (Collins, 1985, pp. 79–80). The first is that people viewed education as a means of entering into an elite status culture. Second, political decentralization or separation of church and state made establishing schools and colleges much easier than in previous eras. Third, technical changes were also responsible for the expansion of education because the rapid industrialization of society reduced the need for unskilled workers and increased the demand for highly skilled technicians and professionals. Notwithstanding these three conditions, Collins observes:

> Once higher levels of education become recognized as an objective mark
> of elite status, and a moderate level of education as a mark of respectable
> middle-level status, increases in the supply of educated persons, and pre-
> viously superior levels become only average. (p. 80)

This meant that high-prestige organizations had to raise their educational requirements to maintain the high status of the upper-level executives and the relative respectability of the middle-level managers.

According to Collins (1979), high-prestige professions discourage vertical occupational mobility by requiring credentials—diplomas, licenses, and certificates—for entrance into these positions. Thus, educational requirements and credentialing serve as a major dividing line between high-status occupations, such as managerial positions, and such lower-status jobs as manual labor (pp. 46–47). Moreover, because educational requirements and credentialing are the major sources of socioeconomic inequality, "elimination of educational requirements [including credentialing] for jobs would be a necessary step in any overall restructuring of the occupational world to produce greater income equality" (p. 202). The abolition of credentialing is possible if training sequences and rotation of position-related duties are integrated into professional activities. For example, university students could be asked to do secretarial work as part of their education while secretaries could be allowed to receive academic training as part of their work (p. 202). In this way, secretaries can eventually become members of a better-paying occupation. Eliminating credentialing would no doubt change the structure of power in our society, but Collins does not expect this radical change to occur in the near future. On the contrary, he anticipates credentialing to expand with a continuing threat of class struggle. Unless we find a means more rational than the use of the educational system for controlling our institutions, he warns, our society may "undergo convulsions from forces beyond [our] control, as in the Reformation" (p. 204).

Limitations of Conflict Theory

According to conflict theorists, socioeconomic inequities result from educational inequities in capitalistic society. They maintain that the domination of the lower working class by the wealthy upper class is maintained by having the schools reproduce the hierarchical class structure inherent in capitalist society. Not all conflict theorists agree about how capitalist society perpetuates its class structure. For example, Marxists argue that the class structure is maintained because schools teach social relationships of production. On the other hand, neo-Marxists contend that domination of the lower working class by the wealthy upper class is accomplished through schools teaching status culture to their students.

In spite of the differences already mentioned, both Marxists and neo-Marxists are convinced that the root cause of inequities in capitalist society is the school's reproduction of the hierarchical class structure. They are also persuaded that educational as well as socioeconomic inequities will persist as long as capitalism continues to exist. Yet when we examine the range of factors related to both educational and social inequities in our society, the Marxist and the neo-Marxist views, even at best, only partially explain the causes of inequities. Social classes of the young alone do not explain how well or poorly children perform in school and work. In addition to social class backgrounds, a myriad of biological, environmental, and psychological factors—and even luck— enter into people's intellectual, social, economic, and political achievements. Moreover, there is no assurance that educational and social inequities would cease to exist if capitalism were abolished, for such inequities persist in societies that no longer allow private ownership of industry.

Whether the responsibility of educating the citizens of a society is left in the hands of schools, community, or workplace, transmitting societal norms and values is inescapable and indispensable. After all, no society can hope to survive without a means of transmitting and perpetuating its fundamental norms. Accordingly, educational institutions, whether formal or informal, are bound to reflect the social structure and norms of the larger society. Moreover, the hidden curriculum serves as an effective indirect means of transmitting society's norms and values of capitalist, Marxist, neo-Marxist, socialist, and many other forms of society. For example, assuming that the neo-Marxist explanation of schooling is sound, schools in Marxist or socialist society also will teach status culture. Given such a relationship between education and society, how is genuine educational reform possible? Some conflict theorists' suggestion that we do away with school may be an interesting notion, but it is hardly a plan that can be implemented. Even if we were successful in disestablishing the school, this change would not bring about educational equality, for the children of the poor are simply not as effective as their wealthy counterparts in utilizing educational resources and opportunities.

Critical Theory

Critical theory encompasses a series of theoretical ideas about the course of 20th-century history that appeared in Germany in the 1920s and 1930s (Held, 1980). Some of the well-known members of this school of thought are Max Horkheimer (1895), Theodore Adorno (1903–1969), Herbert Marcuse (1898–1979), and Jurgen Habermas (1929). Though varied in certain specific aspects, their thoughts, generally categorized as the Frankfurt School, represent an attempt to reevaluate capitalism and the Marxist explanation of class domination and to reformulate the meaning of human emancipation. Because both capitalists and Marxists view schools as agents of socialization, what the critical theorists have to say about how class structure is reproduced and class domination is maintained has significant implications for the role of schooling. In recent years, the thoughts of the Frankfurt School have stimulated Stanley Aronowitz, Paulo Freire, Henry Giroux, and other educational theorists to work toward developing a critical theory of education (Giroux, 1983).

Because critical theorists sided with Max Weber's position (functionalism) rather than the Marxist perspective, a brief discussion of the Weberian notion of rationalization may be helpful in understanding the general thrusts of the critical theory. According to Weber (1947), people in preindustrial societies were educated to lead their lives by learning to perform tasks related to their particular positions. But as societies became more industrialized, schools increasingly were required to train individuals for new specialized roles. Accordingly, modern technological societies moved toward *rationalization,* institutional organization based on specialized knowledge and skills. The individuals for these roles were selected on the basis of credentials and examinations. Thus, modern society became an organization of specialists and modern government a bureaucracy occupied by experts. This meant that schools had to produce "specialists" rather than "cultivated people." Weber further pointed out that modern schools teach values and norms of the high prestige positions, that is, status cultures. Members of the specialist bureaucracy control not only people's lives; they also control schools to maintain their domination over the working class as well as the gender, race, ethnicity, and even age-related groups. In this way, Weber's notion of rationalization leads not to rationality but to technological authoritarianism. Hence, class domination goes beyond economic domination of the working class by the capitalist class. Now, let us examine the ideas of the critical theorists in relation to these Weberian concepts.

Unlike Marxists, the critical theorists of the 1920s and 1930s did not believe that domination of the working class by the capitalist class is achieved by perpetuating the economic class structure alone. Nor did they think that there is only one form of human domination (i.e., economic class domination). For example, in spite of their differences, Horkheimer and Adorno both argued that people's individuality, uniqueness, and creativity would become obliterated by what Adorno called the *mass culture.* Adorno pointed out that the mass culture—movies, TV shows, and even commercials, for example—contains the norms and values of the dominating groups and, as such, distorts reality to perpetuate the ruling group's interests. Consequently, individuals become unable to think critically about themselves or their society.

In a similar vein, Marcuse contended that as modern society becomes a society of technological experts, people with unique individuality are replaced with "one dimensional [people]" who think neither reflectively nor creatively. Horkheimer, Adorno, and Marcuse agreed that the increasing intrusion of the state into people's lives leads to technocratic authoritarianism, which controls citizens' attitudes, behaviors, and thinking. Even critical thinking is defined within the confines of the dominating group's interest. Habermas (1971) maintained that the interests of the dominating class are legitimized and the most vital and indispensable aspects of human life become threatened when the problems of living are defined as issues with which only specialists can deal. Hence, if human beings are to be emancipated from domination by the authoritarianism of experts, we need to reaffirm the need for self-reflection, critical inquiry, and self-understanding. Further, we must "penetrate beyond the level of particular historical class interests to disclose the fundamental interests of mankind as such" (p. 113).

Although Paulo Freire (1985, 1993), a contemporary Brazilian social and educational reformer, is not considered a critical theorist in the strictest sense, he echoes the critical theorist perspective when he argues that there is no single form of class domination. Just as society includes divergent types of social relations, it also harbors many different forms of domination and oppression.

> The dominated are human beings who have been forbidden to be what they are. They have been exploited, violated, and violently denied the right to exist and the right to express themselves. This is true whether these dominated people represent a unique people, a social group (like homosexuals), a social class, or a particular gender (like women). (Freire, 1985, p. 192)

For Freire, education is more than a process in which the student simply accepts bodies of information provided by the teacher. Education, of which schooling is one part, is a struggle to overcome dominations of all sorts so that each person can grasp the meaning of his or her personal existence and future life. It is the process of self-emancipation. The kind of knowledge that will enable our young people to emancipate themselves from domination and oppression is not verifiable scientific knowledge. Rather, it is radical knowledge through which the young and the oppressed can learn about the conditions responsible for their dominated and subordinated positions (Freire, 1993, p. 32). Only this kind of radical, or critical, knowledge can help students analyze how the dominant society legitimates (justifies) its norms and values. At the same time, young people can also see the possibility of alternative cultural practices, ways of thinking, and social orders. Such knowledge "would function to help students and others understand what this society has made of them (in a dialectical sense) and what it is they no longer want to be, as well as what it is they need to appropriate critically in order to become knowledgeable about the world in which they live" (Aronowitz & Giroux, 1981, p. 132). Helping students, teachers, and others to acquire critical knowledge as a tool of analysis is to help develop critical literacy, which will enable them to raise questions about the nature of knowledge and its justification, modes of discourse, and school organization that "reduce learning and social practices to narrow technical dimensions" (pp. 132–133).

Giroux (1983) insists that the development of critical literacy is hampered by the fact that the values and norms of the dominant social classes are incorporated into school curricula. Hence, the dominant group's cultural practices, modes of thinking and knowing, lifestyles, language patterns, learning and communication styles, and even political principles are transmitted both overtly and insidiously. A fundamental flaw in the traditional approach to schooling is that it stresses knowledge, social practices, and modes of thinking that have been historically handed down to us. What is necessary in schooling is an emphasis on critical literacy skills that will enable students "to recognize what this society has made of them and how it must, in part, be analyzed and reconstituted so that it can generate the conditions for critical reflection and action rather than passivity and indignation" (p. 231).

Schools need to challenge the established practices, institutions, and ways of thinking and conceive new and alternative possibilities. "Teachers and other educators [need] to reject educational theories that reduce schooling either to the domain of learning theory or to forms of technocratic rationality that ignore the central concerns of social change, power relations, and conflicts both within and outside of schools" (Giroux, 1983, p. 62). Only in this way can schools highlight the human potential and struggle and expose the discrepancies between society as it exists and as we envision it (p. 36).

Dilemmas of Critical Theory

As the proponents of critical theory have pointed out, our society contains many different forms of domination. More often than not, the many and varied conditions responsible for human oppression and exploitation are rooted in the social structure and the cultural norms and conditions of the society. Hence, schools as social institutions reflect the conditions that lead to domination. A dilemma of the conflict theorists is that if teachers and other educators are products of schools controlled by the dominating group, how can they help students develop critical literacy to emancipate themselves? One proposal is to do away with schools and place the control of education in the hands of parents and local communities. However, there is no assurance that families and communities will not work toward perpetuating their own class culture nor is there a guarantee that the powers of the upper class will not nullify the efforts of lower-class families and communities.

Yet another dilemma faces advocates of critical theory. On one hand, Giroux (1984) wants to "develop a real defense of schools as institutions which perform a public service." He also insists that educators work with community groups to develop pockets of cultural resistance and to help students become reflective about their life, status, and society. This means that our universities should produce teachers who can encourage students to analyze the assumptions underlying the existing social order and cultural practices and envision alternative forms of society. In spite of Giroux's idea about how our schools should develop critical literacy among the young, he also argues that we cannot rely on existing schools for radical educational reform to promote emancipatory change. The power of schools to control what can and cannot be debated, the disrespect they have toward the oppressed, and their willingness to act against their opponents simply make them unreliable agents for social change (Giroux, 1984). Now, if, as the critical theorists contend, schools reproduce the dominant ideology, who would educate teachers to become emancipating agents? Insofar as schools cannot escape from the influence of the values and norms of the larger society, the critical theorists' demand that schools help students to question and reject the existing system is tantamount to asking teachers and students to pick themselves up by their own bootstraps.

The Interpretivist Perspective

As we have seen, the functionalists, the conflict theorists, and the advocates of critical theory arrived at their views by analyzing the relationship between education and the structural elements of the social class system. However, the interpretivists maintain that an understanding of the relationship between school and society requires an analysis of interactions between students, teachers, administrators, and various peer groups. They urge us to understand the schooling-society relationship by interpreting the meanings of interactive patterns between these groups, curriculum, and school achievements. At the same time, we are admonished not to impose our own preconceived philosophical or theoretical framework on our observation of school and society. In their approach to research, the interpretivists attempt to integrate the structural study of society with analytic studies of interactions among students and school personnel, the nature and contents of school curricula, as well as the consequences of direct and hidden approaches to teaching. Consequently, the interpretivists utilize the findings regarding the linguistic basis of cognition (symbolic interactionism), the role of shared meanings in social situations (ethnomethodology), and the experiential or common-sense views of reality (phenomenology).

According to the interpretivists, social structure consists of a system of class inequality that the family perpetuates by transmitting linguistic codes or patterns of communication to the young (Karabel & Halsey, 1977, p. 63). Thus, although the school is a principal instrument of socialization, it is not the basic agency in which socialization begins. Children learn to play the "game" of living by interpreting the meanings of various rules of behavior, sanctions, lifestyles, and other appropriate norms through speech patterns determined by the family's social position. The child's future class status in society is in turn affected by the communication patterns acquired from the family. Not unexpectedly, the school directly and indirectly expects all children to acquire the dominant linguistic and cultural competencies—those originally produced by families belonging to the dominant class. The lower-class children are required to function according to linguistic and cultural patterns that are alien to them.

> The educational system demands of everyone alike that they have what it does not give. This consists mainly of linguistic and cultural competencies

and that relationship of familiarity with culture which can only be produced by family upbringing when it transmits the dominant culture.
(Bourdieu, 1977, p. 494)

Because the school reproduces the dominant culture, it creates serious discrepancies between what the lower-class children know and the school norm
(Bernstein, 1977, p. 483; Bourdieu, 1977, pp. 493–494). It is not surprising
that children from lower socioeconomic classes do poorly in school, for they
cannot readily develop those dominant linguistic and cultural abilities needed
for academic or socioeconomic success.

   According to Basil Bernstein (1977), a leading interpretivist, socialization is the process by which the child, a biological being, is made into a specific cultural being. It is a complex process that gives distinctive form and
content to the child's cognitive, affective, and moral tendencies (p. 476).
Through socialization the child becomes aware of the various orderings of the
society and the roles he or she may be expected to play. Bernstein holds that,
of the many factors, the family's social class has the most formative influence
on the child's education and future work. Further, it is the class system that
controls the distribution of knowledge in the society so that knowledge and
the modes of thinking available to the upper class become inaccessible to
lower-class individuals. This control of knowledge "has sealed off communities from each other and has ranked these communities on a scale of invidious
worth" (p. 477). For this reason, the communication and behavioral patterns
of the lower class are often considered inferior to those of the higher social
classes.

   Through the social control of knowledge the class system has affected
not only the distribution of material wealth but also communication patterns
of different social classes. According to Bernstein, communication patterns of
working-class children are much more situation-specific, or particularistic,
and restricted than those of the middle- and upper-middle-class children,
who are given more elaborated, or universalistic, communication patterns in
which meanings are not imbedded in specific local situations. Bernstein
(1977) explains that "where [the speech] codes are elaborated, the socialized
has more access to the grounds of his own socialization. . . . [However,] where
the codes are restricted, the socialized has less access to the grounds of his
socialization" (p. 478). In other words, individuals with universalistic, elaborated communication patterns are able to respond more flexibly to new and
different social situations than those who have particularistic and restricted
speech patterns.

   The particularistic and restricted nature of the lower-class communication patterns become a barrier for working-class children in dealing with situations that go beyond their social class experiences. Further, these children
are less able to handle abstract thoughts and generalizations. Socioeconomic

inequities in society are maintained because families reproduce the communication patterns and speech codes that are specifically connected with their social status. In addition, higher-status positions require those communication patterns that are reproduced by families belonging to the dominant class. These conditions leading to societal inequities are exacerbated by the fact that schools consider only the universalistic, elaborated communication patterns as acceptable norms. Moreover, they view any pattern that deviates from the dominant norms as "devalued, and humiliated within schools or seen, at best, to be irrelevant to the educational endeavor" (p. 484).

Bernstein asserts that the school is primarily interested in transmitting universalistic speech codes. Hence, serious discrepancies are bound to arise between what the school attempts to accomplish and the communication patterns of the lower-class children. Accordingly, if we are to reduce the amount of social inequities in society, the school must purge all built-in class biases from its curriculum and pedagogy and its conception of educability. Moreover, the school should not try to get lower-class families to provide their children with linguistic and cultural knowledge and skills that these families do not possess. Rather, the school should focus on how it can help these children bridge the gap between their own skills and those that the larger society demands within the context of schooling.

Limitations of the Interpretivist Theory

Interpreting the meanings of various interactive relationships between students, school personnel, the curriculum, and pedagogy is essential in understanding the role of schooling, for schooling occurs among people mediated by curriculum and instruction. The use of this approach in studying the school-society relationship requires that we become participant-observers, just as ethnographers study an alien culture by living in it. One of the difficulties with this ethnomethodological approach is that when the investigator becomes involved in the process or event being studied, the degree of involvement may easily affect the outcome of the study. In addition, because the investigator's focus is on interactions among people and various aspects of the school, not enough attention is paid to the influences of the larger social, political, and economic contexts in which individuals function. For these reasons, the interpretivists are often criticized for not having conducted enough rigorous empirical studies to support their claims with hard evidence. This criticism raises further questions about the nature of the criteria interpretivists use to determine the soundness of their claims.

Another limitation of interpretivism is that although this theory offers an insightful description of the class system and its impact on social inequities, it does not provide a viable plan to resolve class conflicts. Nor does it offer realistic plans to eliminate or even substantially reduce social inequities in society.

Postmodern Perspectives

Undergirding the functionalist, critical, and interpretivist perspectives are *modernist* assumptions. Key among these is the idea that social phenomena are characterized by fixed structures and systematic underlying relationships. So, for example, we cannot understand a teacher's activity without examining how that fits together with broader aspects of schooling and society such as the expectations of the curriculum, the social class of the students, and the regulations of the bureaucracy. From the modernist perspective these relationships are regular and predictable. It is possible to uncover these systemic relationships and thereby understand the social world. Modernism in its functionalist form places great emphasis on the rationalization of the social world. That is, that through the establishment of clear, objective procedures and through efficient, unbiased management, social institutions can fairly serve all people. In both its functionalist and critical forms, the modernist perspective places great faith in the human ability to control humankind's future and to shape a better world.

The postmodern, or poststructural perspective, calls these assumptions into question. Poststructuralism, in its contemporary forms, is rooted in the writings of Michel Foucault (1972) and Jacques Derrida (1972). Foucault is interested in the ways in which social and political institutions produce and reproduce ideas about truth and knowledge. Derrida challenges the idea that meaning is fixed. Meaning is only fixed through a consensus of readers and will change, or shift, over time. From the postmodern perspective, what has passed for reason and objective knowledge has in fact been the knowledge, norms, and expectations of those in power. What has been seen as objective truth is defined by postmodernists as a master narrative in which those who hold power determine what passes for knowledge. Henry Giroux (1993) describes the postmodern perspective succinctly:

> Postmodernism rejects a notion of reason that is disinterested, transcendent and universal. Rather than separating reason from the terrain of history, place and desire, postmodernism argues that reason and science can only be understood as part of a broader historical, political, and social struggle over relationships between language and power. (p. 53)

Western culture has defined a privileged canon, a body of literature and ideas that is seen as true and good. This canon has ignored or marginalized the voices and ideas of those with little or no power. The writing and thinking of the oppressed and the poor, for example, have not been seen generally as having equal worth with the voices of the dominant culture. Postmodernists argue for the need for multiple narratives. Rather than one way of knowing and understanding, there are many. Subordinated and excluded groups are given voice and opportunity to discover their worlds and histories.

Postmodernists further argue that it is necessary to examine or *deconstruct* meanings that we tend to take for granted. That is, language is not simply a medium for transmitting ideas and meaning; it is, in fact, a reflection of existing power structures. Rather than being value-neutral and fixed, meanings are constructed and reconstructed as society and social structures change.

> Some people speak with authority, while others listen as consumers, because power infiltrates language we inherit, the meanings of our words, utterances, and discourses, and the institutions and practices which shape their use. (Cherryholmes, 1988, p. 50)

Postmodernism has implications for the ways we think about education. Textbooks, for example, generally introduce key words with their definitions and examples. Rarely do they indicate that there is likely to be more than one definition. The word *identity*, for example, is likely to have several different meanings and particularly different meanings in different cultures. Further, textbooks make authoritative claims about what is or is not knowledge, with little indication that the claim is controversial or contested. Textbooks determine what knowledge is important or not important by what they include and what they leave out.

Critiques of Postmodernism

Postmodernism raises many important questions about what counts as knowledge and whose voice gets heard in the construction of knowledge. It has been criticized for the very questions it raises. Does the postmodern invitation to open up the curriculum to multiple voices and perspectives threaten the cohesion of our society? Even those who agree with the need to analyze the power assumptions embedded in the curriculum question the postmodern critique, which sees the struggle for democracy as based on a politics of difference and power rather than on deliberation and reason (Giroux, 1993, p.48).

A Review and Critical Estimate of the Four Perspectives

Before we discuss a critical estimate of the four perspectives, it may be useful to briefly review these ideas because, in spite of their differences, they contain several overlapping views (see Table 5.1).

A Review

As we have already seen, the advocates of the structural/functionalist theory believe that as a social system the school is an integral part of society. A central role of the school is to pass on the cultural norms of the society to the young so that they can function effectively. Through schooling and other means of

TABLE 5.1
Four Perspectives Toward the Role of Schooling

| | Functionalist | Critical | | Interpretivist | Postmodern |
		Conflict Theory	Critical Theory		
Leaders	Durkheim, Parsons & Dreeben	Bowles & Gintis, Collins	Freire, Giroux	Bernstein	Derrida, Foucault
Present Role	Transmit culture and maintain social order	Reproduce the existing economic order	Legitimize oppression and reinforce the roles of the oppressed through uncritical acceptance of social order	Teach various roles through curricula and learning activities with class bias	Transmit knowledge as defined by those in power
Future Vision	Teach the young to function effectively in society	Provide economic equality through participation in class struggle	Develop critical literacy	Analyze interactions among school participants with a view toward eliminating cultural and class bias from school experiences	Deconstruct taken-for-granted meanings and knowledge; enable multiple voices and perspectives to be recognized

education the society is able to maintain social order and perpetuate itself. Critics argue that schools transform culture for the purpose of "helping students meet the institutional requirements of their credentialing" (McNeil, 1986, p. 13). McNeil explains that schools transform culture into pieces of school knowledge and units of courses and sequences that conform to the school's bureaucratic processes. She goes on to say that

> after being processed through worksheets, list-filled lectures and short-answer tests, the cultural content . . . comes to serve only the interests of institutional efficiencies. Its forms may have some utility but its substance has been depleted. (p. 13)

Unlike the functionalists, those who assume a critical perspective take a critical stance toward the status quo of schooling. Conflict theorists argue that the school is an instrument of domination used by those in power to preserve and extend the existing social order. This practice results in an inequitable distribution of wealth, power, and educational opportunities. A new social structure emerges from struggles between the poor and the rich to achieve a more egalitarian distribution of wealth and power. According to critical theorists, there is a genuine need to reconsider the meanings of domination and emancipation because people can be dominated through learning the kind of knowledge, culture, and history that legitimize domination and reinforce the roles of the subjugated. We need to "break the grip of all closed systems of thought and to counter an unreflected affirmation of society" (Thompson & Held, 1982, p. 2). Our reflection about domination must "penetrate beyond the level of particular historical class interests to disclose the fundamental interests of mankind as such" (Habermas, 1971, p. 113). Educationally, schools must help their students learn modes of inquiry, knowledge, and skills to enable them to think critically about how their society may have shaped their positions and prevented them from realizing goals that go beyond the prescribed status. Through such schooling the young should be able to "affirm and reject their own histories in order to begin the process of struggling for the conditions that will give them opportunities to lead a self-managed existence" (Giroux, 1983, p. 38).

The functionalist and critical perspectives seek to understand the role of schooling based on analyses of the relationship between schools as structural aspects of society and society. But is it possible to adequately understand human society without having sound knowledge regarding human behavior? Interpretivists note that to gain such knowledge we need to examine the norms with which people interpret their experiences and other events in life by assigning significance and values to them. If we grant that culture consists of a system of norms for ascribing meanings and worth to the events in individuals' lives, then those who live in the same culture will tend to give generally similar interpretations to various occurrences. Variations in interpretations are still possible because of the differences in personal experiences and socioeconomic class. In educational terms, the interpretivists are interested in analyzing interactions among students and various school personnel. To these theorists, student behaviors cannot be understood unless we know about their goals and the norms that guide school activities. Children learn the rules and standards that determine their roles and status in school. Hence, schools should evaluate the effects of class bias in teaching, curriculum, and other school-related activities.

The postmodern perspective argues against efforts to strive toward objectivity. What has been defined as school knowledge, as universal and true, has, in fact, been defined by those in power. From a postmodern perspective, it is necessary to deconstruct both those power relationships and the canon of knowledge that has emerged from them. Only by seeing knowledge and language within historically constructed contexts can we begin to know. Only by attending to diverse voices can we really begin to understand the world and our lived experiences within it.

A Critical Estimate

These perspectives toward the role of schooling represent four interpretations of the same educational and sociocultural processes found in all human societies. Each of the four perspectives attempts to explain the relationship between schooling, culture, and social structure and proposes different educational measures to make human society more egalitarian. As important as these theories are in helping us analyze the relationship between school and society and class structure and social inequities, all of the theories leave certain aspects of social reality unexplained. For example, social inequities continue to exist in socialistic or Marxist societies. At the same time, educational opportunities are accessible to many more groups of people in the United States than in other capitalistic or even noncapitalistic countries. In the area of their proposed programs for social change and educational reforms, they are intellectually compelling but practically not achievable. In fact, hardly any of the measures proposed by those who hold a critical, interpretivist, or postmodern perspective have had significant impact on how schools are run and children are educated.

At least two possible reasons explain why these theories have had little direct influence on how children are educated. One is the fact that the relationship between education, schooling, and social stratification is extremely complex and multidimensional. Any reform programs based on a theory that is rooted in a single concept, for example, class domination or transmission of communication patterns, will inevitably be inadequate. The impact of such measures will be limited if not superficial. What is needed is the development of a multidisciplinary theory of education that utilizes the findings and methods of a wide range of biological, physical, and social sciences as well as our lived experiences. This does not suggest that these four theories should be discarded, for they do provide insight into certain aspects of the relationship between schooling, culture, and society.

Secondly, the failure of educational theorists to make a genuine difference in the actual business of educating people may be attributable in large part to the fact that the theorists are outside of the world of educational politics. The theorists become "outsiders" because they are preoccupied with developing and reproducing their own unique languages, which are not accessible to those who do not belong to the same intellectual "class." Since educational politicians and practitioners have their own ordering of meanings that are not open to the theorists, the theorists have very little, if any, power to affect educational establishments and their practices. For the theoretical ideas to make any difference at all, the theorists must become more actively involved in political movements of the larger educational community. Perhaps they should take seriously the following admonition:

> If one is concerned to establish a more human society, then he ought to work to establish that society in the very places where people live and work. If one is intent on having man's work and his machines serve real human needs, then he ought to see to it that a man's work serves his human need and not assume this to be an inevitable by-product of letting talent rise to the top. And if it is believed that the requirements of technology and the nature of work are destroying the humanizing and educative functions of the family and the community, then one should reexamine the requirements of technology and the nature of work. (Feinberg, 1975)

CASE STUDIES

Mrs. Clark teaches remedial reading at a school in an economically depressed lower-middle-class neighborhood with about 1,200 families. The following is a description of one of Mrs. Clark's six classes in remedial reading.

THE HIDDEN CURRICULUM

> The class meets five days a week for one-half hour. Each day the children enter the reading room, usually one at a time, and silently take seats around a small rectangular table which comfortably accommodates the four children and the teacher. "Greeting conversations" are rare; when they occur they are usually initiated by Mrs. Clark, and the topics are limited. . . . Occasionally one child, Jack, asks whether this is to be "game day." The children then wait a minute or two in silence while Mrs. Clark assembles materials for the day's business at hand, and then the lesson begins.

Mrs. Clark is fully sensitive to neighborhood conditions, and in response to these she has developed what she calls her "educational philosophy." . . .

In keeping with that philosophy, she has devised a teaching strategy. Instruction unfolds in two forms: she introduces a new skill (e.g., synonyms, nouns, vowel sounds); then on subsequent days the children practice the skill and practice it again until the slowest child knows it. . . . During most of these activities Mrs. Clark watches for "frustration cues" and tries to cause the child to slow down whenever these are evident. . . . [A]t least once a week there are games. . . . All these games are structured so that each child waits for his or her individual turn; all involve reading skills, but a child wins or loses through chance, the roll of the dice or the draw of the cards.

On one day, Mrs. Clark may introduce a new reading skill to the children—for example, synonyms. She defines "synonym," discusses the idea, and gives several examples of synonyms and their use. Then she asks a question and the first child who can calls out an answer; other children usually echo the answer; then a second question, and so on. During lessons of this kind the children do not raise their hands and she almost never calls on a specific child. The next day may be devoted to practicing the same skill. . . . She defines the rules of the drill, then says, "I am thinking of a synonym for _." Children raise their hands to be called on and one child is selected; that child points to a card and reads it, with help from Mrs. Clark if necessary, which often includes the pretense that a wrong answer (for example, reaching toward the wrong card) was not really an answer; having answered correctly, the child may then take the card from the table and keep it. . . .

Friday is usually "game day." On these days, the winners get points which are accumulated over time and earn small prizes. On a game day the children come in a bit excited, but as before they sit down and wait silently while their teacher gets the game set up. A favorite game is "bundles." Mrs. Clark shuffles a deck of cards (almost every card has a word on it; a few have only a picture of a sack tied closed with a rope, called a "bundle"). The deck is placed face down in the center of the table. A child is selected to start the game, draws the card on top, and places it on the table so that everyone else can see the word. With help if necessary, the child reads the card and keeps it; then the next child on the left, who has been waiting more than participating, can take a turn; and so on. A child who draws a "bundle" card gets to take all of the cards the child to the right has accumulated. When the last card has been played, the child who holds the most cards wins, and this means points added to his or her total. . . .

In general, the efforts seem to work. The children seem to read, and they seem to enjoy their sessions.

Source: Reprinted by permission of Waveland Press, Inc. from George Spindler, *Doing the Ethnography of Schooling: Educational Anthropology in Action.* (Prospect Heights, IL: Waveland Press, Inc., 1988). All rights reserved.

QUESTIONS

1. What attitudes and behaviors do you think Mrs. Clark's approach would encourage and/or reinforce in her class? For example, how would the following aspects of Mrs. Clark's teaching affect her students' affective, cognitive, and behavioral domains?

    Each child waiting for his or her turn

    Responding to Mrs. Clark's statement, "I am thinking of a synonym for _____"

    Pretending that a wrong answer was not really an answer

    Playing the "bundles" game

2. The report indicates that Mrs. Clark's "educational philosophy" was developed out of her understanding of the neighborhood condition. What do you think her educational philosophy is? Does she have a set of stereotypic status roles for her children? What might they be? What do you think is the relationship between Mrs. Clark's educational philosophy, her teaching approach, and the norms of the dominant culture?

3. How would the functionalists, the conflict theorists, the critical theorists, and the interpretivists assess the impact of Mrs. Clark's teaching on reducing or eliminating socioeconomic inequalities in our society?

4. Which one of the four theories discussed in this chapter best represents Mrs. Clark's perspective on the role of schooling? Discuss your rationale. Would you suggest that Mrs. Clark change any aspect of her teaching approach? What suggestions would you make and why?

● ● ●

OTHER CASES OF THE HIDDEN CURRICULUM

The teachers were in the lunchroom discussing the introduction of fractions. They were exchanging ideas about how to explain how fractions work and how to demonstrate in several ways how fractions function and appear. One of the teachers said, "Adding and subtracting aren't much of a problem. Just wait till you have to teach multiplication and division to three Hispanic students you have. Those kids don't know top from bottom, can't memorize their tables, and they'll just bring down your classroom's score." The rest of the teachers proceeded to give examples about how Hispanic children do not understand English, do not speak English, and as one summarized, "Can't do."

Source: Ortiz, 1988, p. 78.

QUESTIONS

1. What stereotypic views of Hispanic children are reflected in the attitudes of the teachers? How might such stereotypic views affect the academic performance of Hispanic children?
2. How might the teachers' stereotypic views influence the self-image of the Hispanic children?
3. If you were the principal of the school described, what could you do to help the teachers change their views of Hispanic and other minority children?
4. According to each of the four theories discussed in this chapter, what role of schooling is reflected in the teachers' attitudes toward the Hispanic children as given in this case?

* * *

"When you sing in our school choir, you sing as proud Negro children," boomed the voice of Mrs. Benn, my fifth-grade teacher. "Don't you know that Marian Anderson, a cultured colored woman, is the finest contralto ever? Haven't you ever heard Paul Robeson sing? It can just take your breath away. We are not shiftless and lazy folk. We are hard-working, God-fearing people. You can't sing in this choir unless you want to hold up the good name of our people."

It never occurred to me in those days that African Americans were not a special people. My education both at home and at school reinforced that idea. We were a people who overcame incredible odds. I knew that we were discriminated against but I witnessed too much competence—and excellence—to believe that African Americans didn't have distinctly valuable attributes.

Source: Ladson-Billings, G. (1994). *The Dreamkeepers: Successful Teachers of African American Children*, pp. 9–12. Copyright 1994 by Jossey-Bass Inc., Publishers. Used with permission.

QUESTIONS

1. In what ways did the implicit or hidden curriculum function for this author to contradict stereotypic views of African-American children? What appears to have been Mrs. Benn's ideas about the role of schooling for her students?
2. How might this incident be viewed from the perspective of each of the theories discussed in this chapter?

REFERENCES

Apple, M. W., & Weis, L. (1983). *Ideology and practice in schooling*. Philadelphia: Temple University Press.

Aronowitz, S., & Giroux, H. A. (1981). *Education under siege*. South Hadley, MA: Bergin & Garvey.

Bernstein, B. (1977). Social class, language and socialization. In J. Karabel & A. H. Halsey (Eds.), *Power and ideology in education* (pp. 473–486). New York: Oxford University Press.

Bourdieu, P. (1977). Cultural reproduction and social reproduction. In J. Karabel & A. H. Halsey (Eds.), *Power and ideology in education* (pp. 487–510). New York: Oxford University Press.

Bowles, S. (1977). Unequal education and the reproduction of the social division of labor. In J. Karabel & A. H. Halsey (Eds.), *Power and ideology in education*. New York: Oxford University Press.

Bowles, S., & Gintis, H. (1977). IQ in the U.S. class structure. In J. Karabel & A. H. Halsey (Eds.), *Power and ideology in education* (pp. 137–152). New York: Oxford University Press.

Cherryholmes, C. H. (1988). *Power and criticism: Poststructural investigations in education*. New York: Teachers College Press.

Collins, R. (1979). *The credentialing society*. New York: Academic Press.

Collins, R. (1985). Functional and conflict theories of educational stratification. In J. H. Ballantine (Ed.), *Schools and society: A reader in education and sociology* (pp. 60–87). Palo Alto, CA: Mayfield.

Counts, G. S. (1932). *Dare the school build a new social order?* New York: John Day. The writings of John Dewey, John Childs, William Heard Kilpatrick, and Harold Rugg in the journal, *The Social Frontier,* published in the mid-1930s, represent the early social reconstructionist position.

Derrida, J. (1972). Discussion: Structure, sign and play in the discourse of the human sciences. In R. Macksey and E. Donato, (Eds.), *The structuralist controversy* (pp. 247-272). Baltimore: Johns Hopkins Press.

Dreeben, R. (1968). *On what is learned in school*. Reading, MA: Addison-Wesley.

Durkheim, E. (1985a). Definition of education. In J. H. Ballantine (Ed.), *Schools and society: A reader in education and sociology* (pp. 19–22). Palo Alto, CA: Mayfield.

Durkheim, E. (1985b). Moral education. In J. H. Ballantine (Ed.), *Schools and society: A reader in education and sociology* (pp. 23–29). Palo Alto, CA: Mayfield.

Durkheim, E. (1961). On the learning of discipline. In T. Parsons, E. Shills, K. D. Naegele, & J. R. Pitts (Eds.), *Theories of society* (Vol. 2) (pp. 860–865). New York: The Free Press of Glencoe.

Feinberg, W. (1975). *Reason and rhetoric: The intellectual foundations of 20th century liberal educational policy*. New York: John Wiley & Sons.

Foucault, M. (1972). *The archeology of knowledge*. New York: Harper Colophon Books.

Freire, P. (1993). *Pedagogy of the oppressed*. London: Penguin Books Ltd.

Freire, P. (1985). *The politics of education* (D. Macedo, Trans.). South Hadley, MA: Bergin & Garvey.

Giroux, H. A. (1983). *Theory and resistance in education*. South Hadley, MA: Bergin & Garvey. *Education Under Siege* (1981), by Stanley Aronowitz and Henry A.

Giroux, and *Critical Pedagogy and Cultural Power* (1987), by David W. Livingstone, et al., South Hadley, MA: Bergin & Garvey, respectively, are useful books in this area.

Giroux, H, A. (1984). Marxism and schooling: The limits of radical discourse. *Educational Theory, 34*(2), 113–136.

Giroux, H. A. (1993). *Border crossings: Cultural workers and the politics of education*. New York: Routledge.

Habermas, J. (1971). *Towards a rational society: Student protest, science and politics* (J. J. Shapiro, Trans.). London: Heinemann.

Held, D. (1980). *Introduction to critical theory*. London: Hutchinson & Co. This book presents a scholarly discussion of the thoughts of several major figures of the Frankfurt School from Horkheimer to Habermas.

Karabel, J., & Halsey, A. H. (1977). Educational research: A review and an interpretation. In J. Karabel & A. H. Halsey (Eds.), *Power and ideology in education* (pp. 1–85). New York: Oxford University Press.

Katz, M. B. (1971). *Class, bureaucracy, and schools*. New York: Praeger Publications. For a description and analysis of bureaucracy, see Max Weber's *The Theory of Social and Economic Organization*, edited by Talcott Parsons.

McNeil, L. M. (1986). *Contradictions of control*. New York: Routledge and Kegan Paul.

Ortiz, F. I. (1988). Hispanic-American children's experiences in classrooms: A comparison between Hispanic and non-Hispanic children. In L. Weis (Ed.), *Class, race, and gender in American education* (pp. 63–86). Albany: State University of New York Press.

Parsons, T. (1961). Introduction to symbolic processes and the cultural heritage. In T. Parsons, E. Shills, K. D. Naegele, & J. R. Pitts (Eds.), *Theories of society* (Vol. 2) (pp. 997–998). New York: The Free Press of Glencoe.

Parsons, T. (1985). The school class as a social system: Some of its functions in American society. In J. H. Ballantine (Ed.), *Schools and society: A reader in education and sociology* (pp. 179–197). Palo Alto, CA: Mayfield.

Thompson, J. B., & Held, D. (1982). Editors' introduction. In J. B. Thompson & D. Held (Eds.), *Habermas: Critical debates*. London: The Macmillan Press Ltd.

Weber, M. (1947). *The theory of social and economic organization* (A. M. Henderson & T. Parsons, Trans.; T. Parsons, Ed.). Glencoe, IL: The Free Press. For an instructive description and analysis of bureaucracy the readers are referred to this work. For an analysis of bureaucracy in schools see *Class, Bureaucracy, and Schools* by Michael Katz.

6

Culture and Educational Development of the Learner

Educational development as a process implies changes in the learner's intellectual competencies, social and sensorimotor skills, emotional dispositions, and moral reasoning. Clearly, these changes are influenced by a wide range of biological, social, cultural, and other environmental factors. Yet current research studies in educational development are predominantly psychological in nature. These efforts usually lead to psychological theories that give us partial insight into the nature of educational development and, occasionally, useful educational strategies. Educators need to have a broadly based interdisciplinary perspective both in their research and in their practice because education is a value-laden enterprise that always takes place in specific social, cultural, and political contexts. The worth of certain cognitive abilities, social skills, and attitudes are determined within these varied contexts. Accordingly, this chapter is primarily concerned with the centrality of culture in the learner's educational development.

EDUCATIONAL DEVELOPMENT AND PSYCHOLOGICAL ANTHROPOLOGY

Educational Development

From a societal perspective, educational development represents the movement of young people toward becoming full-fledged members of society, which implies changes in many different domains of the learner. But as

Edwards and Ramsey (1986) point out, "it is not just any type of change; it is change toward greater differentiation, inclusiveness, and powerfulness of ideas. It involves progress toward more advanced or mature forms of reasoning, judgment, and action" (p. 15). Hence, educational development entails growth in cognitive competencies, acquisition of knowledge and social skills, cultivation of certain attitudes, and the formation of moral values and attitudes. Also essential is the ability to make sound judgments about moral, social, and intellectual issues and maintain competent interpersonal relationships.

Although there have been numerous empirical findings and theories about educational development, none have attracted more attention from educators than Jean Piaget's theory of cognitive development and Lawrence Kohlberg's moral development theory. Because of their widespread influence among educators, a brief description of these theories will be useful as a preface to our discussion of the need for psychological anthropology in understanding educational development.

Piaget's Developmental View

Central to Piaget's theory of cognitive development is the premise that learning involves the learner's active participation in relation to objects or to social relationships. Knowledge, rather than being transmitted, has to be constructed and reconstructed by the individual learner. Hence, learning, the development of intelligence, is a continuous process of assimilating the external facts of experience and integrating them into the individual's internal mental categories, or schemata. Consequently, activity is indispensable to learning. To know something is not merely to be told about it or to see it, but to *act* upon it.

Now, if learning and knowing involve the structuring and restructuring of what has been acquired, how do they occur? According to Piaget, the processes of biological and cognitive development occur through the organization and adaptation of the organism to the environment. Intellectual development also results from organization and adaptation. Organization is the tendency of living organisms to integrate experiences and activities into a coherent system. Thus, organization is said to have occurred when a child is able to perform two originally separate acts, such as grasping and looking, at the same time. Adaptation refers to the organism's ability to interact with its surroundings. In human beings, it is this interaction that leads to the development of an increasingly complex mental organization.

For Piaget (1963), cognitive development takes place as children go through four invariant stages, which are innate and fixed for all children in all cultures. The precise age at which a specific stage emerges varies from child to child according to individual capacities and culture. The first of the four stages is the *sensorimotor stage,* in which children learn motor behavior. In general, this first stage develops between birth and 2 years of age. The *preoperational stage,* wherein children acquire the ability to conceptualize and use language, develops between the ages of about 2 and 7. Children's ability to apply logical thought to concrete problems manifests itself in the *stage of concrete operations,* which appears between the ages of approximately 7 and 11. The fourth is the *stage of formal operations,* which takes place between the ages of 11 and 15. In this stage, children learn to apply logic to problems of all sorts. Each of these stages leads to the emergence of the next one.

Although the developmental stages are fixed and unaffected by culture, they are influenced by organic growth, exercise and acquired experience, and social interaction (Piaget & Inhelder, 1969, pp. 154–158). Organic growth refers to maturation of the nervous and endocrine systems. Although maturation is an essential aspect of cognitive development, the influence of the child's physical and sociocultural environment becomes increasingly more important as the child grows older. Exercise and experience of acting upon objects is a critically important factor in cognitive development, for neither assimilation nor accommodation can take place unless children interact with their environment.

Social interaction is particularly important in the development of concepts that cannot be gotten by the child alone. In other words, children cannot construct abstract concepts such as love, loyalty, and courage by looking at corresponding objects. They must develop them through interaction with other individuals and interchange of ideas. For educators, Piaget's view implies that learning requires the child to actively interact with others and with the learning environment. Piaget and his contemporary followers further insist that the most important goal of education is thinking. For this reason, although language in the forms of reading and writing are important, we should not become preoccupied with them at the expense of learning to think. Consequently, children should be helped to grow by constructing their own knowledge and moral standards through their own thinking and judgment.

Kohlberg on Moral Development

Following Piaget's perspective, Lawrence Kohlberg studied how people reason in dealing with their moral conflicts. Like Piaget, he found that moral development occurs in an invariant sequence. Moreover, although the rate of development may vary among individuals, stages are universal and unaffected by social or cultural conditions. According to Kohlberg (1971, 1984), moral development proceeds in six stages. In the first stage, *punishment and obedience,* "right" conduct is viewed as obedience to authority and avoidance of punishment. In the *instrumental-relativist stage,* right action consists of acting to achieve one's own goals while recognizing the interests of others. The *good boy-nice girl* is the third stage, in which right conduct involves having good intentions and acting according to socially defined roles. In the fourth, the *law and order stage,* meeting one's responsibilities and contractual obligations for the good of the whole constitutes the morally right deed. In stages five and six the individual makes moral choices based on a *social contract* (the legalistic orientation) and a *universal ethical principle,* respectively. In both of these stages, right conduct is thought of as following a set of consciously chosen principles. These principles may be rooted in legalistic or philosophical concepts of virtue and justice.

These six stages of moral development do not tell us which specific moral beliefs people have in various stages. Rather, they represent how individuals in different developmental stages reason to resolve their moral dilemmas. From Kohlberg's perspective, the educator should encourage the learner to think through conflicting moral situations by presenting realistic ethical issues rather than imparting ready-made solutions. However, learners should not be expected to reason at a level beyond their developmental stage. For example, a child who is at the good boy-nice girl stage ought not be asked to deal with moral issues in terms of abstract and universal principles of justice and morality.

Table 6.1 shows the relationship between Piaget's and Kohlberg's theories.

Discontinuity and Culture in the Developmental Process

The theories of Piaget and Kohlberg are based on two fundamental assumptions: (1) the belief that the developmental process occurs through continuous transformation of earlier stages and (2) the notion that these stages are

TABLE 6.1
Relationship Between Cognitive and Moral Development Theories

Stages/Ages	
Piaget's Theory	**Kohlberg's Theory**
Sensorimotor (0–2)	
Preoperational (2–7)	Punishment and obedience (7)
Concrete operational (7–11)	Instrumental-relativist (7–10)
	Good boy–nice girl (10–13)
Formal operational (11–15)	Law and order (13–16)
	Social contract (16+)
	Universal ethical principle

invariant because the process of development is fundamentally biological and genetic in nature. In other words, although the contents of each developmental stage may be culturally bound and unique to each individual, the order of the stages is the same for everyone and is unaffected by culture. Other theorists such as Jerome Bruner, Jerome Kagan, and Kieran Egan dispute these assumptions; their observation and empirical evidence indicate that both cognitive and moral development often occur in spurts or sudden appearances of certain skills or orientations and that these phases are not invariant. This would mean that individuals in different cultures may not go through the same set and sequence of developmental stages.

In recent years, even those who concur with Piaget's perspective often use the terms *skills, skill levels,* and *tiers* in referring to Piaget's stages. For example, William Damon (1983) found that children not only performed certain cognitive tasks at inconsistent levels, but they often regressed in their developmental levels in understanding concepts. To put it differently, children who can think abstractly often think only in concrete terms in some areas. Kurt Fischer (1980), another Piagetian psychologist, discovered that cognitive development proceeds unevenly and that children almost never perform at the same skill level in all areas. Abstract thinkers do not always use their abstract thinking skills evenly in all subject areas. In the area of moral reasoning, the findings of Damon and Fischer imply that individuals who can think about ethical issues according to universal principles may deal with some moral dilemmas in terms only of rewards and punishments.

Discontinuity in the Developmental Process

According to a Harvard psychologist, Jerome Kagan (1984), Western views on human development as a continuous process are based on the assumptions that (1) "each child must step on every link . . . as he or she journeys into maturity" and that (2) a particular adult personality is a necessary product of the past (p. 110). These two beliefs suggest that by looking at an infant, we can get a glimpse of what he or she is going to be like in the future. Kagan argues that grounds that challenge these claims are found both in biology and psychology (p. 111). For example, in the growth of the fetal nervous system, the cells surrounding the future spinal cord move around to various locations in the embryo. Certain cells become part of the heart, the eyes, and the intestine; others end up serving still other organs. Once the cells become part of various organs they are no longer changeable. Whether a particular cell becomes a part of the eye or the heart has to do with what the cell encounters or where it ends up rather than the unfolding of some innate capacity to become this or that organ. Similarly, in the development of an individual there are many points at which the person can move in one of many possible directions. The effects of each "choice" or event modify the individual's future. These choices and events can range from traumatic events at birth to choosing academic majors and occupational fields. "Once a choice is made, the child will resist being detracted from the path" (p. 111).

Though each individual has been genetically programmed in very broad terms, the specific ways in which such programs become manifested are closely related to what the person encounters in various developmental phases and what special demands those phases make of the individual. "Hence, some of the past is inhibited or discarded. The new pattern may contain none of the elements of the earlier," excepting some functionally similar competencies (Kagan, 1984, p. 91). Kagan is not insisting that there are no elements of continuity in human development; he is suggesting that major changes in people's cognitive skills, social behavior, and emotional dispositions occur in response to certain life situations and cultural conditions that require special competencies. He is further pointing out that every change in human behavior or attitude does not always contain every part of the earlier developmental phases.

In support of his position, Kagan refers to Paul Bates of the Max Planck Institute in West Berlin (Kagan, 1984, pp. 91–92). According to Bates, both early and later aspects of our development are influenced not only by genetically programmed changes in our central nervous systems but also by a host of other environmental conditions. Such conditions include our society's cultural norms, new inventions ranging from computers to video games, major historical events such as wars and economic depressions, natural catastrophes like major floods and earthquakes, as well as such other unexpected events as divorce, illness, and accidents. These circumstances in our journey toward maturity demand special skills and attitudes; as a result, new competencies may appear and some old abilities and attitudes may disappear abruptly. As Kieran Egan (1979) suggests, educational development "goes by fits and starts, by stages which involve quite sudden shifts of focus and kinds of understanding" (p. 103).

Culture in the Developmental Process

The view that the developmental process is characterized by both continuity and "fits and starts" implies that the special demands of each person's unique social relationships and cultural environments play a key role in influencing how and in which direction that individual will grow. This perspective is consistent with Bruner and Haste's (1987) position that the child is a social being who "acquires a framework for interpreting experience, and learns how to negotiate meaning in a manner congruent with the requirements of the culture" (p. 1). Studies in social psychology (Moscovici, 1984; Tajfel, 1981; Williams & Giles, 1978) indicate that children grow intellectually, socially, and morally by giving meanings to personal experiences through the use of the language and culture that represent the world in which they live. Even Damon (1981), a Piagetian psychologist, points out that children do not acquire their knowledge in social isolation. Rather, they "co-construct" their knowledge with others through innumerable social exchanges and the social context in which all knowledge is presented and created.

According to Haste (1987), a dynamic relationship exists between the individual's development and the norms reflected in the folkways and mores of their particular culture (p. 188). Hence, concept development depends on the resources available within the culture, because "it is difficult, if not impossible for a child to develop a concept that does not have an expression within her culture of origin" (Bruner & Haste, 1987, p. 6). A child develops by finding appropriate ways of acting and thinking in various situations through negotiations (transactions) with others. This means, "it can never be the case that there is a 'self' independent of one's cultural-historical existence" (Bruner, 1987, p. 91). From this perspective, the Piagetian theory is inadequate because, although it describes how children's ability to reason changes, it is silent on the ways in which cultural factors affect the developmental process.

Charles Harrington (1979), a leading psychological anthropologist, suggests that the very method of conducting cross-cultural studies of Piaget's theory precludes the possibility of discovering what differences might exist in the developmental processes of culturally different children (pp. 28–30). According to Harrington, transcultural research on Piaget's theory is done by translating the standard tasks associated with Piaget's fixed developmental stages into a foreign language and administering them to children of various ages. A typical finding of such studies is that although the stages are validated, the nonoriginal group is found to be "slower" (p. 29). Because these studies are based on the assumption that the developmental stages are fixed regardless of culture, no amount of research could show whether or not the stages vary in different cultures. Unfair and distorted judgments about educability, intelligence, and learning achievements result from psychological and educational practices based on the belief that the development of all children, regardless of their social and cultural backgrounds, follows invariant stages.

Carol Gilligan (1982, 1990) at Harvard University has called into question the universality of Kohlberg's stages. She and her colleagues argue that women generally think differently from men about moral issues. In Kohlberg's work, morality is defined as justice, and higher-level reasoning involves the resolution of moral dilemmas through an objective consideration of abstract principles of justice. Contractual rules and individual rights are key concepts in the development of higher levels of reasoning. Gilligan proposes another way of viewing moral dilemmas, which she terms the ethic of care. Her studies suggest that women are more likely to conceive of moral dilemmas in terms of human relationships and connections. Higher-level moral reasoning, in this model, involves the responsibility to care for others and for oneself. The resolution of moral dilemmas comes not from stepping back and objectively applying abstract principles, but from "stepping into . . . the situation and by acting to restore relationships or to address needs, including those of oneself" (Gilligan et al., 1990, 42).

THE NEED FOR PSYCHOLOGICAL ANTHROPOLOGY

Historically, much of the research work on teaching, learning, and educational development has been psychological in nature. This is unfortunate, because preoccupation with the psychological aspects of education gives a one-sided view of how people learn, teach, and grow educationally. As has already been suggested in earlier chapters, the psychological processes underlying human behavior and learning may be essentially the same. However, the specific ways in which these processes manifest themselves are culture bound. For example, human beings tend to avoid situations in which they are punished, but they tend to repeat those behaviors for which they are rewarded. However, the meanings of reward and punishment are culture specific. For this reason, "yelling" at the child is likely to have a much more punitive or aversive meaning to white middle-class children than to Asian youngsters, who are relatively more accustomed to being "yelled at" by their parents while growing up. Because education and schooling always occur in a specific social context, developing effective instruction must take into account the profound influence culture has on how people learn, teach, and develop. It is for this reason that the field of psychological anthropology is particularly pertinent in education. But what is psychological anthropology?

Psychological Anthropology, Education, and Ethnicity

According to Francis Hsu (1972), an authority in the field, psychological anthropology "deals with human behavior primarily in terms of ideas which form the basis of the interrelationship between the individual and his society" (p. 6).[1] This discipline is also concerned with the characteristics of societies and the ways in which they relate to the wishes, fears, and values of a majority of the individuals of these societies. To put it differently, psychological anthropology is interested in understanding how the norms of a society influence the modes of relationship among its members as well as the manner in which the societal norms and structure affect the hopes, fears, and attitudes of its

---

[1]See Triandis and Heron (1981), Harrington (1979), and Spindler (1978) for additional discussion of the aims of psychological anthropology.

people. Thus, psychological anthropology not only considers human beings as a source of culture; it also views culture as having a cause-effect relationship with personality. When we consider that education is the process by which individuals become members of a society through learning its culture, the relevance of psychological anthropology in education should be evident.

A key area of study in psychological anthropology is the development of personality in culture, which directly leads to inquiries about how people acquire their attitudes, values, and behavior patterns. Thus, an examination of the learning process itself, which necessarily raises questions about perception and cognition, becomes a central concern. It is nearly impossible to understand how people learn without knowing how they perceive "things" or what meanings they give to their perceptual experiences and how these experiences in turn affect their styles of thinking. Culture plays a crucial role in determining what meanings people assign to their experiences, the contents of what is learned, as well as how learning occurs. Broadly speaking, teaching is nothing more than the facilitation of learning, and learning is at the heart of education. Thus, reliable knowledge about learning, perception, and cognition, and the roles of ethnic, language, and value differences in these processes would be most useful in developing strategies to enable children to learn more effectively. Our discussion will focus on some general findings regarding ethnicity and schooling, which may help us avoid certain pitfalls in working with a culturally diverse school population.

There is no disagreement about the fact that our schools are attended by a culturally diverse population. Nor is there any dispute regarding the projection that the number of culturally and racially different children in our schools will become significantly larger by the end of the 20th century. Yet there is little consensus regarding how the concept of ethnicity should be understood and used. More often than not, a muddled understanding of ethnicity is at the heart of the failure of school personnel to assess and meet the needs of their students. Ethnicity stands for a complex of characteristics that belong to groups of people. Hence, research findings regarding ethnicity are important because the defining characteristics of the concept must relate to those common traits found among various ethnic groups.

Ethnicity is not a single trait or a rigid category. Rather, it is a complex of interrelated factors such as nationality, language, cultural tradition and values, racial characteristics (e.g., skin color), religion, socioeconomic status, and educational level. Individuals usually define their ethnicity on the basis of some combination of these factors that they share with others in the same group. Studies indicate that these factors influence teachers' images, expectations, and evaluations of students from different ethnic groups (Harrington, 1979, pp. 67–86; Levine & Havighurst, 1989, pp. 374–427). To meet the needs of all learners, we need to understand how each child deals with his or her own ethnicity as well as the ethnicity of others. We should also be aware of possible conflicts among the values of various ethnic groups and the norms of the dominant culture according to which the school operates.

Specific knowledge about ethnic groups and their relationship with each other and with the mainstream society has to be acquired through studying individual groups. Nevertheless, school personnel can exercise some general cautions in dealing with young people's ethnicity in school. Although individuals identify with a particular ethnic group on the basis of a combination of factors associated with ethnicity, schools usually categorize minority students into four general groups: blacks, Hispanics, Native Americans, and Asians. Although the criteria by which students are placed in one of the four categories are neither clear nor consistent, the common belief is that the members of each group share common cultural, linguistic, and racial characteristics and needs. Indeed, not all blacks come from the same socioeconomic backgrounds nor do they have the same educational level or a common religion.

The Hispanics as a group consist of even more diverse groups with divergent legal, economic, and social status. For example, those from Puerto Rico, the Dominican Republic, Mexico, and Cuba may speak Spanish. But all Puerto Ricans are American citizens, whereas some of the others may be recent immigrants or illegal or undocumented aliens. Parents of Puerto Rican children may be more likely to participate in school functions than others, if for no other reason than their legal status in this country. The Native American group too consists of individuals from diverse cultural, linguistic, and religious heritages. Asian Americans as a group include those who came from China, India, Japan, Korea, the Philippines, and several Southeast Asian countries. Like the Hispanics, Asian Americans also have greatly varying kinds of legal status, sociocultural history, educational backgrounds, language patterns, and economic achievements.

In spite of the fact that wide variations in the backgrounds of individuals exist even in a single ethnic group, evidence suggests that school personnel often relate to their students by inferring erroneous conclusions based on a single or a very limited number of factors (Harrington, 1979; Levine & Havighurst, 1989). For example, teachers tend to assume that youngsters who speak a nonstandard dialect are intellectually inferior, and children with light skin color are treated more favorably than those with darker skin. There is also an indication that children of highly educated parents tend to receive special attention from teachers and other school personnel. In a different vein, one of the authors recalls a case of a U.S.-born Asian-American child who received a D on a well-written essay. When the child's father pressed the teacher to explain the grade, the teacher responded, "I thought that someone else had written the paper for her because, being an Asian, I assumed that she would naturally have problems in writing an English essay."

There are two primary purposes for citing these examples. One is to stress the view that a person's ethnicity consists of several factors and that the individual's own perception of his or her ethnicity should play a part in placing the person in a particular group. This point is particularly important because how we conceive and use the concept of ethnicity, as well as our image of ethnic groups, influence the ways in which we work with and evaluate ethnic children. The second purpose is to point out the need for our school personnel to learn about the cultural values of different ethnic groups and the manners in which these values influence the children's performance in school. Not all cultural or ethnic groups have the same view of education, schooling, or learning. Thus, it is essential for educators to know how or at what point the values held by the various ethnic groups may come into conflict with school goals. With this knowledge, students from various ethnic groups may be helped to apply these values appropriately according to different cultural contexts. For example, schools reward students for individual competence, achievements, and involvement. On the other hand, Navajos are said to prize group harmony and hence conformity to the group norm. In this situation, a Navajo child may be helped to learn to function differently in school and in the Navajo community.

The wide gap between the school's view of extracurricular activity and that of Asian-American parents is another example of how two different views of education can conflict with each other. In general, our school personnel see schooling as a process of developing the whole person. Hence, nonacademic school activities are considered an important part of the child's education. However, Asian-American parents tend to view schooling as the process of training the child's intellect only and, consequently, regard nonacademic activities as distractions. Teachers may be able to persuade these parents to encourage their children's involvement in school activities by discussing with them the notion of school as a microcosm of the larger society wherein children learn to live and grow socially, intellectually, and emotionally.

To help culturally different young people learn more effectively, we must be aware of the cultural and value differences among various ethnic groups and the school. Further, teachers and administrators need to have specific information about those cultural and linguistic variables that are likely to affect the teaching-learning processes. But such specific data are difficult to obtain without some systematic study of and experience with different cultural groups. This suggests that teacher education and in-service programs should include how divergent value systems, child-rearing practices, thinking styles, and patterns of communication influence children's learning patterns. In addition, schools need to (1) increase the diversity of educational environments so that children can find an environment in which they function more effectively, (2) nurture the legitimacy of multiple educational outcomes that foster cultural diversity without reinforcing discrimination based on social class, and (3) develop the kinds of curricula that incorporate the examination of what goes on in school as part of a larger context, such as children's lives, the larger society, and so on. (Harrington, 1979, p. 100). For Charles Harrington, these "programs" reflect some of the pressing concerns of psychological anthropology in education.

Finally, much of our discussion about ethnicity has been centered on nonwhite ethnic groups. However, ethnicity is no less important in the lives of such cultural groups as the Irish, the Poles, the Italians, and the Jews. Divergent patterns in social norms, linguistic forms, cognitive and communication styles, as well as approaches to learning, are found among members of both the dominant and ethnic minority groups. As educators, we should not categorize individuals into certain ethnic or cultural groups on the basis of one or two characteristics they possess. Rigid and stereotypic labeling of the learner is likely to result in an unfair assessment of his or her educability, which in turn may limit the child's social and intellectual growth.

Rather than becoming preoccupied with categorizing children into various cultural, ethnic, age, or gender groups, we should be concerned with how each learner's unique social, linguistic, and attitudinal patterns influence educational development. For example, we need to determine the extent to which the child's use of a nonstandard English dialect or bilingualism may influence academic performance. We must also examine how the learner's docility and conformist attitude based on respect for authority may affect the teacher-pupil relationship. Whether these abilities and attitudes become assets or liabilities for the child depends on the nature of his or her goals and the contexts in which they are to be achieved. One's unwillingness to express personal opinions and feelings or to assert one's rights may even be a virtue in certain ethnic or cultural environments, but these same attitudes can become liabilities in many academic and social situations in the larger society. A central responsibility of educators is to help learners achieve their goals by utilizing appropriate knowledge, skills, and attitudes in divergent social and cultural environments.

How we use our knowledge of the learner's needs, aspirations, and sociocultural background in facilitating the child's educational development depends on our conception of the nature of childhood. That is, if we regard children as little adults with immature judgments, we may view their needs and aspirations as childish or foolish desires to be suppressed. On the other hand, if children are considered individuals traveling through a natural and necessary phase of their life process, their wishes and future goals may be thought of as legitimate and important aspects of their development. In this sense, childhood is no more an abnormal state than adulthood. In a very real sense, all educational models, theories, and practices are based on either implicit or explicit beliefs about the child (Cleverley & Phillips, 1986). The following sections will examine today's conceptions of the nature of childhood and their educational implications. For this discussion, the terms *childhood* and *youth* will be used interchangeably to refer to the phase of life from birth to late adolescence.

CONCEPTS OF CHILDHOOD AND EDUCATIONAL DEVELOPMENT

Early Concepts of Childhood

Concepts of childhood are formulated by societies at various times and in different contexts. Hence, the meanings of the nature of childhood vary from one historical period to another and from culture to culture. Historically, the idea of childhood as a state distinct from adulthood did not always exist in most parts of the world. In the medieval Western world, children participated in the work and play of adults as soon as they were able to live without the help of an adult. Hence, children were viewed as miniature adults who, by the age of 7, became participating members of adult society (Packard, 1983, p. xv; Suransky, 1982, p. 6). The recognition that infancy was an early stage of life was implicit in this perspective. However, no clear distinctions were made between childhood and adulthood, for children and adults shared common types of work, games, and even clothes. An interesting contrast to the Western images of children is the conception of children found in many Eastern cultures, which have been heavily influenced by the Confucian ideal of filial piety. In these cultures, children are not only taken for granted, but their importance is minimized (Hsu, 1981, pp. 80–84). In the area of the parent-child relationship, parents are more concerned about what children can do for them than what they can do for their children. Consonantly, although parents may be amused by childlike behaviors and attitudes, their children's worth is based on the extent to which they conform to adult norms.

The concept of childhood as a distinct state did not appear until the 17th century. Even then the idea of childhood as a period requiring prolonged training and preparation for adult life was associated only with the children of the nobility (Suransky, 1982, p. 7). Childhood as a separate state did not apply to working-class children. In this way, the concept of childhood became a phenomenon linked with a social class. In the late 17th century, games and play for adults and nobility were delineated from those of children and the poor. This is how "the lower classes were infantilized, and the concept of childhood became linked to subservience and dependency" (Suransky, 1982, p. 7). Unlike in the preceding eras, childhood was seen as something separate from adulthood in 19th-century America. During this period, children were viewed as having economic value not only because they represented an important source of the labor force but also because they were useful in the household division of labor. But with the recognition of childhood as a distinct state and the rise of schooling came a growing trend toward the separation of children from adults (Packard, 1983, p. xviii).

Contemporary Concepts of Childhood

Children as Victims

In the United States, child labor laws and compulsory education introduced in the early 20th century to protect children from economic exploitation gradually led to the transformation of the conception of American children from economically useful to economically useless but emotionally priceless (Zelizer, 1985). Children are to be kept off the labor market and the streets. Frequent reports in today's mass media of physical, sexual, and emotional abuse of children and public policies protecting children from abuse seem to support the image that children are indeed victimized by their elders. In *Pricing the Priceless Child*, Viviana A. Zelizer (1985) argues that American children became objects of sentimentalization regardless of social class. And "the new sacred child occupied a special and separate world, regulated by affection and education, not work or profit" (p. 216). In this way, the United States is considered a uniquely child-centered society. Yet, as Suransky (1982) insists, we separated childhood from adulthood so completely that we have failed to recognize the significance of our children's contribution to the "cultural forms of everyday life" (p. 8). Children are seen neither as meaningful participants in their society nor as possible contributors to certain human problems. We do not see children as thinkers and doers. Rather, we consider them sheltered and victimized members of society who are immature, incompetent, and manipulable for their own good (Boulding, 1979).

Children as Adults

According to Postman (1981), in the United States we have returned to the pre-17th-century notion of the child as a miniature adult by "adultifying" children (p. 174). Children have been prematurely pushed into adulthood by merging their taste and style with those of adults in almost every aspect of their life. Postman insists that children's interests, language, dress, or sexuality as portrayed in television shows, TV commercials, and movies do not differ significantly from those of adults (pp. 120–125). Even in the areas of alcoholism, substance abuse, sexual activity, and crime, distinctions between childhood and adulthood become less and less clear.

The fading differentiation between childhood and adulthood is aggravated by the fact that adulthood is often represented by "childified" or childlike adults. For example, consider the childlike traits of the main characters in such popular television shows as "The Simpsons," "Married With Children," and "Roseanne." For Postman, the rapidly fading distinction between childhood and adulthood—the disappearance of childhood—made the compulsory nature of schooling seem arbitrary by the early 1980s (p. 140). Because they were already adults, there was nothing left for the children in school to become. For this reason, educators became uncertain about what to do with schoolchildren and they were willing to accept "education for the entry into the marketplace" (p. 140). This meant that learning history, literature, and art became less and less worthwhile.

Notwithstanding Postman's (1981) discouraging view, he does think that two social institutions—the school and the family—can stem the tide of disappearing childhood. He points out that the school can help maintain the distinction between childhood and adulthood by teaching children to be literate and allowing them to grow as children. But this task is difficult for the school to accomplish because it tends to reflect the social trends rather than direct them. However, the family can do much more than the school by "conceiving of parenting as an act of rebellion against American culture" (p. 152). More specifically, parents should remain married so that their children can learn the meaning of kinship. They should also insist that their children learn the discipline of delayed gratification, deference to their elders, self-restraint, modesty, and the value of hard work. Parents should also limit the quantity and the quality of media programs to which their children are exposed. Postman claims that by doing these things the family can fight against the disappearance of childhood by opposing every harmful social trend in our society (pp. 152–153).

The family, like the school, exists and functions in a particular cultural context. Hence, it is doubtful that the family as one institution can resist "the spirit of the age" any more than the school can, for it too reflects the social trends more than directs them. But Postman is correct in observing that children are being rushed into adulthood, and the nature of childhood as we understood it in previous eras has declined, if not disappeared. If Postman is correct, or at least on the right track, the current trend in adultification of children will lead to a distorted view of childhood and unfair judgment of our children's capabilities and contributions to the larger society. There is little doubt that this view of childhood will impede children's educational development. Even if Postman's view is not sound in any definitive sense, his perspective gives educators important caveats in helping children grow as children on their way to becoming adults.

Children as Undeveloped Adults

The conceptions of childhood discussed thus far have all been descriptions of the nature of childhood derived from the experiences and observations of adults. As Montagu (1981) insists, these images of childhood are preconceptions of what adults believe the nature of childhood ought to be (p. 121). From such a biased point of view, adults are bound to fail in what the child is trying to become, "to develop not as an adult, but as a child—in other words, to realize the promise of the child" (p. 121). Thus, if we are to understand the meaning of childhood and its significance for educational development, we need to gain an insight into the child's experiences as he or she views them. Although we cannot see the world as a child might interpret it, we could infer the child's-eye view of the world from children's own reports of their experiences and studies of child-rearing practices and socialization of the young. The *culture of childhood* is an expression used by Mary Ellen Goodman (1970), an anthropologist and the author of *The Culture of Childhood*, to get at the child's-eye view of children's experiences (Goodman, p. 2; Suransky, 1982, pp. 27–28).

According to Goodman, the image of childhood held by American adults differs radically from children's view of themselves in that the former is based on two mistaken assumptions. She finds that these assumptions underlie American pedagogy and child-rearing practices (pp. 2–3). One is the fallacy of universal age-stage linkage and the other is the underestimation fallacy. The first is reflected in the belief that adolescence anywhere at any time is necessarily a period of storm, stress, and confusion. Hence, adults characterize adolescent behavior as confused whenever it deviates from the adult norm. The second assumption suggests that children and adolescents are incapable of appreciating interpersonal relations and unable to cope with their frustrations, tensions, and problems. Hence, when the child does not behave according to the demands of adults he or she is thought to have symptoms of behavioral or emotional problems. Consequently, children and adolescents are thought of primarily in terms of incapacities and inabilities.

Because the notion of age-stage linkage and the underestimation fallacy are so widely held by adults, the behavior and value patterns of the young are often described as senseless, irrational, confused, irresponsible, and insensitive. For this reason, "children and adolescents are usually treated with a kind of amiable tolerance; little is expected of them in the way of learning, control or responsibility" (Goodman, 1970, p. 11). In other words, the behavior and belief systems of children and adolescents are not seen as functionally viable means of coping with their problems. Adults in our society have rejected the notion of the culture of childhood and adolescence just as the mainstream culture has rejected minority and ethnic patterns as different but legitimate means of dealing with problems of living.

In a similar vein, Ashley Montagu (1981) points out that the belief in "stages" is educationally damaging because stages are generally correlated with chronological age, which is then considered an indicator of a specific developmental stage in which the child is expected to function in a particular way (p. 125). The fact that every child has his or her own rate of development is likely to be ignored because the age-stage linkage leads us to believe that children of the same age are at the same stage of development in all respects. Montagu warns that it is unreasonable and destructive to expect a child to do equally well in all areas of growth because the rates of developing aptitudes and learning different subjects and skills vary significantly.

What is implicit in the views of Goodman and Montagu is that what the young can accomplish in the areas of cognitive, social, and even motor skills is determined not only by maturation and training but also by the level of culturally patterned expectations. The lower the expectation, the less the achievement. For example, in our society we have minimal expectations with respect to the kinds of social responsibilities and cognitive skills the young are to achieve. Consequently, if children or adolescents lack "social grace" in relating to older people, they are usually excused because adults believe that "kids are kids and they can't be expected to behave and talk properly."

The fact that children and adolescents in other societies work and behave at a much more sophisticated level is due largely to the high level of culturally patterned expectations. For example, in a 3-year study of 564 Korean-American early adolescents and adolescents (grades 5 through 12), the youth attributed their high aspiration and achievement in academic performance to the high level of their parents' expectations (Pai & Pemberton, 1987). The study participants also viewed their parents' expectations as unreasonably high. In the area of "what I want in life," more than 79% of those studied reported that "doing well in school" is "very important" to "at the top of the list" (p. 63). In comparing these Korean-American youth with their counterparts in a similar study of 7,000 early adolescents conducted by the Search Institute, more than 70% of the Korean-American youth and 56% of the Search group indicated that they worry "quite a bit" to "very much" about school performance (Search Institute, 1984). Although we cannot discern a clear cause-effect relationship between the levels of parental expectations and young people's academic performances, they do give us useful clues regarding the cultural conditions that are closely related to culturally established expectations and young people's performance levels.

In "Cultural Influences Shaping the Role of the Child," Solon Kimball (1974) argues that American adults place their children in a difficult and confusing world. On the one hand, they expect little from their children. But on the other hand, they evaluate them according to the adult norm. More specifically, the grown-ups in America expect their children to have a strong commitment to change and to desire constant progress and improvement (pp. 91–92). They are expected to seek to achieve goals higher than what they have already accomplished. In addition to committing themselves to constant improvement and self-fulfillment, they are also required to assume a posture of perpetual optimism (pp. 92–93). Our culture demands that they maintain this euphoric facade. These three criteria of evaluation coupled with our underestimation of children's ability to deal with their problems present young Americans with an unresolvable dilemma, because although they are not expected to act like adults, they are judged according to adult standards.

Valerie Polakow (1992) argues that childhood has been eroded by the imposition of adult agendas and rigid planning on the lives of children. In the absence of national social policies for working mothers, families find themselves increasingly relying on institutional childcare. In Polakow's study of childcare centers all over the country she found that children in general experienced a dulling of curiosity and the regulation of imagination and exploration.

> In short I saw the fostering of a leveled landscape of compliance and the bureaucratization of young children's experiences. Stripped of the power to play and invent, children were denied the opportunity to become meaning makers in their own small worlds. (p. 203)

Few of us would disagree that Americans are preoccupied with and anxious about their children and uncertain about how to deal with them. Thus, on the one hand, we claim to respect the rights and dignity of the young as intrinsically worthwhile, but on the other hand, we evaluate them according to the criteria used for adult members of the society. It would appear that American adults implicitly assume that children's behavior and belief patterns are deficit forms of adult norms. From this kind of deficit view, children are treated as undeveloped adults who must depend on "real adults" for a prolonged period of time. Hence, grown-ups are unable to recognize children's problem-solving capabilities and their potential contribution to the family or the larger society. For Montagu (1981) the child surpasses the adult by the wealth of his possibilities.

> Infants and children implicitly know a great deal more about many aspects of growing than adults. . . . Children have a world of their own for us to know. (p. 197)

The "Culture of Childhood" and Education

The conceptions of childhood we have discussed represent three very different perspectives regarding the nature of childhood. Whether children are seen as victims, miniature adults, or undeveloped grown-ups, all three images underestimate the potential of young people. If, as Montagu argues, children know a lot more about growing than adults do, they are also well aware of their own abilities. Studies of the culture of childhood or the child's-eye view of his or her own culture (Goodman, 1970; Kimball, 1974; Boulding, 1979; Montagu, 1981; Kurth-Schai, 1985) indicate that young people are conscious of the ways in which the contradictory expectations of the adult world make their social participation and contribution difficult.

For the present as well as the future of our society, we need to revise our conception of childhood, for, as Margaret Mead (1970) once pointed out, grown-ups can learn to cope with a rapidly changing world more effectively by observing the young. We need to have the young "ask the questions that we would never think to ask, but enough trust must be re-established so that the elders will be permitted to work with them on the answers" (p. 95). Our youth are less fettered by excess historical baggage to imagine and explore a much wider range of social alternatives than their elders. For the future, it is essential that we reconceptualize the nature of childhood in terms of children's own views of their world or the culture of childhood rather than by the degree to which they conform to or deviate from the adult norm. We need to redefine children as thinkers, doers, creators, and sharers of knowledge and arts, as well as participants in promoting human welfare. Once the nature of childhood is defined in this way, education should be the art and science of helping the child to realize his or her potentialities. Accordingly, education should (1) emphasize the personal meaning and social significance of children's learning experiences, (2) promote critical evaluation of knowledge claims and integration of knowledge and experience, (3) encourage reflective inquiry into the moral implications of what is learned, and (4) stimulate the exploration of new and different ways of knowing and valuing.

CULTURAL INFLUENCE IN PSYCHOEDUCATIONAL ASSESSMENT OF THE LEARNER

If we conceive education as the art and science of aiding the child to fulfill his or her promises, an accurate and unbiased assessment of the child's needs, abilities, and aspirations becomes critically necessary. From this perspective, psychoeducational assessment is much more than administering standardized intelligence, achievement, or aptitude tests to obtain such global indicators as IQ or percentile scores on children.

What Is Psychoeducational Assessment?

Broadly speaking, psychoeducational assessment is a process of obtaining information about the learner and communicating it to the intended users for making the best possible decisions about the learner's education (Shellenberger, 1982). For most young people who do not have apparent behavioral, emotional, or learning difficulties, the assessment process usually does not go beyond the use of a limited number of standardized intelligence and achievement tests and pupil evaluations done by classroom teachers. In general, student performance on teacher-made achievement tests and more or less systematic observations of pupil's behaviors by other school personnel constitute the classroom teacher's assessment of the child. The teacher shares information obtained through this process with the parent in making decisions about the child's educational program.

Ideally, a systematic and comprehensive psychoeducational assessment includes but is not limited to the use of standardized intelligence and achievement tests, evaluation of the child's social or adaptive behaviors, and tests of sensorimotor and cognitive skills. Observations of classroom teachers, counselors, principals, school psychologists, social workers, physicians, and other psychological and educational specialists are an integral part of the process. The learner's parents are also viewed as active participants in assessing the child's needs, abilities, and goals. We can safely say that all of the elements in this assessment process may be affected by a wide variety of cultural factors. Consequently, if the assessment is to be both comprehensive and nondiscriminatory, we must guard against possible biases of the assessor, the instrument, and the assessment process as well as the environment or context in which the assessment is to take place (Hillard, 1977; Lutey & Copeland, 1982; Torrance, 1982). Following a brief discussion of assessment models, we will examine how the cultural aspects of these key assessment process components may influence the outcomes and their uses.

Assessment Models and Culture

Approaches to psychoeducational assessment can be grouped into five conceptual models: (1) the medical model, (2) the social system model, (3) the ability training model, (4) the task analysis model, and (5) the pluralistic model, or system of multicultural pluralistic assessment (SOMPA) (Mercer & Ysseldyke, 1977; Torrance, 1982, pp. 489–491).

The Medical Model

The medical model is based on the belief that learning difficulties are caused by some biological conditions. Hence, the sociocultural characteristics of the person with behavioral or learning difficulties are thought to be irrelevant in the assessment process. Treatment programs for the learner would be based on assessing physical factors. Although this model is not believed to be culturally bound, it may become culturally discriminatory if certain behaviors caused by physical conditions are erroneously viewed as resulting from cultural conditions. For example, inappropriate and even harmful educational programs may be prescribed for a minority child if reading difficulties caused by neurological conditions are judged as stemming from the child's cultural background.

The Social System Model

According to the social system model, the learner is evaluated in terms of the extent to which the child meets the expectations of the group in which he or she functions at the time of assessment. In the context of schooling, deviant or undesirable behaviors are those that do not conform to the expectations of the school and its rules and policies. The child's failure to learn the necessary role behaviors as defined by the school is considered primarily responsible for the child's poor academic performance. Although many conditions contribute to the child's failure to master the necessary social norms, conflicts between values of the learner's culture and those of the school and the lack of opportunity to learn the necessary role expectations need to be examined carefully.

From the social system's perspective, educational "treatment" involves helping the child learn the norms of behavior for various roles in the school. Such an educational strategy is useful insofar as the role expectations to be learned fit a particular social setting, for example, school. However, the social system's approach becomes culturally biased if the norms of one group are taught as universal norms to be adopted by all groups and at all times. To many culturally different children, this attitude may lead them to believe that only the mainstream or the school norms are legitimate. But after all, role expectations vary from group to group, and we do not always act according to only one set of norms at all times.

The Ability Training Model

The ability training model is based on the premise that children learn differently and that academic failures occur as a result of certain disabilities or deficits existing within the child. The primary objectives of this model are to identify the underlying causes of failure through testing and to help children improve their school performance by teaching them the necessary skills. Within the ability training model, deviations from average or model performance levels are considered deficits or disabilities according to which children are labeled.

The ability training approach to assessment relies heavily on children's performance on norm-referenced tests, which are given to a large and representative group of individuals who presumably have comparable academic and cultural backgrounds. Hence, a child's score on a norm-referenced test tells us about where he or she stands in relation to others who took the same test. The score does not indicate how much the child has learned in relation to a specific educational objective. Most standardized intelligence and achievement tests are norm-referenced instruments. This means that minority children's scores on these tests will not give us unbiased information about their abilities and achievements as individuals, only their abilities as members of a representative group. Because minority children are compared with mainstream children with whom they do not share comparable intellectual or sociocultural backgrounds, a heavy use of norm-referenced tests frequently results in discriminatory assessment and placement of minority children. Many suggest that this practice is partly responsible for the overrepresentation of black and Hispanic children in educable mentally handicapped (EMH) classes and underrepresentation in gifted programs.

The Task Analysis Model

For advocates of the task analysis model of assessment, the main concern is analyzing specific skills that make up certain terminal behaviors or educational objectives. Because the primary focus of this assessment model is integrating identified individual skills into desired objectives, there is a minimal concern for disabilities or deficits based on a group norm. In the 1990s, a resurgence of interest in this approach appeared in the form of *mastery learning*. Based on earlier work of Benjamin Bloom (1968), mastery learning is based on the assumption that all children can learn, given sufficient time on task. Some students may require more time than others and instruction must be modified to meet individual differences. Mastery learning advocates stress the importance of assuring that students experience success at each level of instruction. Another approach that gained popularity in the 1990s, *Outcomes Based Education* (OBE), also places emphasis on the clear identification of outcomes and the construction of individual knowledge through mastery.

This assessment model stresses the use of criterion-referenced instruments to evaluate children's progress. Unlike norm-referenced tests, criterion-referenced instruments measure how much a child has learned in relation to a particular educational objective. Once a child's strengths and weaknesses are assessed in relation to a specific goal, instructional objectives are written to enable the child to reach his or her goal by developing necessary skills. This test-teach-test process can be repeated until the individually planned educational programs are successfully achieved. Because each child is treated as an individual rather than being judged in relation to others, the assessment process is less likely to be biased or discriminatory. However, educators need to capitalize on the different ways children think and learn so that each child can be helped to reach his or her goals effectively.

The Pluralistic Model

The pluralistic model, also known as the system of multicultural pluralistic assessment (SOMPA), pioneered by Jane Mercer, represents an attempt to estimate "learning potential in a manner which is not racially or culturally discriminatory" (Mercer & Ysseldyke, 1977, p. 85). Even though more than 20 years have elapsed since its initial development in 1973, many still find this model to be particularly useful with black, Hispanic, and other culturally different American children, for example, poor Appalachian children. The popularity of this model derives from the fact that it takes into account the possible impact of sociocultural and health factors on the measurement of learning potentials (Torrance, 1982, p. 490). SOMPA is based on two basic premises.

One is the belief that learning potential is similarly distributed in all racial and cultural groups. The other is the view that all tests used for estimating learning potential are culturally biased. Hence, individuals whose cultural backgrounds are similar to those of the persons who belong to the group used for test standardization (the norm group) tend to perform better on such tests than those who have different cultural heritages.

Within the pluralistic model, well-established standardized intelligence tests as well as culture-specific tests (for example, the Black Intelligence Test of Cultural Homogeneity) are used to evaluate the child in terms of the cultural materials with which he or she is familiar. The child's role performance in the family, the neighborhood, and the school and his or her perceptual-motor development and health conditions are assessed. The assessment is accomplished through an interview with the child's parents or guardian and direct examination of the child. Once the specific skills the child needs to learn have been identified, he or she is taught those skills and then tested to estimate the amount of growth gained as a result of the teaching. In this context of test-train-retest, intelligence is viewed as the child's ability to profit from experience (Mercer & Ysseldyke, 1977, p. 83). Similarly, educability of the minority child should be seen as his or her ability to learn new cultural patterns. Mercer points out that the measures of minority children's learning potential obtained according to the pluralistic model tell us about how well these children performed in specific cultural groups. These measures may suggest probable potential of minority children for learning new skills and knowledge in mainstream groups when appropriate instruction is given.

In reviewing the five assessment models (see Table 6.2), we find that each model can yield information about some specific aspect of the child. For example, the medical model can tell us about the physical factors related to the child's performance in school. The task analysis model can yield information about what specific skills the child needs to develop in order to master a particular subject matter. On the other hand, the pluralistic model can give us a measure of the child's learning potential in terms of the cultural heritages within which he or she has been reared. It would appear that nondiscriminatory assessment for educational development requires an approach that can utilize the unique techniques and methods of a wide variety of disciplines such as counseling psychology, anthropology, social psychology, psychometry, ethnography, social work, certain health sciences, and even subject matter specialization. Parents' observations of the child and the child's self-perception, as well as his or her optional performance of untested skills, can also provide valuable information for fair assessment and sound educational planning.

In general, the multidisciplinary staff conference is held for evaluating and placing special education students. This conference usually involves the parents, psychologist, school personnel, social worker, and at times the child.

It would seem desirable that similar meetings involving a smaller number of individuals could be held to assess both the mainstream and minority students who experience minor difficulties or desire special educational guidance.

Cultural Factors in Psychoeducational Assessment

All approaches to psychoeducational assessment share at least three common components: (1) the person who is doing the assessing, (2) the instrument used for assessment, and (3) the person who is being assessed. These components contain certain cultural elements that may contribute to biased assessment and discriminatory decisions leading to harmful influence on the educational development of the child.

The Assessor

Beliefs, values, and biases of the person responsible for carrying out the assessment can make a significant difference in the outcome, the interpretation, and the use of the data. One of the major issues regarding the interactions between the assessor and the child being evaluated is the concern that the assessor's attitudes toward minority cultures, the opposite sex, and the aged may negatively affect the outcomes of testing. The assessor's ethnocentrism as well as his or her failure to understand the child's culture, values, cognitive styles, language usage, and unique approach to interpersonal relationships may influence the assessment results adversely. The child may have similar difficulties in understanding the assessor's attitudes and behavior patterns. When we consider the fact that most minority children are evaluated by white assessors, it is not difficult to see how poor performance on standardized tests can result from poor communication and misunderstanding between the assessor and the assessed. The negative influence of these factors on how tests are administered, scored, interpreted, and used can lead to biased assessment, which in turn can result in unfair and inappropriate placement. Most school personnel, including school psychologists and counselors, are monocultural in both experience and education. Unless they have had special training in cross-cultural studies they are most likely to interpret the attitudes and behaviors of minority children in terms of the mainstream culture. Hillard (1977) insists that, "when the [assessor's] frame of reference is imposed on the experience of people alien to him [or her], confusion and invalid interpretation are almost certain to result" (p. 108).

Evidence to date regarding the relationship between the assessor's attitudes and evaluation outcomes appears to be inconclusive (Lutey & Copeland, 1982, pp. 131–133). However, it would be prudent for psychoedu-

TABLE 6.2
Summary of Assessment Models

			Models		
	Medical	Social System	Ability Training	Task Analysis	Pluralistic
Learning Difficulties	Biological or physical deficits	Not behaving according to the school norm	Lack of abilities to do schoolwork	Lack of specific skills to achieve terminal behaviors	Not having certain culture-specific skills to do schoolwork
Assessment	Physical and/or neuro-logical conditions	Degree to which the child meets the school's expecta-tions at the time of assessment	Norm-referenced measures used to compare with the norm group	Criterion-referenced measures used to determine how much the child has moved toward a target behavior	Standardized IQ tests, culture-specific IQ tests, sociocultural and health factors, and personal interviews
Treatment	Remedy physical or neurological conditions	Teach the behavioral norms for various roles in school	Teach skills to reach the group norm	Develop specific skills to master a subject matter; test-teach-test	Develop culture-specific skills necessary to do well in school; test-train-retest
Discriminatory Effects	Behaviors resulting from physical conditions may be viewed as stem-ming from cultural backgrounds	Deviation from dominant norms viewed as deficits or pathological conditions	Only the dominant group norm is used to define educability	Less discriminatory because learned skills are specifi-cally related to a learning objective	Least discriminatory because socio-cultural factors are considered in defining educability

197

cational assessors to know as much about their own attitudes and values, other cultural norms, and the cultural biases built into all forms of testing instruments and processes as possible. After all, assessment is a form of social interaction among individuals whose values and worldviews are bound to affect how they think and what they do.

The Assessment Instrument

One of the most frequently made criticisms against the use of standardized intelligence and achievement tests is the claim that the contents of these tests are biased in favor of white middle-class Americans. For example, neither black nor Hispanic cultures give minority students opportunities to be exposed to many commonly used test items. Moreover, because the norms are established by testing predominantly white students, the culturally different tend to do poorly on these tests. The use of minority children's test scores for placement purposes is said to be unfair and unsound, because these norm-referenced measures of intelligence and academic achievements do not indicate how much minority children have learned in an alien culture, the school. Even for white middle-class children, the use of IQ scores and percentile scores on standardized tests for educational placement may be inappropriate because the scores on these tests only indicate where the youngsters are in relation to others who took the same test.

Another area of concern in the use of standardized tests for minority children has to do with their cognitive styles and language usage. For example, studies indicate that many black and Hispanic children are not concerned with the details of a concept or a situation or with "hurrying" to do a job (Hillard, 1977, pp. 114–115; Carter & Segura, 1979, pp. 83–89, 97; Grossman, 1984, pp. 175–186). However, timed standardized tests require that analytic and detail-specific responses be given within a fairly short period of time. It is generally known that even among white children, urban children do much better on timed tests than rural children because rural residents tend to place less emphasis on a time-oriented lifestyle than urban city dwellers. In addition, the fact that minority cultures may consider certain test items as simply unimportant may also contribute to poor test performance by minority children.

A most serious barrier to nondiscriminatory assessment is the lack of appropriate instruments for assessing minority children's learning potential, personality characteristics, and social behavior. This problem is believed to be rooted in the differences in concepts, behaviors, values, and measurement techniques that exist between mainstream American and minority cultures (Koh, 1988, p. 7). Tong-He Koh, Research Director of the Bureau of Child Study of the Chicago Board of Education, reports that when the Minnesota Multiphasic Personality Inventory (MMPI) was administered to Koreans who recently immigrated to the United States, they were found to have a highly elevated level of depression and other psychological disturbances (Koh, Sakauye, Koh, & Liu, 1986). However, such a level of depression and other psychological disturbances were considered common or "normal" among Japanese in Japan and Chinese in China (Clark, 1985; Song, 1984). On the other hand, when another well-established psychiatric interview schedule was given to Koreans in Seoul, Korea, and to Chinese in Taiwan and Shanghai, the subjects were found to have significantly lower levels of psychological disturbances than Americans in the United States (Koh, 1988, p. 8). Koh concludes that diametrically opposing findings can come from established and well-translated assessment instruments because of their cultural contents and the contexts in which the instruments were administered. It is quite likely that Asians prefer not to disclose their own problems to others or tend to give socially acceptable responses in face-to-face interview situations. These research findings suggest that a person's performance on an assessment instrument varies with the cultural contents of the instrument and culturally induced ways in which the individual responds to written or oral questions. This has important implications for assessor-subject, teacher-pupil, and counselor-client relationships. Some of these ramifications will be discussed in the following chapter.

Finally, all of this is not to suggest that standardized norm-referenced instruments are useless, for they can give us information about where a particular person or a group stands in relation to a larger norm group. But a central point of our discussion is that each child's unique learning potential or attitudinal characteristics cannot be determined on the basis of the child's scores on norm-referenced instruments alone. The emergence of efforts toward *authentic assessment*[2] is, in part, a reaction to the criticisms of standardized, norm-referenced testing. Authentic assessment seeks to engage students in assessment tasks that are more clearly reflective of articulated goals and emphasize process as well as products. Rather than choosing from predetermined options, the emphasis is on having students create or construct responses. For example, if the expectation of students is that they be able to analyze and think critically about a work of literature, the assessment should give students the opportunity to demonstrate that ability rather than respond to a multiple-choice test. Expectations and standards for success are to be made clear to learners at the outset and instruction is focused around the attainment of those goals; however, different learners may be able to demonstrate their attainment of particular goals in somewhat different ways. Students are not assessed against one another, but rather against the attain-

---

[2]The terms *performance assessment* and *alternative assessment* are also frequently used to refer to similar kinds of assessments.

ment of clear goals. Both mainstream and minority children's learning potential can be estimated without comparing their learning rates with those of others.

The Assessed

When we consider the complex nature of the psychoeducational assessment process, it is not surprising that anyone about to undergo an evaluative experience might be apprehensive. As compared to mainstream youth, most minority students face much more severe psychological stresses at the prospect of having to be evaluated because, for them, the evaluation represents an alien cultural setting. However, studies indicate that not all forms of anxiety have a negative effect. Of the two types of anxiety, trait and state anxieties, only the latter tends to adversely influence test performance (Lutey & Copeland, 1982, p. 130). According to Lutey and Copeland, *trait anxiety* is a pervasive condition that affects the person's daily life. On the other hand, *state anxiety* is brought on by the person's emotional reaction to immediate conditions. It is this state anxiety that tends to disrupt test performance. Although it is not unusual to be apprehensive in a testing situation, the assessor needs to be aware of the potential adverse influence of state anxiety. Anything that the assessor can do to establish a positive rapport with the assessed may help reduce negative effects of state anxiety.

Findings regarding the effect of bilingualism on test performance seem mixed (Lutey & Copeland, 1982, pp. 129–130). For example, Spanish-English speaking children tend to do significantly better on the verbal section of the Spanish version of the Wechsler Intelligence Scale for Children (WISC) than on the English version. However, when another intelligence test was given to black children in black dialect, their performance did not vary significantly from the scores of black children who were given the standard English version of test. Other studies dispute these findings. However, there appears to be enough data to suggest that children seem to do significantly better when they are assessed by those whom they see as most like themselves. In any event, this is an area that requires much more intensive and extensive study.

Finally, children's own worldviews, values, attitudes, and perceptions of their roles are likely to have direct and/or subtle effects on the assessment outcomes because evaluation processes invariably involve interactions among many different people. For example, black and Hispanic children's preference for dealing with people rather than things (Hillard, 1977; Carter & Segura, 1979; Grossman, 1984) may influence how these children respond to test items. The deferential attitude toward adults and authority figures held by Asian, black, and Hispanic children could have a significant impact on how these young people relate to the assessor (Hillard, 1977; Carter & Segura, 1979; Hsu, 1981). Changes in the assessor's perception of minority cultures may in turn affect the evaluation results and their interpretations as well as how they are used to make educational decisions.

Educators need to keep in mind that the primary purpose of psychoeducational assessment is to gather information that can be used to make the most appropriate decisions for the child's educational development. This process goes beyond obtaining quantitative scores on a variety of standardized devices that are incapable of providing insights into the child's problems, needs, aspirations, and other constraints in his or her life. The test data give us limited information about certain aspects of the child. Interpretation of test scores should be enriched with an understanding of the complex sociocultural milieu in which the child has been reared and now lives. On the basis of the author's own involvement in the psychoeducational assessment of minority children, the experience of having lived in both the mainstream and the child's own culture adds immensely to understanding him or her. Yet the insights one derives from such experiences are neither quantifiable nor describable in precise empirical language. Perhaps literary depictions of other cultures can give educators a sense of what it feels like to live in two or more cultures at the same time.

The importance of learning about the more technical aspects of the assessment process should not be minimized. Indeed, school psychologists, counselors, administrators, social workers, school nurses, classroom teachers, and other subject matter specialists must be competent in their own fields of specialization and appropriate professional "crafts." But they should also be required to do ethnographic, observer-participant studies of other cultural groups found in their communities. Psychoeducational assessment without the experiential ingredient can become a mechanical means of classifying students according to predetermined categories from which children, particularly the culturally different, may never escape.

Torrance (1982) provides two categories of "solutions" related to psychoeducational assessment of children (pp. 485–486). One consists of the first-order solutions and the other includes the second-order solutions. First-order solutions, also called the more and better of the same solutions, involve such changes as reducing the teacher-pupil ratio and providing smaller classes, more teaching aides, and paraprofessionals. Second-order solutions involve working collaboratively with principals, teachers, other school personnel, children, parents, community agencies, and special consultants to bring about genuine alterations in the system. Torrance points out that second-order solutions, rather than the more and better of the same, are more effective in dealing with the special needs and problems of the culturally different. The creative use of ethnic, cultural, and other special resources in the community is essential in making second-order changes truly effective.

In principle, what needs to be done to make the assessment process nondiscriminatory and educationally enriching is no different from what we have to do to make our culturally diverse classroom and schools more effective and humane.

CASE STUDIES

The following Bill of Rights, which originally appeared in an Ann Landers column, represents one child's reactions to the various ways in which he or she is viewed and treated by adults. For the sake of discussion, assume that these views are held by most children. Read each of the rights and discuss the suggested questions.

ONE KID'S OWN BILL OF RIGHTS

Dear Ann Landers: Us kids have rights, too. Too few adults are willing to recognize this fact. I hope you will print the Bill of Rights for Kids so every parent who reads your column can see it. It's time we were treated like people.

1. I have the right to be my own judge and take the responsibility for my own actions.
2. I have the right to offer no reasons or excuses to justify my behavior.
3. I have the right to decide if I am obligated to report on other people's behavior.
4. I have the right to change my mind.
5. I have the right to make mistakes and be responsible for them.
6. I have the right to pick my own friends.
7. I have the right to say, "I don't know."
8. I have the right to be independent of the good will of others before coping with them.
9. I have the right to say, "I don't understand."
10. I have the right to say, "I don't care."

Source: Permission granted by Ann Landers and Creators Syndicate.

QUESTIONS

1. The 10 rights may be seen as children's reactions to certain adult attitudes about children. Discuss the types of adult views of and behaviors toward children to which you are inclined to attribute each of the rights. Discuss your rationale.
2. Discuss your reasons for agreeing or disagreeing with each of the 10 rights.
3. Do the rights as a whole represent a particular concept of childhood? If not, do they provide some hints for formulating a concept of childhood that may be most sound and appropriate for democratic education?

4. If you accept the 10 rights, what implications do they have for teachers and other educators?

•   •   •

The report that follows was given by an actual fourth-grade teacher. Comments regarding the outcome of this situation are given after the discussion questions.

ABOUT DANA

When Dana entered my fourth-grade class, the principal gave me a bulging cumulative folder and much information about Dana's previous undesirable behavior and nonlearning experiences. He had been retained in the third grade and had run away from school on frequent occasions. He had a severe speech problem; he stuttered so badly that he was most difficult to understand. As expected, reading was a problem but arithmetic was average.

It was difficult at the beginning because the children didn't accept him and they were tempted to mimic him. [However, in a number of class activities he showed considerable abilities.]

Source: From "Identifying and Capitalizing on the Strengths of Culturally Different Children" by E. P. Torrance. In C. R. Reynolds & T. B. Gutkin (Eds.) *The Handbook of School Psychology* (p. 487). Copyright © 1982 by John Wiley & Sons, Inc. Reprinted by permission of John Wiley & Sons, Inc.

QUESTIONS

1. If you were Dana's teacher, what procedure would you follow in assessing Dana's needs? What are the pros and cons in receiving the child's cumulative folder and other reports about the child's behavioral and learning difficulties?
2. If your observation or estimate of Dana did not agree with what is in his cumulative folder or what other teachers said about him, how would you use (or not use) the latter sources in assessing Dana and making educational decisions about him?
3. What are some second-order solutions you might try?

OUTCOME

Dana's teacher did not push the reading skills and let him enter the discussion group in reading at his own choice. The teacher talked the principal out of requiring extra help in addition to the speech therapist, who was a kind man who had a good relationship with Dana.

The teacher discovered Dana had a talent for art during a hand puppet show. He later became "art director" for the reading group and also assumed the position of "art consultant" for the classroom. More self-confident now, Dana gave many new ideas for the class. His attendance was perfect and he worked hard in every subject. Dana moved to another school before the end of the school year and was expelled from the school for having a behavior problem (Torrance, 1982, p. 487). What do you think are some possible reasons for this unfortunate ending to Dana's school experience?

*   *   *

JENNIFER IN LA VICTORIA

[La Victoria] consists of no more than 17,000 people with an average family income of less than $17,000, and a lower net household income for Chicanos than for non-Chicanos. Over 40% of La Victoria residents were Chicanos who had resided in the Southwest for over five generations. . . . The majority spoke only English in their family. Isolated Spanish words accented family conversations but no detection of an accent was heard which indicated that Spanish was not a frequent medium among family members. . . .

A major concern within the Chicano community in La Victoria was the lack of quality education for Chicano youth evidenced by the consistently high dropout rates. Of Chicanos between the ages 16-25, at least 33% had not completed high school. . . .

In La Victoria, no single motive could be cited for leaving school nor is there a single model of a student dropout. Parents who both worked in the school as nurses, secretaries, and teachers' assistants and who lived in the community concluded that tracking of students was one of the worst problems and one that began in the elementary school. The tracking system ostensibly followed the students throughout their schooling years. [According to one teacher, everything is geared towards the mainstream culture.] . . .

[Jennifer consciously decided to] leave La Victoria High School when she could not keep up with her classes in the tenth grade. She tells,

> As I got to be a sophomore they [classes] got to be boring. The classes were harder, and like in Geometry, I kept telling the teacher that I didn't understand, but he didn't try to slow down, so then I just gave up. He kept telling me to keep up but I needed more help. I didn't want to put up with anything like pressure in classes. I was flunking the classes because I didn't go. I would go to school, but I wouldn't go to class. I would just ditch.

Jennifer . . . experienced a vague disturbing boredom in the classroom. Jennifer, like her brother, Bob, had always been placed in accelerated or advanced classes. In Jennifer's transition from junior high school she became interested in her social life. Her boredom in school and new interest in boys led Jennifer to become pregnant.

Jennifer felt self-conscious about continuing in the high school program although the school did have a program for pregnant girls and teenage mothers. Jennifer's mother did not pressure her to stay in school but she told her . . . that if she did not attend school, she had to get a job especially now that she had a child to support.

Source: Reproduced by permission of the American Anthropological Association from ANTHROPOLOGY & EDUCATION QUARTERLY 19:4, 1988. Not for further reproduction.

QUESTIONS

1. How would you go about identifying Jennifer's problems and needs? How helpful do you think some of the standardized instruments (tests) would be in making educational plans for Jennifer?
2. What do you think are some key conditions that led to Jennifer's decision to leave school?
3. What recommendation(s) would you make to Jennifer's mother? Discuss your rationale. Should Jennifer be allowed to leave school and find a job? How about having Jennifer enroll in the program for pregnant girls and teenage parents? Would the school district's alternative school be more appropriate for Jennifer? One student in the alternative school made the following comment about the school: "The teachers tell you what you have to do there . . . and they help you. The teachers in the regular school talk to the whole class. The classes are also smaller in the alternative school and I guess that's how the teachers can help you a lot" (Delgado-Gaitan, 1988, p. 369).
4. Can you think of some programs the La Victoria High School can introduce to make the school experiences more culturally relevant to its students?

OUTCOME

Jennifer decided to go to the alternative school, where the barriers to her learning were reduced. The following is a brief description of the alternative high school (AHS) in La Victoria:

The classroom usually provided a casual and relaxed environment for the student in the AHS. The halls were lined with bulletin boards announcing employment, dances, and concerts in the neighboring cities. The language arts classroom, for example, had seven round tables, newspapers, and student compositions scattered all over; a couple of soda cans sat on top of the teachers' desk and a can of hair spray on top of a girl's desk. An Aztec Calendar with 20 days drawn up, hung on a large board. On the blackboard a few written statements appeared as story starters using local vernacular, for example, "Yesterday was a real drag . . . ," which the teacher used as a way to open up dialogue during the first part of class as she walked around the room. Although this was a language arts class, the teacher explained the need for using the reading and writing tools to learn about science, history, and other subjects. Thus, students brought their books from other classes which lay open on various desks. . . .

In La Victoria, the Alternative High School existed to accommodate students who could not succeed socially or academically in the [La Victoria High School]. . . . Students were able to work the necessary hours to help their family while completing their requirements to graduate. They could work at their own pace without the fear of failure, and they could work faster with the appropriate teacher support. . . . Social and academic competition became manageable because it was not the force governing the school. Rather, the school was based on caring, individualized instruction, and alternative academic and skill training programs.

REFERENCES

Boulding, E. (1979). *Children's rights and the wheel of life*. New Brunswick, NJ: Transaction Books.

Bruner, J. (1987). The transactional self. In J. Bruner & H. Haste (Eds.), *Making sense* (pp. 81–96). New York: Methuen.

Bruner, J., & Haste, H. (1987). Introduction. In J. Bruner & H. Haste (Eds.), *Making sense* (pp. 1–25). New York: Methuen.

Carter, T. P., & Segura, R. D. (1979). *Mexican Americans in school: A decade of change*. New York: College Entrance Board.

Clark, L. A. (1985). A consolidated version of the MMPI in Japan. In J. N. Butcher & C. P. Spielberger (Eds.), *Issues in personality assessment*. Hillsdale, NJ: Lawrence Erlbaum Associates.

Cleverley, J., & Phillips, D. C. (1986). *Visions of childhood: Influential models from Locke to Spock*. New York: Teachers College Press. This book deals with how various conceptions or paradigms of childhood have influenced "the way humans have understood, cared for, and educated their young" (p. 141).

Damon, W. (1981). Exploring children's social cognition on two fronts. In J. H. Flavell & L. Ross (Eds.), *Social cognitive development* (pp. 162–163). Cambridge: Cambridge University Press.

Damon, W. (1983). *Social and personality development: Infancy through adolescence*. New York: Norton.

Delgado-Gaitan, C. (1988). The value of conformity: Learning to stay in school. *Anthropology and Education Quarterly, 19*(4), 354–381.

Edwards, C. P., & Ramsey, P. G. (1986). *Promoting social and moral development in young children*. New York: Teachers College Press.

Egan, K. (1979). *Educational development*. New York: Oxford University Press.

Fischer, K. W. (1980). A theory of cognitive development: The control and construction of hierarchies of skills. *Psychological Review, 87,* 473-531.

Gilligan, C. (1982). *In a different voice: Psychological theory and women's development.* Cambridge: Harvard University Press.

Gilligan, C., Lyons, N. P., & Hanmer, T. J. (1990). *Making connections: The relational worlds of adolescent girls at Emma Willard School.* Cambridge: Harvard University Press.

Goodman, M. E. (1970). *The culture of childhood: Child's-eye views of society and culture.* New York: Teachers College Press.

Grossman, H. (1984). *Educating Hispanic students: Cultural implications for instruction, classroom management, counseling and assessment.* Springfield, IL: Charles Thomas.

Harrington, C. (1979). *Psychological anthropology and education.* New York: AMS Press.

Haste, H. (1987). Growing into rules. In J. Bruner & H. Haste (Eds.), *Making sense* (pp. 163–195). New York: Methuen.

Hillard, A. G. (1977). Intellectual strengths of minority children. In D. E. Cross, G. C. Baker, & L. J. Stiles (Eds.), *Teaching in a multicultural society: Perspectives and professional strategies* (pp. 97–120). New York: The Free Press. This chapter discusses ways in which cultural factors influence several key aspects of the process of assessing minority children's intellectual abilities. It also examines how biases against minority cultures can lead to unfair and erroneous placement of children.

Hsu, F. L. (Ed.). (1972). *Psychological anthropology.* Cambridge, MA: Schenkman.

Hsu, F. L. (1981). *Americans and Chinese* (3rd ed.). Honolulu: University of Hawaii Press.

Kegan, J. (1984). *The nature of the child.* New York: Basic Books.

Kimball, S. T. (1974). Cultural influences shaping the role of the child. In S. T. Kimball (Ed.), *Culture and the educative process* (pp. 85–98). New York: Teachers College Press.

Koh, S., Sakauye, K., Koh, T. H., & Liu, W. T. (1986). *Mental health and stress in Asian-American elderly.* Chicago: University of Illinois, Pacific and Asian American Mental Health Research Center.

Koh, T. (1988, June). *Cognitive and affective adaptation of Korean-American school children: Service and research priorities.* Paper presented at the invitational conference on Asian-American research priorities funded by the Pacific and Asian American Mental Research Center and held at the University of Illinois—Chicago.

Kohlberg, L. (1971). Stages of moral development as a basis for moral education. In C. M. Beck, B. S. Crittenden, & E. V. Sullivan (Eds.), *Moral education: Interdisciplinary approaches.* Toronto: University of Toronto Press.

Kohlberg, L. (1984). *Essays on moral development: The psychology of moral development* (Vol. 2). New York: Harper & Row.

Kurth-Schai, R. (1985). *Reflections from the hearts and minds of children: A Delphi study of children's personal, global, and spiritual images of the future.* Unpublished doctoral dissertation. University of Minnesota, Minneapolis.

Levine, D. U., & Havighurst, R. (1989). *Society and education.* Boston: Allyn & Bacon.

Lutey, C., & Copeland, E. P. (1982). Cognitive assessment of the school-age child. In C. R. Reynolds & T. B. Gutkin (Eds.), *The handbook of school psychology* (pp. 121–155). New York: John Wiley & Sons. This is a helpful discussion of the goals

of assessment, evaluations of tests, aspects of the testing process, and interpretation of test results in schoolchildren's cognitive assessment.

Mead, M. (1970). *Culture and commitment*. New York: Doubleday.

Mercer, J. R., & Ysseldyke, J. (1977). Designing diagnostic-intervention programs. In
T. Oakland (Ed.), *Psychological and educational assessment of minority children* (pp.
70–90). New York: Bruner/Mazel.

Montagu, A. (1981). *Growing young*. New York: McGraw-Hill.

Moscovici, S. (1984). The phenomenon of social representations. In R. Farr & S.
Moscovici (Eds.), *Social representations*. Cambridge: Cambridge University Press.

Packard, V. (1983). *Our endangered children*. Boston: Little, Brown & Co.

Pai, Y., & Pemberton, D. (1987). *Findings on Korean-American early adolescents and adolescents*. Kansas City, MO: School of Education, University of Missouri—Kansas
City.

Polakow, V. (1992). *The erosion of childhood*. Chicago: The University of Chicago Press.

Piaget, J. (1963). *The psychology of intelligence*. Paterson, NJ: Littlefield, Adams.

Piaget, J., & Inhelder, B. (1969). *The psychology of the child* (H. Weaver, Trans.). New
York: Basic Books. (Original work published 1966).

Postman, N. (1981). *The disappearance of childhood*. New York: Delacorte Press.

Search Institute. (1984). *Young adolescents and their parents: Project report*. Minneapolis,
MN: Author. More than 80% of this study population consists of white middle-
and upper-middle-class children.

Shellenberger, S. (1982). Presentation and interpretation of psychological data in educational setting. In C. P. Reynolds & T. B. Gutkin (Eds.), *The handbook of school
psychology* (pp. 51–81). New York: John Wiley & Sons. This is a technical discussion of a wide variety of issues related to gathering, interpreting, and reporting
psychological evaluation data for the purpose of making educational recommendations.

Song, W. Z. (1984). A preliminary study of the character traits of the Chinese. In W. S.
Tseng & D. Y. H. Wu (Eds.), *Chinese culture and mental health*. New York: Academic Press.

Spindler, G. D. (Ed.). (1978). *The making of psychological anthropology*. Berkeley: University of California Press.

Suransky, V. P. (1982). *The erosion of childhood*. Chicago: University of Chicago Press.

Tajfel, H. (1981). *Human groups and social categories*. Cambridge: Cambridge University
Press.

Torrance, E. P. (1982). Identifying and capitalizing on the strengths of culturally different children. In C. R. Reynolds & T. B. Gutkin (Eds.), *The handbook of school
psychology* (pp. 481–500). New York: John Wiley & Sons. Implications of the cultural characteristics of the assessor, the assessed, and the assessment instrument
and process, and the context of assessment are discussed.

Triandis, H. C., & Heron, A. (Eds.). (1981). *Handbook of cross cultural psychology* (Vols.
1–6). Boston: Allyn & Bacon.

Williams, J., & Giles, H. (1978). The changing status of women in society: An intergroup perspective. In H. Tajfel (Ed.), *Differentiation between social groups*. New
York: Academic Press.

Zelizer, V. A. (1985). *Pricing the priceless child*. New York: Basic Books.

7

Culture and the
Learning Process

Today numerous psychological theories explain how human beings and other animals such as monkeys, mice, and even flatworms learn. Educationally and in the context of schooling, these theories may be classified into three broad types or models: (1) guided learning, (2) discovery learning, and (3) learning as information processing (Spindler & Spindler, 1987, pp. 64–66).

Guided learning begins by breaking down a learning objective into a set of specific skills or bodies of information. By mastering each of the components according to a carefully prearranged sequence, the learner is able to achieve the objective. The guided learning model is frequently called behavioristic because the component skills and knowledge must be stated in behavioral terms. This view of learning has been advanced by B. F. Skinner, Robert Gagne, and David Ausubel in somewhat varied ways.

Although not new in concept, the modern version of *discovery learning* was formulated by Jerome Bruner. According to Bruner (1966), learning is the process of discovering regularity and relatedness by ordering and organizing one's experiences for solving problems. In other words, the more one tries to work out solutions to problems and independently figure things out, the more one gains new insights. Hence, greater emphasis is placed on the process of discovering than on mastering knowledge and skills.

As a model, *learning as information processing* is based on the view that a goal-oriented problem-solving process helps the learner cope with simplified models of real problems, as with a computer (Simon, 1979). The working of the computer is viewed as similar to the ways in which children organize and structure newly acquired knowledge and skills. The data that the child has interpreted and organized by using such skills as attention, encoding, and comparing with other information are either immediately used to solve problems or stored in long-term memory. From this perspective, the process of learning a subject cannot be analyzed into individual components, because the learner has to understand the interrelationships among different parts and may have to revise what has been learned earlier. Hence, proponents of the learning as information processing model do not focus on the outcomes of instruction. Rather, they are more concerned with cultivating skills that will enable them to (1) represent their problems schematically and (2) identify relations among the problem elements and recombine them into new patterns (Kneller, 1984).

CULTURAL CONDITIONS FOR LEARNING

The preceding discussion may give the impression that these types of learning represent three distinct and perhaps incompatible processes; on the contrary, these models do have certain overlapping aspects. Thus, some guided learning may be necessary in helping children raise appropriate questions for discovery learning, and learning as information processing may require that the learner discover new relationships among things he or she already knows. As an illustration, the child may see that 2 x 3 = 6 is another way of stating 2 + 2 + 2 = 6. However, learning is not purely a psychological phenomenon, because it almost always takes place in some social and cultural setting. Many complex physical as well as cultural factors affect how people learn. Accordingly, regardless of one's own conception of learning, any attempt to understand the learning process must deal with questions about the relationships among the learner, the teacher, the context, and the purposes for learning certain knowledge or skills. These queries inevitably lead to questions regarding the role of social relationships among a wide range of individuals related to the learning environment.

In their article on primate learning and educational thought and policy, Marion Lundy Dobbert and Betty Cooke (1987) suggest that four kinds of factors affect the learning process (pp. 106–113). They are (1) observation and modeling, (2) social experience, (3) social conflict, and (4) play. In observation and modeling, the individual learns by "watching" others doing things and attempting to repeat them. This process usually occurs within a group that provides a supportive climate, allowing the learner to try things out. Learning through observation and modeling is not an act the learner does alone. On the contrary, a supportive and perhaps affectionate social relationship between the individual and others is an important condition.

Learning in a formal or informal educational setting involves other people. Hence, the learner's ability to maintain complex relationships with others influences how he or she learns. Such an ability, as well as the learner's own sense of personal identity and roles, is developed through social experiences of associating with others. As social experience is an essential aspect of learning, so is social conflict. Through encounters with interpersonal conflicts, an individual may learn to work cooperatively with others to resolve various problems stemming from aggression, competition, and struggle for power.

For young children, play is neither a trivial nor a useless activity because it contains most of the physical, cognitive, and behavioral elements of adult life. By experimenting with varied combinations of these elements in their play, children learn to solve problems, work cooperatively with others, cope with conflict and competition, and maintain complex social relationships. Through play, they also learn their own culture. Not surprisingly, we can often find out about the norms of another culture by observing the rules according to which children communicate, behave, and learn in their play. For example, "playing house" involves trying out different roles, role reversals, punishing bad behaviors, rewarding good deeds, and the various means of dealing with conflicting interests. For this reason, "the more children play freely, the more experience they build up and the more likely they are to be able to solve complex problems in later life" (Dobbert & Cooke, 1987, p. 108).

Dobbert and Cooke's discussion of observation and modeling, social experience, social conflict, and play gives us useful insight into the roles these factors play in learning. But whether one agrees with Dobbert and Cooke's classification of learning mechanisms or not, their view does point out a fundamental aspect of the learning process. Although there are psychological conditions for learning, their significance cannot be known unless we understand what meanings they carry in different cultural contexts. For example, psychology tells us that rewarding is reinforcing and punishing leads to avoidance behavior. But it cannot tell us whether or not giving a hug to a person is equally rewarding in all cultures. Nor can it inform us about how punitive the act of yelling at a person is in one culture as opposed to another, because specific acts or events have no inherent meaning unless seen from a particular cultural perspective.

Like all human behavior, learning must be viewed in the context of the total sociocultural setting in which it takes place. The specific values, attitudes, norms of behavior, ways of thinking, styles of communication, and modes of interpersonal relationships the larger society expects from its young become the bases of formulating the school's policies, procedures, curriculum, and pedagogy. These norms of the dominant society and the changing conceptions of childhood are the cultural factors that influence how and what people learn.

In a society as diverse as the United States, students come to school with many distinct cultural backgrounds. The ways in which these young people think, interact, and communicate with others, as well as their value priorities, often clash with those of the school and its personnel. These cultural differences or discontinuities often become a source of misunderstanding and conflicts. These unfortunate consequences of cultural differences may in turn lead to inappropriate educational evaluation of and planning for culturally different young people. For this reason, the remainder of this chapter will (1) discuss the relationship between social structure, communication styles, and the teaching-learning processes and (2) examine cross-cultural implications for practitioners.

SOCIAL STRUCTURE, COMMUNICATION STYLES, AND THE TEACHING-LEARNING PROCESSES

The concept of social structure can be defined in many different ways. However, for the purpose of our discussion, the school's social structure will be seen as that complex of formal and informal role relationships that exist among students, teachers, counselors, administrators, and other school personnel. Integral to this structure are the school's academic, social, and behavioral expectations. The social structure of the school functions as an official agent of the dominant society. It defines and rewards culturally approved values, skills, and attitudes; punishes deviance; and provides opportunities for the young to learn various adult roles (Sieber & Gordon, 1981). However, the learner must function not only within the social structure of the school but also within that of his or her own family and community.

For most white middle-class children, the social structures of the school and their families share essentially the same characteristics. However, most minority children will find the school's social structure to be radically different from that of their family or ethnic community. Consequently, to many minority children, going to school means having to function according to two divergent social structures with fundamentally different sets of rules. Hence, the effectiveness with which the child can function and learn in school depends on the degree of discontinuity between the school and the family environment. The greater the differences between the norms of the school and the culture of the child's family, the more difficulties he or she is likely to encounter in learning. For example, in general, white middle-class children are more likely to interact with adult members of their family in a way very similar to the manner in which they relate to teachers and other adults in school. However, minority children who have been reared to be docile and conforming to grown-ups' demands may find it difficult to meet the school's expectation that good students be more assertive in exchanging their views with other students and the teacher.

According to a study of Native American and non-Native American youngsters' classroom participation patterns (Philips, 1972), Native American children tended to become involved more effectively in classroom activities that did not require a great deal of teacher control. On the other hand, non-Native American middle-class children participated more effectively in typical classroom activities. The Native American children's participation patterns appear to be a result of growing up in a cultural environment in which peer relationships were more important than the hierarchical relationship between adults and children. However, the non-Native American children's patterns of classroom participation seem to be attributable to growing up with role-differentiated relationships between children and their elders. Other studies of minority youth not only support these findings but also suggest that the learning failures of Native Americans (Erickson & Mohatt, 1988), blacks (Kochman, 1972), and Hawaiian Americans (Au, 1980) are attributable to differences in the participation structures of these ethnic communities and their schools. These studies amply illustrate the kinds of difficulties minority students may encounter when they move from the social structure of their own ethnic communities to that of the school.

Frequently, a child unable to perform according to school norms receives poor evaluations and is unfairly labeled, a result not only of academic performance but also of his or her interactional patterns (Rist, 1985). Unfair labeling often contributes to the teacher's minimal academic expectations from minority students. These lower expectations become self-fulfilling prophecies when the labeling is accepted by students. White middle-class children, too, may be affected adversely by unfair labeling practices and self-fulfilling prophecies. One of the crucial problems of cultural discontinuities between the school and minority students is that these differences "trigger implicit evaluations which in intricate ways reinforce larger institutional patterns of unequal treatment" (Collins, 1988, p. 309).

To minimize, if not eliminate, unequal treatment of schoolchildren and help them learn optimally, the school needs to take into account the negative impact of cultural discontinuities between the social structures of the school and ethnic communities in assessing the educability of the culturally different. In addition, the school can initially provide the kinds of learning environments to which minority children have been accustomed so that they can learn successfully. Following their successes in such supportive school conditions, the culturally different children can be guided to function equally well in a social structure that operates according to the norms of the mainstream culture.

Styles of Communication

Forging and maintaining appropriate relationships within a social structure is achieved through effective communication. In this sense, communication is neither a simple matter of transmitting a body of information to another person nor receiving messages from others. Rather, it is a process by which people try to influence one another by "interpreting one's own and others' actions, and . . . performing actions that will be interpreted" (Pearce & Kang, 1988, p. 25). Here, the term *actions* refers to both verbal and nonverbal behaviors. Certain principles or norms of interpreting other people's actions emerge when individuals act by adjusting themselves to the behavioral patterns of others (Carroll, 1981). Individuals who share these norms have certain expectations of behavior for each other. For example, in the United States, waving one's hand to another person in a particular manner is understood as "Good-bye," because most of us share a common set of criteria for interpreting this behavior. However, to persons from a different culture or social structure, such a behavior may carry an opposite meaning, such as "Please come here."

All individuals and groups have distinct communication modes that include style of speech, varied forms of language, and such nonverbal behaviors as postures and gestures. However, which mode or modes of communication one uses in a given situation depends on the nature of the social relationships that characterize a particular social structure or culture. That is, in some cultures social relationships are rigidly hierarchical, whereas in others they are more or less egalitarian. When social relationships are strictly hierarchical, the flow of communication tends to move in one direction, from the top to the bottom. Within such a social structure, individuals are required to use highly formal and ritualized language forms and complex codes of behavior and demeanors appropriate for persons in various positions and status. For example, in Japan, only the emperor is permitted to use the word *ching* in referring to himself. Further, children are required to behave according to correct forms of gestures and language that are consonant with the hierarchical positions of their elders. On the other hand, in a society like the United States, social relationships are egalitarian and people view others more or less as their equals. Accordingly, the language used in communication tends to be less formal and, in general, frequent exchanges of opinions occur among individuals regardless of their status. Moreover, fewer formal codes of behavior relate to people's positions.

As might be expected, the "official" mode of communication in American schools is based on the norms of the mainstream culture (Gay, 1978; Hsu, 1982; Ramirez & Castaneda, 1974; Sue, 1981). People communicate through direct expression and reciprocal exchanges of thoughts and feelings while maintaining direct eye contact, and such exchanges are expected to be carried on serially, that is, each person taking turns in talking and listening. Further, children are expected to think analytically, objectively, and in a detail-specific way so that they can clearly distinguish facts from their feelings about them. This means our schoolchildren are evaluated on the basis of the proficiency with which their thoughts can be clearly and precisely expressed in standard English. However, those who use a nonstandard dialect and gestures that differ from those of the dominant group are likely to be judged poorly and treated unequally. The following discussion of the communication styles of Asian Americans, Black Americans, Hispanic Americans, and Native Americans may help us see how these different modes of communication may help or hinder the educational development of culturally different students in our schools.

A danger in describing characteristics of any one group of people is overgeneralization. In the strict sense, findings of an ethnographic study of a group should apply only to that group. Yet, as Heath (1986) aptly points out, "the public at large uses inclusive labels for groups of people: Chicanos, Native Americans, Indo-Chinese, Asians, Blacks, Hispanics, etc." (p. 153). Little attention is paid to variations of characteristics based on people's age, gender, length of stay in the country, educational levels, socioeconomic status, and regional locations, as well as their religious affiliations. For the sake of an accurate understanding of another ethnic group, subdivisions of the group ought to be studied separately. Notwithstanding the wide variations found within a racial or ethnic group, some broad characteristics are more or less ascribable to groups as a whole. For example, the deferential attitude young people have toward their elders may be common to all Asian Americans as well as to Hispanic and Native American groups. What is important in this discussion is that educators should recognize the legitimacy of divergent styles of communication, thinking, and learning so that children who exhibit non-mainstream patterns are not judged as possessing pathological conditions. As stressed in early chapters, this is not to suggest that every communication style is as functional as every other style, for some modes may be more effective than others for certain purposes. Thus, rather than attempting to have all learners use only the mainstream style of communication, educators ought to help each child use the mode most appropriate for achieving his or her educational goals.

Asian Americans

Cultural values and worldviews have significant influence on behaviors and communication styles. Thus, the fact that Asian Americans come from a strongly family-centered tradition with a rigidly hierarchical interpersonal relationship has a strong impact on their communication style (Hsu, 1982; Sue, 1981; Suzuki, 1980). Within the hierarchical social structure of Asian-American communities the roles of individuals are defined according to age, sex, and status. Further, individuals are expected to deal with problems indirectly so as not to offend others. Docility, respect for authority, and restraining of strong feelings are encouraged, while direct expression of feelings or thoughts is strongly discouraged. Because communication flows from higher to lower positions in the hierarchy, it is considered inappropriate for children to participate in adult conversation or decision making. Accordingly, elders frown upon children asking "why" questions.

Clearly, radical differences exist between these traits of Asian Americans and the school's emphasis on assertiveness, informal social relationships, spontaneity, direct communication, and active involvement in various activities. Because of these differences Asian Americans are frequently judged as less autonomous, less assertive, more conforming, less expressive, and hence "inscrutable." Although these are general and stereotypic descriptions of Asian Americans, these characteristics do manifest themselves in the behaviors of Asian-American young people. For example, in general, Asian-American students are not likely to participate actively in classroom discussions, seek explanations or other forms of help from teachers, or become involved in open discussions about academic matters or personal problems. On the other hand, their deferential attitude toward teachers and willingness to conform to the rules of the school and the classroom may lead teachers to see them as either shy or "model students." This image often hides other underlying emotional, social, or even academic problems, which are usually disclosed to family members or intimate friends only.

African or Black Americans

Although Black Americans have a very strong oral/aural tradition of story-telling with an emphasis on stylish delivery, nonverbal behaviors are also considered important elements in their mode of communication. Elsie Smith (1981) points out that blacks are prone to spend much time unobtrusively observing people to see "where they are coming from." Moreover, they do not have to maintain direct eye contact while talking to each other. School personnel often interpret this behavior as an indication of disinterest, fear, or lack of self-confidence. Similar interpretations are given to this nonverbal behavior of Asian-American, Hispanic-American, and Native American children. In a cross-national comparison of black cultural forms in schools, Solomon (1988) found that blacks in U.S. schools use both Black English and standard English as a means of communication as well as a symbol of their identity (p. 256). Many black students respond to their teachers in standard English but communicate with their peers in Black English. Claudia Mitchell-Kernan (1985) is probably correct in reminding us that the use of Black English does "symbolize a spirit of liberation in the black community, and the separatist function of Black English has become more explicit" (p. 209). However, in the area of nonverbal behavior, teachers and counselors often interpret black youngsters' stylized sulking gestures and body movements as an expression of resistance and a challenge to the school authority. Not surprisingly, black students who display such a "bad attitude" are frequently denied opportunities for participating in special enrichment or honors programs (Solomon, 1988, p. 257). This is only one illustration of how differences in communication styles can result in unequal education because "attitude" is considered more important than academic achievement.

Hispanic Americans

The Hispanic-American category includes several different ethnic groups with many varied historical, linguistic, cultural, and even legal backgrounds.

However, studies suggest that the following general communication characteristics would apply to all of the groups in varying degrees (Carter & Segura, 1979; Heath, 1986; Levine & Havighurst, 1988; Ramirez & Castaneda, 1974).

In general, Hispanic children are socialized to observe and emulate adults, who do not usually give them specific instructions. Nor do children orally report what they are doing. As is the case with Asian Americans, communication flows from adults to children generally in the form of commands and demands. Children are expected to follow or conform to these commands or demands without questioning. The young rarely initiate social conversations with adults, who neither consider children as conversational partners nor accept them as active participants in decision making. In the area of thinking, Hispanic children are much more sensitive to the global or overall view of a situation or a concept than to its component parts. Moreover, because these young people are more concerned with social or interpersonal relationships and opinions of others than with impersonal facts, they tend to mix the cognitive with the affective aspects of their experience. Of course, whites also are interested in social and interpersonal relationships; however, in school children are encouraged to separate expressions of personal feelings from reports of factual information.

Not surprisingly, the school requires that students think objectively and analytically and express their ideas in a logical and detail-specific way. In addition, the young are expected to respond promptly to their teachers' questioning and to frequently express their thoughts and feelings in public. When Hispanic children are judged solely in terms of these school norms, they are likely to be seen as having little interest in education and as intellectually inferior to white middle-class children. A key point of this discussion is not to argue that either the way of the school or of Hispanic children should be discarded, because each has its own strengths and weaknesses. Much more important is the responsibility of educators to help these children learn to communicate effectively by using the most appropriate means of relating to others. This may be accomplished by having Hispanic children become involved in a new mode of communication by working through a carefully planned sequence of social and cognitive activities. But this requires that the teacher be able to appreciate the "lived" culture of the child.

Native Americans

The Native American group includes many different nations, each with a unique historical and cultural heritage. A dearth of research studies have reported the communication styles of these groups in relation to education. Hence, many of the characteristics of Native American communication style have to be gleaned from information about other aspects of Native American cultures and described in rather general terms. According to Edwin H.

Richardson's (1981) comparative study of Native American and mainstream norms, several Native American values have significant bearing on their communication style. The Native American emphasis on personal humility, respect for elders, learning through storytelling or legends, intuitiveness, preference for a low-key profile, concern for group harmony, having few and flexible rules, and simplifying problems would directly influence communication style. This tendency toward intuitiveness, learning through storytelling, simplification of problems, and preference for few and flexible rules may contribute to the global rather than analytic character of the Native American cognitive style. This inclination combined with concern for group harmony and desire to maintain a low-key profile would make Native Americans avoid public and direct expression of their feelings and thoughts to others.

A study of Sioux and Cherokee children (Dumont, 1985) revealed that Sioux children have an extremely complex system of communication, combining both verbal and nonverbal behaviors. They seem to communicate with each other excitedly and more frequently in the absence of an adult Sioux or white supervisor. Moreover, they tend to hesitate and restrain themselves when they are speaking to persons outside of their family or when they are singled out to read or answer questions. Not surprisingly, when these children perform a task at the teacher's request, they seem to be neither interested nor excited about their involvement. According to Dumont, the Cherokee believe that the ways in which people relate to each other verbally or nonverbally are a form of moral transaction (p. 364). Hence, how something is said is as important as what is said.

Like others, Native American children communicate with verbal and nonverbal behaviors, but their attention is also focused on actions and visual elements related to words. This implies that exercises that analyze meanings and sentence structure are likely to have very little meaning to Native American children. John (1985) reports that Navajo children may be attentive to the teacher's voice, but they are likely to watch his or her actions (p. 334). On the basis of what the mainstream society and the school consider the "normal" and proper mode of communication, we may considerably underestimate the Native American children's educability, intellectual ability, motivation, and interest in formal education. Such misjudgment is bound to hinder these children's educational development.

Styles and Genres of Language Uses

All people use both verbal and nonverbal behaviors to communicate. However, not all groups rely on written, spoken, and body language with equal emphasis. Even in the use of language, some use certain styles and forms more often than others. The frequency with which one style or form is used more frequently than another may be related to the purpose of the person's communicative act. On the other hand, the individual may simply be more accustomed to using one particular style or form because of his or her cultural background. Like individuals, groups, including schools, vary in their uses of language. Thus, major discrepancies between the linguistic styles of the school and those of culturally different students may contribute to the latter's serious academic as well as interpersonal difficulties.

Styles of Language Uses

In *The Five Clocks*, Martin Joos (1967) names five major styles of language: (1) the intimate style, (2) the casual style, (3) the consultative style, (4) the formal style, and (5) the frozen style. The *intimate style* is used by those who have especially close personal relationships—husbands and wives, boyfriends and girlfriends, and lovers. Thus, the intimate style contains jargons and private "codes" understandable only to the communicants. The *casual style* is used by individuals who share a close but not intimate personal relationship. These individuals use certain expressions understood only by "insiders." Telling "inside jokes" is a good example of the use of the casual style. The style often used by peers or acquaintances to convey specific information and instructions to accomplish a particular task is called the *consultative style*. In this style, the listener often becomes involved in the communication process by injecting such expressions of acknowledgment as "I see," "I understand," or "OK." Unlike the styles already mentioned, the *formal style* does not allow for listener participation, for it is the style most frequently used in prepared lectures and speeches. The *frozen style*, which is used solely for print, does not involve active interaction between the writer ("speaker") and the reader ("listener").

The styles commonly used in school tend to be more formal and frozen than intimate, casual, or even consultative. Many black, Hispanic, and Native American students are likely to find learning through the exclusive use of formal and frozen styles to be difficult because these styles do not permit meaningful interactions between students and their teachers. On the other hand, teachers who prefer to relate to their students through the intimate or the casual styles might find that Asian-American young people appear to be reticent or uncomfortable. Each of the five styles serves unique and special functions, but not all groups use them with equal emphasis. Thus, schools may be able to help their students learn more effectively by using a wider variety of styles, which are at once familiar to students and appropriate for certain instructional purposes. Indeed, there is no good reason to believe that only the formal and frozen styles are educationally sound and desirable.

Genres of Language Uses

In addition to the different styles of language uses, there are also divergent forms of language that are related to varied linguistic functions. According to Shirley Brice Heath (1986), *genres* are synonymous with forms, schemas, or molds of language uses that stand for "maps or plans for stretches of discourse" (pp. 166-167). Heath describes (1) label quests, (2) meaning quests, (3) recounts, (4) accounts, (5) eventcasts, and (6) stories as basic genres of uses of language (pp. 168–171). Each genre has its own set of rules, which are organized so that initial clues enable listeners to predict the nature of the coming discourse. For example, one would anticipate a joke from an opening phrase like "A Chinese, an Indian, and a Mexican . . . "; whereas "When I was your age . . . " would clearly suggest that a lecture about one's behavior might be coming.

As cultural groups differ in their uses of language styles, so do the range of genres and the extent to which certain genres are used by these groups and families vary. Similarly, schools use some oral and written genres more frequently than others. This suggests that the proficiency with which children can effectively use the genres valued highly by the school can profoundly influence their school success.

According to Heath, the *label quests* and the *meaning quests* are the two genres most frequently used in school learning activities. The remaining four genres are used by children as they integrate and expand the first two genres in their acquisition of language.

The language activities related to the *label quests* are asking questions about the names and the properties of objects, places, persons, and body parts. These questions generally begin with such words as *what, where,* and *who.* In school, students, particularly those in early primary grades, are asked to give names and properties of things found in their learning environment. When the *meaning quests* are used, children are asked to give meanings or interpretations of words, events, behaviors, pictures, and combinations thereof. Moreover, adults often explain their interpretations of children's own behaviors. Uses of the meaning quests are illustrated in the teacher's requests that students explain an author's intended meaning of his or her work or interpret the meanings of certain written passages. In school, teachers of reading, literature, and other humanities courses frequently rely on this pattern.

In the use of the genre called *recounts,* a person retells certain events or repeats information already known to the teller and the listener. A child may be asked to repeat a story read in a book or recount something that happened while playing with others. In a school setting, students may be asked to summarize a class discussion, a lecture, or a chapter they have just read. Proficient use of this genre is particularly important in doing well on tests that require accurate recounting of materials read, heard, or discussed. Studies of Chinese- and Mexican-American families by Heath (1986) reveal that recounts occur rarely in these groups (pp. 172, 173). Given the hierarchical nature of the parent-child relationship and the predominant communication styles of Black American, Native American, and Asian-American families, we might reasonably suspect that adults in these groups infrequently request recounts from their children.

Children telling their parents about what happened at school or at a party or a spouse explaining the details of an automobile accident are examples of the *accounts genre*. The use of the accounts genre is initiated by the teller for the purpose of conveying new information or reinterpretations of known events (e.g., an insurance adjuster's description of how the accident "really occurred") to the listener. Characteristic uses of the accounts genre in school occur in creative writing classes, show-and-tell sessions, and advanced classes that require students to interpret what they have learned on the basis of their personal experiences.

In *eventcasts*, the speaker gives a running description of an event in progress, as a media correspondent might explain what is going on at a senate hearing or a sportscaster might cover a Super Bowl game. The eventcasts genre consists of giving an account of future events. For example, making statements such as "After dinner, we'll go bowling" or "After I finish my homework, I'll go to the movies" are good illustrations of the use of this genre. Children as well as adults often use the eventcasts genre by talking aloud to themselves while they are engaged in play or other activities. These speech acts either describe what the speakers are doing or refer to something they will do after completing their current activity. Teachers provide eventcasts by explaining their semester plan in a particular course to students or by giving step-by-step instructions to those who are about to engage in a physical exercise activity in the gym.

Stories as a genre involves telling stories about certain facts, which are elaborated or exaggerated to make them interesting to the listener. Uses of the stories genre frequently involve the listener's imagination, as children often imagine when they listen to bedtime stories. In school, historical studies or science lessons are sometimes supplemented with historical fictions, docudramas, and science fiction tales to clarify and illustrate key points and infer certain ethical implications from them.

These six genres of language uses by no means exhaust all possible uses of language. However, they appear to be the patterns most frequently employed by middle-class families and the school in teaching children the uses of language (Heath, 1984). Heath explains that when a mainstream child is asked to "read" a book with only pictures, the child is asked to *label,* give *meanings* of events portrayed by the pictures, *recount* the story, and compare it with personal *accounts*. In art classes, children are requested to give an *eventcast* by explaining what they are doing or may do in the future. They are further asked to illustrate and clarify the important points of their work by providing *stories*.

Patterns of Language Uses and the School

The school, as well as other institutions in the larger society, requires the use of all six or more genres of language uses. Hence, much of our children's success in school and in their future workplaces depends largely upon the degree of proficiency with which they can use a wide range of these genres. However, not all cultural groups use the same range or kinds of genres with equal emphasis. Although the school as a whole values and utilizes a much larger repertoire of linguistic genres than individual families, the number of different patterns used in individual classrooms tends to be quite limited. For this reason, it is important for teachers to help children practice as many different patterns of language uses as possible, both within and outside of their classroom setting. By cooperating closely with families and ethnic communities, schools may be able to help children learn genres not commonly used in their own cultural groups. This can be accomplished through youth group activities, community service projects, and church programs, in conjunction with formal and informal school offerings. Heath (1986) is correct in pointing out that "it is the responsibility of the school to facilitate expanded language uses in English and other languages for students from all sociocultural and class backgrounds" (p. 179).

CONNECTING CULTURALLY WITH STUDENTS

> Come for a moment to the playground of the Franklin Elementary School in Oakland, where black girls like to chant their jump-roping numbers in Chinese. "See you mañana," one student shouts with a Vietnamese accent. "Ciao!" cries another, who has never been anywhere near Italy. And let it be noted that the boy who won the National Spelling Bee . . . was born in India . . . and speaks Tamil at home. . . . Graffiti sprayed in a nearby park send their obscure signals in Farsi. . . . The Los Angeles County court system now provides interpreters for eighty different languages from Albanian and Amharic to Turkish and Tongan. (Friedrich, 1985, p. 36)

This excerpt from Otto Friedrich's portrait of an elementary school clearly reflects the range of cultural diversity found in our schools today. It also reinforces the need for the contemporary American school to find effective means of dealing with a myriad of special needs and problems of children from divergent sociocultural and ethnic groups. Teachers and other school personnel need to know about and appreciate minority cultural patterns represented in school, but they should also be aware of the assumptions underlying their own worldviews, values, and attitudes.

Cultural Differences Between Mainstream Society and Shared-Function Groups

To work effectively with culturally different children, we must know about their cultural backgrounds and their historical heritages. In addition, we must be sensitive to the degree of conflict these children may be experiencing in relating to the cultures of the mainstream society and their own community. Some young people live in families that have been almost completely assimilated to the norms of the dominant culture; others come from traditional families in which their own ethnic ways are strictly practiced. Many from the latter environment often must deal with contradictory expectations; they literally have to live in two distinct worlds. To help culturally different students cope with disparate cultural forces in school and society, teachers and counselors must be cognizant of the cultures of the mainstream society and several ethnic groups in the United States. As a helpful guide, some of the basic characteristics of the mainstream and shared-function groups—Asian Americans, Black Americans, Hispanic Americans, and Native Americans—are listed in Table 7.1 and Table 7.2 in very broad terms.

Unfortunately, the characteristics listed in Table 7.1 are very broad generalizations that do not give us a picture of how such general traits are manifested in disparate cultural groups. Hence, intragroup distinctions are pro-

TABLE 7.1
Cultural Differences Between the Mainstream Society and Shared-Function Groups

	Mainstream Culture (Norms of the American School)	Shared-Function Groups
Worldview	Person-centered world See others as equals Informal human relationship	Human-relationship-centered world Hierarchical and formal human relationships
Values	Emphasis on individual rights Stress assertiveness and competitiveness	Emphasis on personal duties Respect for authority Group harmony and conformity
Learning	Through personal involvement Emphasis on active communication	Through docility Emphasis on observation and emulation
Identity	Based on personal competence Emphasis of self-motivation	Based on group membership Motivation derived from group
Cognitive Style	Objective, analytic, and detail-specific thinking Separating facts from feelings	Global approach to conceptual thinking Combining facts with feelings
Communication Style	Reciprocal (give-and-take) mode Direct expression and exchanges Serial exchanges (taking turns in speaking and listening)	Hierarchical (commands and demands) Indirect expression Spontaneous expression

TABLE 7.2
Intragroup Distinctions Among Asian-, Black-, Hispanic-, and Native American Groups

	Asian Americans	Black Americans	Hispanic Americans	Native Americans
Worldview	Hierarchical and formal human relationships with complex rules of behavior and language use	Focus on people and their activities rather than on things	Subjugation to nature Present-time orientation Time is to be enjoyed Obedience to will of God Sensitive to the opinions of authority figures	Mother Earth belongs to all Everything belongs to all people Life is to be enjoyed Few rules are best; be simple
Values	Emphasis on personal duties Respect for authority Value formal education Conformity to established role expectations	Concern for others Attach importance to creativity, freedom, and justice	Preference for conformity to status quo Humility Achievement defined in terms of interpersonal relationships Work for present needs Sharing	Group harmony Respect for nature Respect the elderly for their wisdom Sharing; all belong to the Great Spirit Accept others Be carefree
Learning	Docility: follow instructions Listen, observe, and emulate	Words and actions Responds to social rather than nonsocial or object stimuli	Use words and actions Use humor, narration, personal experience, and fantasy Cooperative work	Through storytelling and the use of legends Simplify problems Cooperative work

224

Identity	Group membership (status) Group-based motivation (e.g., "Get all A's for my family")	Position in a group Motivation derived from group	Membership in a group Group-derived motivation (work for and with a group)	Membership in a group Group-derived motivation (work for and with a group)
Cognitive Style	Global or overall approach to conceptual thinking Less emphasis on detail-specific thinking Combine the cognitive with the affective (facts with feelings)	General or overall approach to conceptual thinking Less emphasis on detail-specific thinking Combine the cognitive with the affective (facts with feelings)	Global and overall approach to conceptual thinking Combine the cognitive with affective (facts with feelings)	Global and overall approach to conceptual thinking Combine the cognitive with affective (facts with feelings)
Communication Style	Indirect expression Emphasis on discretion Restrain strong emotions Use of formal or ritualized language	Verbal and nonverbal behaviors Stylized speech and delivery Spontaneous expression	Verbal and nonverbal behaviors Spontaneous expression Emphasis on being a good listener	Verbal and nonverbal behaviors (not language dependent)

Note: Information was synthesized from Carter and Segura (1979); Gay (1978); Hsu (1982); John (1985); Levine and Havighurst (1988); Ramirez and Castaneda (1974); Richardson (1981); Ruiz (1981); Smith (1981); Solomon (1988); and Sue (1981).

vided in Table 7.2 so that a clearer understanding of individual groups can be had. However, the reader should be warned that even these distinctions are very general descriptions of complex beliefs, attitudes, values, and cognitive styles of various cultures. With this caveat in mind, we will now examine some of the major differences among Asian-American, Black American, Hispanic-American, and Native American groups.

As can be seen in Tables 7.1 and 7.2, the mainstream society as well as the school view the individual person as central to the world. Consequently, rights of the individual and asserting these rights occupy a crucial place in the mainstream culture. Since individuals see one another as equals in the person-centered world, relationships among individuals tend to be less formal. The codes of behavior and uses of language are not inclined to be complex. When each person is seen as having a central place in the society, people are encouraged to demand their rights and compete with each other for just rewards for their accomplishments. The same qualities are fostered among schoolchildren. They are encouraged to learn their social roles as well as academic subjects by becoming actively involved in classroom activities and schoolwide programs. For both children and adults, their identity is rooted in individual competence and actual achievements. Consonantly, the qualities of autonomy and self-reliance are valued by the larger society and its schools. It is not surprising that a lack of self-motivation is frequently seen as a main cause of the person's failure to achieve in his or her own field of endeavor.

In the area of cognitive styles, the young are taught to think objectively by separating facts from their personal feelings and experiences. Perhaps because the Western world places such importance on science and technology, a child's ability to solve a problem by breaking it down into minute component parts, or *atoms,* is given a very high premium in the school and society. The ways in which our schoolchildren are taught to plan a family trip in their social studies class is a good illustration of this approach to thinking and problem solving. In a project of this sort, students are required to plan their trip by calculating how many miles or hours they must drive each day to reach their destination within a specified period of time. They are also asked to figure out lodging places and how much money to spend on gasoline, food, entertainment, and other unexpected contingencies. Finally, in an egalitarian society, communication flows in both directions so that the young and the grown-ups can freely exchange ideas and opinions. Issues are usually clearly and directly addressed and their resolutions are to be given in an unambiguous manner.

Implications for Teachers

In the context of schooling in the United States, students are judged in terms of their willingness and ability to participate and compete in academic and nonacademic activities as well as their competence in thinking objectively and analytically. They are required to give detail-specific answers without mixing personal feelings with facts. Students are also expected to raise questions to and share their thoughts and feelings with teachers and counselors. The ability to communicate clearly and directly is another essential requisite to being judged a good student. Although the foregoing description of the school's expectations is general, children growing up in white middle-class families are less likely to experience conflicts between their family norms and those of the school.

Unlike the children of mainstream culture, young people from the shared-function groups must deal with at least two different sets of rules and codes of behavior. In general, members of the shared-function groups see the relationships among human beings as central to their world. These relationships are more or less hierarchical, and individuals tend to see each other in terms of the positions they occupy in the hierarchy. Whereas some groups define the rules of behavior and language usage very rigidly, others are more flexible in specifying their role expectations. In any event, the shared-function groups place a much greater emphasis on each person's duties and responsibilities than on rights and privileges. For example, the duties of parents are to nurture and guide their children by making wise decisions. The duties of children are to follow parental decisions without questioning.

Regarding values, respect for authority and concern for group harmony are promoted in the shared-function groups. Members generally express these two qualities by not challenging the decisions made by authority figures and by conforming to the established group norm. For this reason, young people from the shared-function groups are not likely to be vocal in school or to raise questions to teachers, counselors, and administrators. They tend to restrain themselves from having intimate or informal personal conversations or relationships with school personnel. Consonantly, many culturally different children learn by being docile and conforming. That is, they follow the instructions given by their elders and teachers without raising many questions; observation and emulation or "watch and do" characterize their learning style. These young people's hesitancy in sharing their thoughts and feelings with others and in public reflects the cultural norm that encourages discretion and humility. But more often than not, this attitude is viewed by school personnel as a sign of nonresponsiveness or being disinterested in school, or even as an intellectual deficit.

Members of the shared-function groups develop their self-identity not so much in terms of personal competence and achievements but more in relation to their positions in the family and community. In this context, the term *member* should not be understood as meaning an autonomous individual joining a group. Rather, self-identity is inextricably tied to the individual's position in a group. In a real sense, the individual is not only an integral part of his or her group; the group is an indispensable aspect of the individual. From this perspective, one who follows the group norm without questioning should not be viewed as an "outer-directed-person," for the group is an organic part of that person. *Outer* and *inner* are terms that reflect the assumptions underlying the Western concept of a person who is considered an entity separate from the group or nature. For those students whose identity is group-based, motivation to work or study hard comes not so much from the desire for self-improvement as from their concern for how their achievement may affect the group to which they belong. Even competition for high honors may be carried out for the sake of the group. This implies that school failure of culturally different children should not always be attributed to the lack of individual learners' self-motivation.

Of the many cultural differences already discussed, the variations in the cognitive styles of the mainstream society and the shared-function groups may most affect the performance of culturally different young people in the school. In contrast to the importance the school places on objective, analytic, and detail-specific thinking, children from shared-function groups are inclined to think globally about concepts, events, and other subject matter-related activities. In other words, they are more interested in getting an overall or general picture of the objects of their thinking than the minute details and their relationships. Consistently, their responses to queries that require specific, step-by-step answers tend to be rather general. This may be one of the reasons why many students from the shared-function groups encounter difficulties in conceptual analysis or reducing a complex problem into its minute constituent parts.

Communication in groups that emphasize hierarchical human relationships tends to move from higher to lower positions in the form of commands or demands. In such a communication mode, there is little giving and taking of ideas. Moreover, limits are often set as to what individuals in lower positions can say to persons occupying higher positions. For example, in some Asian languages, there are no expressions children can use to directly praise their parents because it is simply not appropriate for children to praise their elders. Although the directness with which people communicate with others varies greatly, members of the shared-function groups generally do not communicate as directly as individuals belonging to the mainstream culture. However, spontaneous and frequent exchanges are commonly practiced with peers in the shared-function groups. This practice radically differs from the implicit school requirement that the speaker must first be recognized by the teacher and that each person take turns speaking and listening. When seen from the school's perspective, spontaneous expression of thoughts by several students at the same time is undisciplined or disorderly conduct. This kind of judgment reinforces whatever negative images teachers and counselors may have about students from certain ethnic groups.

A primary purpose of the foregoing discussion is to point out that learning and behavioral difficulties may arise out of cultural differences. What is necessary for the school and the teacher is neither to dismiss the legitimacy of other cultures nor to encourage the culturally different to tenaciously stick to their own ways regardless of their own purposes or the context in which they must live and work. Insofar as minority children must function as members of the dominant and their own societies, they must acquire the skills necessary for functioning in both environments. Although limited space does not allow us to discuss how teachers and counselors could relate effectively to individuals from several distinct cultural groups, some general suggestions are possible. First, teachers should provide opportunities for the culturally different to display their special skills, talents, or achievements to others in the class so that they may gain group approval as well as self-confidence. One author recalls observing a third-grade teacher asking a non-English-speaking immigrant child to come up to the board to solve several difficult arithmetic problems the class had not yet studied. Her success at this task helped the child win many friends and placed her in an environment that enabled her to participate in many other classroom and school activities. Due to the teacher's sensitivity to the child's emotional and social needs, the child was able to learn both the English language and social skills to become an active and contributing member of her class and the school. What this episode illustrates is that whereas an enriching social environment helps a child to do well in school, social isolation becomes a serious barrier to a child's educational development. To many culturally different children, social isolation is one of the most painful and educationally damaging experiences. Having a teacher who establishes a close personal relationship through expression of approval and support and who uses personalized means of rewarding children's accomplishments is important to all learners. But these measures are particularly reassuring to minority children, who tend to have a sense of fear and uncertainty about mainstream teachers and students as well as themselves.

Students who come from cultures in which hierarchical human relationships, respect for authority, docility, and conformity are prized tend to experience difficulties in loosely structured learning situations. They need step-by-step instructions for carrying out a particular task. For this reason, teachers should be mindful of giving clear-cut explanations of what is to be done and how the work can be accomplished by providing specific instructions. As these students learn to do their work successfully, teachers may gradually relax their instruction-giving practice. In general, students from shared-function groups require a much more tightly structured or directive learning situation than their counterparts in the mainstream culture. We should keep in mind that providing a tightly structured learning situation is not the same as "having stricter disciplinary measures." Learning through modeling (imitating) can be an effective way for children to acquire the necessary skills and eventually develop their own unique ways. This approach is useful not only in performing arts but also in learning new languages and even in essay writing. Finally, having culturally different students in the classroom affords an excellent opportunity for mainstream students to learn about other cultures and about their own as different but legitimate ways of dealing with essentially similar human problems.

CASE STUDIES

Mr. Miller teaches seventh and eighth graders and Mr. Howard teaches fifth- and sixth-grade classes in a school for Cherokee children. Following are descriptions of their classes.

MR. MILLER'S CLASS

They have just finished their spelling. Sue: "Is it a miss if you got a capital where it's suppose to be a small letter?"

Mr. Miller: "Is it Alice's? [sic]"

"Yes."

"She'll probably get enough wrong anyway." Turning to Alice: "Now, we'll just have to correct that. You're old enough. . . . You've been making capital letters lately, Alice, and you're old enough to know not to do that." He becomes more stern, "Now, I'll give you a week to correct that. I want you to correct that by next week." . . .

"How many twelfths are there in a whole?"

Debra has been at the board for some time and is unable to do the problem.

Mr. Miller: "How many thirds in a whole?"

Silence.

"How many halves in a whole?" Since he is getting no response from the rapid-fire questions, he changes tactics. "Did she miss it?"

Bob, who is correcting her papers, murmurs, "Ya."

"Debra, now, how many halves are there in a whole?" She looks toward the board. "It isn't on the board—just imagine. If you divide something twelve equal times, how many parts are you going to have?

"Twelve." It is weak and can barely be heard. She now works the problem with Mr. Miller's help. All he was trying to get her to do initially was to take one away from eight.

Mr. Miller: "Let's try another one. Let's write those numbers large. That helps." She starts the problem and he continues, with each statement more intense and pressuring than the one before. "You have borrowed one whole number. The object is to get this numerator large enough to subtract. You are going to have to change this number . . . you've got to learn to borrow."

He gives her another problem. "Forget about those whole numbers, except you have to borrow from them. Then you will have it licked . . . you may add on this side if you want."

Debra has her hand poised at the board. She is figuring in her head, and her hand makes quick, intense gestures. Mr. Miller stares at her intently. . . .

Mr. Miller, irritated: "Wait a minute. Wait a minute." . . . He erases everything at the board and rewrites the same problem. "We must find the common denominator. What is it, Debra?"

"Twelve" explodes [Debra].

MR. HOWARD'S CLASS

The discussion is about building split-rail fences without nails. Mr. Howard asks John to demonstrate at the board. At first John is reluctant but goes up, shuffling along. He grabs the chalk, turns around, and smiles uneasily.

Problems cover the blackboard, and Kathyrn [sic] says in a stern tone. "Don't erase those problems." The class discusses it, and they decide the first one can be erased.

John begins, starts a triangular figure, erases it, and starts again. He draws some lines very quickly and adds, "Get something to tie the top and the end of the posts there." He goes back to his desk with an uneasy smile.

Kathyrn: "I wouldn't do it that way. You can do it this way." She goes to the board.

Mr. Howard: "Is that the way you would build yours, Harry?"

"Just like John's," Harry states quietly, and then reluctantly goes to the board. He is uneasy, starts several times, erases, and looks around the room with an embarrassed smile. He turns back to the board, shuffles a bit, and then starts to diagram.

Mr. Howard: "Show me an old way."

Harry: "Use nails." He smiles, and I am surprised by his shy humor. He does not know English very well and misses much of what goes on in the class.

John jumps up and draws another diagram. "I think that's the way."

Kathyrn: "I think I know," and she returns to the board.

John: "There's some near Townsend."

From his desk Harry adds, "I know," and returns to the board. All three work on the diagram.

Kathryn: "It looks like this at the top," and she tries to draw it.

Finally they get it, but it is only after a good deal of effort. Throughout the exercise the teacher stayed in the back of the room.

Source: Reprinted by permission of the publisher from Cazden, Courtney B., John, Vera P., & Hymes, Dell, *Functions of Language in the Classroom.* (New York: Teachers College Press, © 1972 by Teachers College, Columbia University. All rights reserved.), pp. 352–354, 362–363.

QUESTIONS

1. What styles and genres of language uses are found in the classes of Mr. Miller and Mr. Howard?
2. How would you characterize the interpersonal relationships among Mr. Miller, Mr. Howard, and their respective classes?
3. In what ways do you think the teacher-pupil relationships in these classes might have influenced the children's learning?
4. What can you infer about the two teachers' knowledge and use of the children's cultural background in their teaching?
5. If you were in Mr. Miller's place, what different approaches might you have tried? Why? Could Mr. Howard have taught differently? How and why?

• • •

SCHOOL CHANGE AND THE COMMUNITY

The school district was about to experience a series of major changes: desegregation, "back to basics," dramatic expansion of due process for students, increase in services for students with special needs, and so on. Generally, faculty and staff seemed very poorly prepared for these changes. Most of the administration had long histories in the school district, and many were close to retirement. These impending major changes precipitated the willingness of the "old guard" to listen to new ideas.

The school psychologist found an opportunity for systemic intervention in the midst of these changes when a group of Mexican-Americans, the Concerned Parents for Equal Education, presented the school board with 20 concerns for the education of their children. The superintendent was instructed by the school board to develop responses to the 20 concerns.

The school psychologist became involved when asked by the superintendent to develop a response to a question about the poor performance of Mexican-American children on academic achievement tests. The total written response was developed and given to the Concerned Parents for Equal Education. The response did not satisfy the committee and they returned to the board. The superintendent summoned his administrators together and asked for additional ideas for rephrasing or redeveloping the responses. Much consideration was given in developing the text of the response. However, the school psychologist suggested that a different approach to the problem might be advisable. He contended that trying to explain away the identified problems might only increase the frustration and anger of the Mexican-American parents. Furthermore, he believed that the parents were interested in being heard and understood. Moreover, parents wanted some voice in attempting to remediate the problems they knew existed in the school district. The psychologist suggested that the key problems be acknowledged. Even more important, he maintained that the parents' question should be interpreted not as a criticism of the district but rather as a genuine expression of concern about such vital issues as low achievement scores of Mexican-American students in special education.

Because the parents' committee included leaders of the Mexican-American community, the school psychologist recommended not writing any more responses. Instead, he proposed that some or all the committee members attend a series of evening meetings to discuss different topics with representatives from different areas within the administration. For example, one night could be set aside for discussion of achievement test scores, another night for discussion of proposed bilingual education programs, another for disproportionate participation in special education programs, and so on.

Source: Snapp, M., Hickman, J., & Conoley, J. (1990). "Systems intervention in school settings: Case studies." In Gutkin, T., & Reynolds, C. (Eds.), *The Handbook of School Psychology,* New York: John Wiley & Sons, 926.

QUESTIONS

1. How would you characterize the communication style and interpersonal relationships that the school psychologist was advocating in this case?
2. How do you suppose the concerned parents would respond to his idea for a series of meetings? What examples of efforts at cross-cultural understanding do you see in the efforts of the psychologist?
3. What recommendations might you make to this school board for dealing with the concerns of this group of parents?

* * *

PETS AND VACATIONS

Some educators suggest that teachers refrain from asking students to talk or write about such topics as "my favorite pet," "our family trip," "my favorite bedtime stories," "what it feels like having my own savings account," and "how many books I own" in a classroom with children of culturally and socioeconomically heterogeneous backgrounds. What do you think are some possible reasons behind this admonishment? Can you think of other topics that may not be appropriate to discuss in a culturally diverse classroom setting? Also, are there ways in which students could deal with these topics without feeling left out? If you were a counselor, what are some questions about which you might need to be cautious raising with culturally different students or clients?

REFERENCES

Au, K. (1980). Participant structure in a reading lesson with Hawaiian children: Analysis of a culturally appropriate instruction/event. *Anthropology and Education Quarterly, 11*, 91–115.

Bruner, J. (1966). *Toward a theory of instruction.* Cambridge: Harvard University Press.

Carroll, T. G. (1981). Learning to work: Adaptive communication of the organization of the organizing principles of work in a suburban elementary school. In R. T. Sieber & A. J. Gordon (Eds.), *Children and their organizations: Investigation in American culture* (pp. 44–57). Boston: G. K. Hall & Co.

Carter, T. P., & Segura, R. D. (1979). *Mexican Americans in school: A decade of change.* New York: College Examination Board.

Collins, J. (1988). Language and class in minority education. *Anthropology and Education Quarterly, 19*(4), 299–326.

Dobbert, M. L., & Cooke, B. (1987). Primate biology and behavior: A stimulus to educational thought and policy. In G. D. Spindler (Ed.), *Education and cultural process* (2nd ed.) (pp. 97–116). Prospect Heights, IL: Waveland Press.

Dumont, R., Jr. (1985). Learning English and how to be silent: Studies in Sioux and Cherokee classrooms. In C. B. Cazden, V. P. John, & D. Hymes (Eds.), *Functions of language in the classroom* (pp. 344–369). Prospects Heights, IL: Waveland Press.

Erickson, F., & Mohatt, G. (1988). Cultural organization of participant structures in two classrooms of Indian students. In G. D. Spindler (Ed.), *Doing the ethnography of schooling* (pp. 133–174). Prospect Heights, IL: Waveland Press.

Friedrich, O. (1985, July 8). The changing face of America. *Time*, p. 36.

Gay, G. (1978). Viewing the pluralistic classroom as a cultural microcosm. *Educational Research Quarterly, 2*, 45–49.

Heath, S. B. (1984). Linguistics and education. *Annual Review of Anthropology, 13*, Palo Alto, CA: Annual Reviews.

Heath, S. B. (1986). Sociocultural contexts of language development. In Bilingual Education Office, California State Department of Education, *Beyond language: Social and cultural factors in schooling language minority students* (pp. 143–186). Los Angeles: Evaluation, Dissemination and Assessment Center, California State University—Los Angeles.

Hsu, F. (1982). *Chinese and Americans.* Honolulu: University of Hawaii Press.

John, V. P. (1985). Styles of learning—styles of teaching: Reflections on the education of Navajo children. In B. Cazden, V. P. John, & D. Hymes (Eds.), *Functions of language in the classroom* (pp. 334–340). Prospect Heights, IL: Waveland Press.

Joos, M. (1967). *The five clocks.* New York: Harcourt Brace & World.

Kneller, G. F. (1984). *Movements of thought in modern education.* New York: John Wiley & Sons.

Kochman, T. (1972). *Rippin' and runnin'.* Urbana: University of Illinois Press.

Levine, D. U., & Havighurst, R. J. (1988). *Society and education.* Boston: Allyn & Bacon.

Mitchell-Kernan, C. (1985). On the status of Black English for native speakers: An assessment of attitude and values. In B. Cazden, V. P. John, and D. Hymes (Eds.), *Functions of language in the classroom* (pp. 195–210). Prospect Heights, IL: Waveland Press.

Pearce, W. B., & Kang, K. (1988). Conceptual migrations: Understanding "travelers' tales" for cross cultural adaptation. In Y. Y. Kim & W. B. Gudykunst (Eds.), *Cross-cultural adaptation: Current approaches* (pp. 20–41). Newbury Park, CA: SAGE Publications.

Philips, S. (1972). Participant structures and communicative competence: Warm Springs children in community and classroom. In B. Cazden, V. P. John, and D. Hymes (Eds.), *Functions of language in the classroom* (pp. 370–394). Prospect Heights, IL: Waveland Press.

Ramirez, M., & Castaneda, A. (1974). *Cultural democracy, bicognitive development and education.* New York: Academic Press.

Richardson, E. H. (1981). Cultural and historical perspectives in counseling American Indians. In D. W. Sue, *Counseling the culturally different: Theory and practice* (pp. 224–227). New York: John Wiley & Sons.

Rist, R. C. (1985). On understanding the process of schooling: The contributions of labeling theory. In J. H. Ballantine (Ed.), *Schools and society* (pp. 88–106). Palo Alto, CA: Mayfield.

Rotter, J. B. (1966). Generalized experiences for internal versus external control of reinforcement. *Psychological Monograph, 80,* 1–28.

Ruiz, R. A. (1981). Cultural and historical perspectives in counseling Hispanics. In D. W. Sue, *Counseling the culturally different: Theory and practice* (pp. 186–215). New York: John Wiley & Sons.

Sieber, R. T., & Gordon, A. J. (1981). Introduction: Socializing organizations—environments for the young, windows to American culture. In R. T. Sieber & A. J. Gordon (Eds.), *Children and their organizations: Investigations in American culture* (pp. 1–17). Boston: G. K. Hall & Co.

Simon, H. A. (1979). Information processing models of cognition. *Annual Review of Psychology, 30,* 363–396.

Smith, E. (1981). Cultural and historical perspective in counseling blacks. In D. W. Sue, *Counseling the culturally different: Theory and practice* (pp. 141–185). New York: John Wiley & Sons.

Solomon, R. P. (1988). Black cultural forms in schools: A cross national comparison. In L. Weis (Ed.), *Class, race, and gender in American education* (pp. 230–248). Albany: State University of New York Press.

Spindler, G. D., & Spindler, L. (1987). Do anthropologists need learning theory? In G. D. Spindler (Ed.), *Education and cultural process* (2nd ed.) (pp. 53–69). Prospect Heights, IL: Waveland Press.

Sue, D. W. (1981). *Counseling the culturally different: Theory and practice.* New York: John Wiley & Sons.

Suzuki, B. H. (1980). Education and socialization of Asian Americans: A revisionist analysis of the "model minority" thesis. In R. Endo, S. Sue, & N. N. Wagner (Eds.), *Asian-Americans: Social and psychological perspectives* (Vol. 2) (pp. 155–175). Palo Alto, CA: Science and Behavior Books.

Epilogue

This is not a book about culture and education. Rather, it is about education as a cultural process. Implicit in this statement is the view that almost every aspect of education and schooling is influenced by culture. Our goals, how we teach, what we teach, how we relate to children and to each other are rooted in the norms of our culture. Our society's predominant worldview and cultural norms are so deeply ingrained in how we educate children that we very seldom think about the possibility that there may be other different but equally legitimate and effective approaches to teaching and learning. In a society with as much sociocultural and racial diversity as the United States, the lack of this wonderment about alternative ways often results in unequal education and social injustice.

In general terms, the late 1960s to the late 1970s represents a period in which a great many attempts were made to provide equal education to the children of minority cultures and lower socioeconomic classes. A wide range of programs in compensatory education, bilingual/bicultural education, ethnic studies, multicultural education, and school desegregation have been tried. Even today, the findings regarding the impact of these measures are inconclusive. Moreover, there are still large gaps between our knowledge of cultural differences and how such understanding can be utilized to help the culturally different learn and live more effectively in their own community and the school. There is little disagreement about the need to do a great deal more research into the ways in which diverse cultural factors influence the processes of learning and teaching in the context of schooling. But schooling always occurs under complex cultural as well as sociopolitical and economic conditions. These conditions in turn affect how well the school can function. Hence, what happens to the American school as a social institution seriously impinges upon how effectively we can utilize our understanding of the connection between culture and education and schooling.

USES OF "CULTURE"

Although the usefulness of the concept of culture has been discussed elsewhere in this book, a brief review of several key points may be helpful in examining the implications cultural diversity has for classroom teachers and counselors. Through the use of our knowledge about cultures of other people we may be able to understand them better and more accurately. Such an understanding in turn breaks down barriers to effective communication, thereby improving our interactions with individuals from different sociocultural groups. Our appreciation of other cultures tends to prevent us from misinterpreting the behaviors of others by putting ourselves in their place. This kind of sensitivity to other cultures may minimize the possibility of making unfair evaluations of culturally different individuals. For example, teachers may be able to see the relationship between Native American children's reluctance to engage in competitive academic activities and their concern for group harmony. School principals and counselors may understand that Asian-American and Hispanic students' avoidance of direct eye contact with them is an expression of respect for adults. Similarly, teachers may consider that the use of Black English by black students is not an indication of lower intelligence but rather an expression of their identity.

A CAVEAT

There are many varied ways of using "culture" to help children learn optimally and develop necessary skills for dealing effectively with a wide range of intellectual, social, vocational, and even emotional needs and problems. However, an oversimplified use of culture and overgeneralization of cultural traits often lead to erroneous and even harmful judgments about individuals from other cultures. Culture represents a complex of patterns of behaviors, interpersonal relationships, attitudes, uses of language, and definitions of roles that reflect the fundamental worldviews of a particular society. Culture also refers to certain general patterns of behaviors, attitudes, thinking and communication styles, and social relationships that a society expects from its members. Hence, no culture specifically spells out how each individual incorporates and expresses cultural expectations in any given life situation.

The extent to which a society's cultural norms are manifested in the daily lives of the people depends on the nature of their circumstances, personality traits, emotional dispositions, socioeconomic factors, and even familiarity with other cultural patterns. We should not assume that every member of a particular culture will act and think in exactly the same way. Our knowledge of another culture can give us only some general clues or a different perspective with which possible alternative explanations of a person's behavior or attitude can be understood. Teachers and counselors should be sensitive to the points of conflict between the cultures of minority groups and the mainstream society. The behaviors of the culturally different should be understood in this context. That is, if a minority child is found hitting another child, this should not automatically be judged as "picking a fight" or an expression of some strange cultural practice. Children in certain minority cultures play with each other by hitting and kicking, and the child's act of hitting may be a non-English-speaking child's way of saying "Let's play together." But such a judgment should not be made without knowing the circumstances surrounding the relationship between the mainstream and culturally different children and the points at which their cultural practices may conflict. Depending on the behavioral patterns of the minority child, his or her act of hitting may indeed be a hostile reaction to a frustrating situation or it may be an invitation to play.

No simple or fixed formulas prescribe how other people's behavior can be understood. Without detailed clinical observations or experiences and in-depth ethnographic (observer-participant) studies of individuals in their life situations, we cannot gain insightful information about the whys and the wherefores of other people's actions and attitudes. For this reason, the education of teachers and other school personnel should include components in which they are asked to observe, encounter, and evaluate cross-cultural experiences. One author recalls reading a teacher's handbook on Southeast Asian students prepared by a state department of education. The handbook explained that people in Southeast Asian countries and Korea always write their last names first. The book then went on to suggest that when a Southeast Asian student initially reports to school, his or her names should be reversed so that the last name will follow the first name. But following this suggestion would be "correcting" a nonmistake because many students from these parts of the world come to the United States with their last names already placed after the given names. A more appropriate procedure is for school personnel to simply ask the child "What is your last name?" or "Which is your last name?" or "Is this your last name?"

CONCLUDING THOUGHTS

As Giroux and others have admonished, we need to educate children of all sociocultural backgrounds, not just give them credentials. We may not all agree with Giroux's conviction that our schools oppress women, ethnic groups, and other minorities by disconfirming and marginalizing their experience. But at the least, educators need to experience the pain and joy of being different from others and to understand how such differences can give us greater options for doing things. In this way we may learn about ourselves and others while discovering new ways of helping all young people to fulfill their dreams.

Index